I0816618

Praise For

The Monastery *of the* Damned

"Nicholas Tobias' book recounts his entry into the French Foreign Legion and what ensued: a story that must be viewed as extraordinary by the vast majority of contemporary Western mankind given the abrupt abandonment of martial values that had persisted since preclassical times, notwithstanding the advent of originally pacifist Christianity. Nicholas did not accept this abandonment and instead looked for an opportunity to test his character in the Legion, which was once the refuge of rogues and is now the refuge of men who aspire to be warriors.

I, too, volunteered to fight, but originally I did so to serve a cause I deeply believe in, and it was only during the ensuing warfare that I discovered that combat is the most seductive of human endeavors, which heightens one's existence to the highest level precisely because it might end it, as Achilles clearly explains in *The Iliad*.

This is no ordinary book, and Nicholas is no ordinary writer."

Edward Luttwak, author of *Coup d'État: A Practical Handbook*, historian, and strategist

"A thoughtful young man deems unworthy the mentality and mores of contemporary America. After Oxford and Princeton, does he turn to drink, drugs, and promiscuous copulation to assuage his estrangement from contemporary life?

No—he enlists in the French Foreign Legion.

This account of his physical and spiritual journey to a new life, filled with deep reflections, will hold meaning for every person who senses there's something a little wrong with our lives today. Join his voyage of self-discovery to insight and wisdom about people, about cultures, and about our age."

Jeffrey Race, author of the military classic *War Comes to Long An*

"The swashbuckling fantasy of joining the French Foreign Legion, once cultivated by millions of teenage boys, is no longer really a 'thing' among the better-safe-than-sorry Millennial generation. Except for a few. Nicholas tells the story of how he joined the Legion in 2008. He started out as a green *engagé volontaire,* survived hazing and rigorous training to become a *Légionnaire de Première Classe*, and eventually served with French forces in Afghanistan. This served as a singular first step for his subsequent career as an infantry officer in the US Army. Also exceptional: Before joining the Legion, Nicholas was comfortably pursuing a doctorate in European history at Princeton. And more unusual still: He converted to Catholicism in his teens after being raised in Texas as an evangelical Protestant.

Mix these elements together, and we have a Millennial Bildungsroman of striking energy, originality, erudition, and wit. Whether describing his forced marches through the French countryside or his conversations with friends, Nicholas is always reflecting on what this all means for his life, for his generation, and for what the French would call *la culture et la civilisation* that belongs to all of us.

Along the way, he touches on two recurring themes. The first is the parochialism of most Americans, and their related inability to learn from how other peoples sometimes manage affairs better than they do. He believes, for example, that excessive adherence to rules and procedures prevents the US military from cultivating the same depth of unit cohesion that he observed in the Legion. The other, which has loomed pendulously over so many young Millennial men as it has over Nicholas, is the mystery of manhood itself. Manhood, he discovers, requires a transformative rite of passage. On this side lies mere bluster and bravado. On the other lies a serenity of soul that can only be earned through great focus, great exertion, and great mastery. He quotes a classic book about joining the Legion with a brutal title, *La Main Coupée*: 'To be. To be a man. And to discover solitude.' That is what I owe to the Legion.

I look forward to reading the next volume of Nicholas' life."

NEIL HOWE, co-author of the bestselling phenomenon *The Fourth Turning: An American Prophecy*; author of *The Fourth Turning Is Here*

The Monastery *of the* Damned

www.amplifypublishing.com

The Monastery of the Damned

The author has tried to recreate events, locales, and conversations from his memories of them. In order to maintain their anonymity in some instances, the author has changed the names of individuals and places, and may have changed some identifying characteristics and details such as physical properties, occupations, and places of residence. Some names and identifying details have been changed to protect the privacy of individuals.

Cover art by Paul Ryding, info@paulryding.com

For more information, please contact:
Amplify Publishing, an imprint of Amplify Publishing Group
620 Herndon Parkway, Suite 220
Herndon, VA 20170
info@amplifypublishing.com

Library of Congress Control Number: 2024926425
CPSIA Code: PRV0825A
ISBN-13: 979-8-89138-067-7

Printed in the United States

PRINCIPI IGNOTO DICATUM

The Monastery *of the* Damned

From the Ivy League
to the French Foreign Legion

Nicholas Tobias

Indi la cima qua e là menando,
come fosse la lingua che parlasse,
gittò voce di fuori e disse:

"....né dolcezza di figlio, né la pieta
del vecchio padre, né 'l debito amore
lo qual dovea Penelopè far lieta,

vincer potero dentro a me l'ardore
ch'i'ebbi a divenir del mondo esperto
e de li vizi umani d del valore...."[*]

Inferno, Canto XXVI
Dante Alighieri

---

* Then, brandishing its tip this way and that / as if it were the tongue of fire that spoke / it brought forth a voice and said: ". . . not tenderness for a son, nor filial duty / toward my aged father, nor the love I owed / Penelope that would have made her glad / could overcome the fervour that was mine / to gain experience of the world / and learn about man's vices, and his worth."

INTRODUCTION

Less than an hour of daylight was left as we stood on the Grand Canal's largest terrace, with commanding views of the bow-to-stern traffic below us. After conversation in midwinter's twilight, our hands clasping glasses of sparkling beverages to include Coca-Cola and industrially produced prosecco—but with no decent cocktail in sight—leisurely, we made our way back into the drawing room adjoining the terrace. To a hush of Germanic solemness, we sat down to listen to a performance on a robust pianoforte.

Two weeks before this intimate occasion I had gone to my first concert sponsored by the German government's research institute at Venice—the *Deutsches Studienzentrum*. It took place at *La Fenice*'s newly restored *Sala Apollinea*. My reasons for attending were to visit *La Fenice* for the first time and to meet two young scholars with whom I shared research interests, both fellows of the *Studienzentrum* for that academic year. As a new arrival to the city, I was eager to hear their thoughts about research possibilities in Venice. We three only had time to shake hands before sitting down for the performance offered by one of the *Studienzentrum*'s guests of honour and former residents, Hans.

For as long as I can remember, I have been a forsworn foe of any *musique savante* created after the deaths of Shoshtakovich and of Prokofieff. I knew this ever since the day I tried to sleep through George Crumb's *Voice of the Whale* as a child. Yet, as I dressed for the concert that evening and made my way to *La Fenice* from my room in the Cini Foundation's residence on the *Isola di San Giorgio*, I told myself that my prior attitudes toward "modern" music were too harsh, and that maybe I was unable to understand such works' complexity as a child. As I sat down next to a well-groomed Italian couple in the *Sala Apollinea*, I repeated to myself that I was too stringent, too austere, too classical, and that I needed to open my mind to the efforts of today's *musique savante*.

It turned out that I could hardly bear the performance, and I weighed the idea of walking out in mid-concert. Of great technical difficulty, the composition included supposedly experimental and daring manipulations of the instruments, all ho-hum by the 2010s. Quite vexed by the concert's end, I spoke briefly with my Germanic colleagues. We promised to meet at the *Studienzentrum* at the next opportunity.

Thus, about two weeks later, I found myself in the drawing room at the *Deutsches Studienzentrum*, housed in the *Palazzo Barbarigo,* after the *aperitivo* on its terrace, where our unmemorable conversation switched between German, English, and Italian. The performer was a Japanese woman named Mieko, who was spending several months in residence at the palace. Before she sat down to play, she explained her piece's meaning, aware that her music would not speak for itself.

I paraphrase her ideas and I reconstruct her broken German, but the gist of her introductory speech was to explain that her composition rejected any attempts to tell a story. Instead, it aimed to capture her impressions of living in Venice and walking its streets every day. These impressions neither led anywhere nor built anything, she claimed, nor did they tie into any larger project or ambition. Instead, for Mieko, they were but moments of beauty, fragments of memory in an otherwise chaotic and meaningless world—where she now lived in exquisite comfort thanks to the German government's largesse. She had undertaken to forge something that offered no theme, no direction, no purpose, no story.

Her work met these goals. Every now and then came a pleasing melody, an interesting series of chords, a tantalizing progression that made me wish to learn what would follow. And yet, at the very moments when her piece was becoming interesting, she backslid into dissonance and percussion—all with the bizarre theatrical movements needed nowadays to lend credibility to any musical creation. I think that few people in the drawing room were genuinely interested in the performance, although all praised its verve and brilliance out of politeness. I found no enjoyment in Mieko's recital, but lasting food for thought.

Since this performance in 2011, I have associated Mieko's work with my own broad generalizations about artistic enterprise in our quickly aging twenty-first century. That evening and many times afterward, I have imagined this composer as she wandered through Venice, knowing little of its history, of its language, and of its customs. How different was she from so many of us as we wander through legacies of worlds past, overwhelmed by compelling comforts and distractions? However much we admire and revere the artistic and cultural treasures of former worlds, bereft of their sufferings, their disciplines, their beliefs, and their tensions, we cannot create—or choose not to create—anything to rival such accomplishments. To justify our impotence, we postulate that historical conditions have changed and that—suspended in some Pasolinian *Dopostoria*—our cultural artefacts can no longer take forms that weathered past millennia.

In my refusal to see much value in Mieko's music or logic that evening, I rejected such ideas, as I reject them today.

To try my hand at capturing memories and impressions in a different form and spirit, I have undertaken to write this account of a consequential period in my life—my prematurely curtailed engagement in the French Foreign Legion from 2008 to 2010. My goal is to reconstruct outstanding memories from the beginning of my enlistment until its end. To check wordiness and to shape this endeavour, I have resolved to write about exactly one hundred distinct moments or subjects from my engagement in the Legion—that "monastery of the damned"—devoting a thousand words to each of them.

In this way, I shall keep a record of these memories as well as uncover—by parsing closely through them in their fragmented states—what story they tell and how and how much these two years in France changed me.

Cartagena de Indias (Getsemaní), Colombia, 16 February 2020

PART I

Enlistment

*L'imagination, la pensée peuvent être des machines admirables en soi, mais elles peuvent être inertes. La souffrance alors les met en marche...quand un être est si mal conformé (et peut-être dans la nature cet être est-il l'homme) qu'il ne puisse aimer sans souffrir, et qu'il faille souffrir pour apprendre des vérités, la vie d'un tel être finit par être bien lassante. Les années heureuses sont les années perdues...Et comme on comprend que la souffrance est la meilleure chose que l'on puisse rencontrer dans la vie, on pense sans effroi, presque comme à une délivrance, à la mort.**

Le Temps Retrouvé (Time Recovered)
Marcel Proust

* "Imagination and thought can be admirable capabilities, but they can also be inert forces. Suffering puts them to work.... When a creature is so disordered (and perhaps in nature this creature is man) that he cannot love without suffering, and that he must suffer to understand basic truths, then the life of this creature ends up being quite tiresome. Happy years are wasted years.... And when one understands at long last that suffering is the best thing that one can experience in life, he thinks of death without fear, and almost as a deliverance."

I

September 2008

It hurt us to breathe.

Inside a small barrack room whose remarkable cleanliness derived from its inhabitants' sweeping, scrubbing, and mopping three times a day, six of us lay down on worn mattresses of wool, with thin cotton sheets to cover us. Yellowish lamplight outside passed through the room's square windows without curtains, mixing with its darkness and recasting our surroundings in grisaille hues.

None of us new recruits could hold in uncontrolled fits of laughter, even as our laughter's movements brought sharp pains to our chests. For over an hour, together we kept each other awake by our unwanted, almost elated hilarity.

About two hours before this, a Korean corporal in his late twenties had commanded our whole platoon to line up in a hallway on the first floor of our company's building. Before he would release us to sleep, to ensure that all were present, the corporal ordered us to stand in a line against the hallway's walls and to sound out sequential French numbers from the first to the last recruit, or *engagé volontaire* in French.* Fewer than half of this new platoon's fifty or so men spoke any French whatsoever, so to fulfil his order was beyond our powers.

After our many false starts and failures, the increasingly angered corporal spurred us to better our French by slamming his clenched fist into each of our chests as we counted from one to about fifty, from the first to the last recruit lined up against the wall. During the corporal's inaugural iteration of intensive French instruction, I was fourth in this dour line and therefore caught an especially sharp blow after crying out, "*Quatre!*" Only months later did I understand that this punch had fractured my sternum.

Engagé volontaire "Blum"—the *nom de guerre* given to him upon his reception into the Legion—was a lanky, black-haired German fitting the mould of the wide-eyed military recruit given to extravagant but quickly deflated enthusiasms, and all manner of tall tales about matters sexual and martial. He held the sixteenth position in line. As the corporal reached him, he cried out loudly, "*Six!*"

"*Quoi??*" shouted the enraged corporal.

"*Six!!*" shouted Blum with more enthusiasm, as his makeshift boldness faltered.

"It's *seize!!*" shrieked the corporal as he cocked back his right arm and landed a powerful punch to Blum's diaphragm.

Blum slouched over and collapsed onto the floor.

Such trooping the lines with physical corrections took place at least four times that evening, perhaps more, as my memory of these days begins to fail me. On that first night in Castelnaudary we learned by repetition and through physical encouragement how to carry out what became ritual practices of accountability for the next four months whenever we slept in our assigned rooms at the Fourth Foreign Regiment, the Foreign Legion's unit devoted to training new recruits.

If I have learnt one thing over a decade of soldiering, it is that God, in His mercy, has indeed placed a limit on physical suffering. Things can only get so bad

* Literally this means "a person who has voluntarily engaged." All new recruits to the Legion are called this until they finish the Képi Blanc march, or *marche du képi blanc*.

until our bodies falter or until imperfect evils or sources of pain tire, stumble, or sow seeds of their own destruction. The Korean corporal lost his spunk and zeal within an hour, long before we could have hoped to count correctly in French as a group. At some point he let us scatter away to our rooms to sleep.

I shared a room with Blum and with four other recruits. One of these was a French citizen of Lebanese origins who had just left behind his struggles as a penniless medical student in Lyon to try to make a better life for himself and for his young wife. With us there was a young Bulgarian with his head shaven bald, who wore thick glasses. He spoke no French, but surprisingly good English. The fifth recruit was an athletic Irishman, one of the first recruits whom I met in Aubagne as I waited to be ushered through the Legion's in-processing regime. I do not remember the sixth recruit with us that night, but never shall I forget our uncontrolled laughter, heightened by the very pain that it spawned in our battered chests. That night we all laughed to exhaustion because then, for the first time, we believed that we had found what we were seeking out in the Legion, each in his own way.

Our ticklish laughter spoke to our dread and enthusiasm for trials that awaited us. There was no denying that we had come into a world far different from those that we had left behind weeks or months before, when each of us had asked to join the Legion at one of its recruitment posts throughout France. For all we knew that evening, the corporal's punches were mere foretastes of greater pains and abuses to come. The spectre of such repeated challenges to our manhood delighted us.

As it turned out, the next day our company leadership punished this corporal for his actions that evening, behaviour characteristic of his former regiment at Calvi but, on the whole, not allowed at Castelnaudary. After that spirited French lesson, I was unable to climb a rope, and I struggled to do pull-ups owing to my fractured sternum. When I brought up these limitations to the Legion's medics, they either mocked me or threatened me.

For weeks afterward, every night I struggled to sleep because it hurt awfully to remain in horizontal positions. Each breath taken as I lay down brought sharp pain to my chest. These pains slowly faded as weeks passed. After two months they were but memories drowned in those of greater challenges and privations. Today, I no longer remember what it was like to ache from breathing as I tried to grasp those few hours of sleep granted to us during basic training's first weeks.

Already by our first night in Castelnaudary, or "Castel" as we soon learned to call it, I knew that I had come to the right place.

II

July 2006

Whenever someone learns that I have served in the Foreign Legion, the most common question is one that the Legion's commissioned and non-commissioned officers never ask its recruits: "Why did you join?"

Within the Legion it is a faux pas to put this question to legionnaires, perhaps in part a taboo inherited from decades past when many recruits had criminal histories or something else to hide. During my own time wearing the képi blanc, hardened criminals were relatively few. About ten of the fiftyish recruits in my basic training platoon were wanted by the law somewhere.

Perhaps a second reason for this discretion within the Legion is the sheer variety of motives that lead men to seek out one of its recruitment centres in metropolitan France, to walk up to its foreboding gates, and to ask to join the Legion's ranks. Such motives were as diverse as the over 140 nationalities that made up the Legion in the twenty-first century's first decade.

Whatever our differences, one common thread stitched us together as *engagés volontaires*. Each successful recruit wished radically to change his life and to steer it down new and uncharted paths. Those who were not serious in this matter rarely made it past the Legion's in-processing at Aubagne.

Many who knew me at the time of my enlistment might have thought that I had taken this unorthodox step owing to successive mishaps with two women—the first a young Russian violinist and the second an impossibly haughty *Versaillaise*. Both were stunning creatures, such that I still think highly of my rarefied tastes in feminine beauty back in those impressionable years.

In truth, foreseeable domestic establishment with either of these young women would probably have been the only thing able to keep me from embarking on a soul-searing journey of some kind. Such establishment would have allowed me to ignore and to flee my worsening thirsts for adventure and for violence and to learn more of the world's realities. I could have succumbed to temptations to cling to a woman and, disarmed by her occasional consolations and occupied by offspring, to try to brave out existence as an academic in times when cuckolded nihilism steers our universities.

It was not to be.

Instead, my path to the Legion began in a small cottage near Oxford.

Oxford was no longer redolent of aquatint when I came to the city for the first time on a shabby bus from Heathrow Aeroport. After well-meaning undergraduates welcomed me at the city's bus station on a sunny afternoon, I hired a taxi to take me to my lodging. On my first day at Oxford, already I understood that it would not live up to my decade-long dreams about this university. To study there, in what I then believed to be the world's foremost seat of learning, would resolve neither my self-doubts nor my disarrayed spiritual quests.

For those determined to make believe that the twentieth century never happened, as was one of my friends at Wadham, it was almost possible to do so in the older colleges. Owing to a twist of fate, I was assigned to a drab twentieth-century college as a new graduate student. I did not have to seek digs or to live in Oxford, however, as a generous private scholarship provided for my lodging on the grounds of a Jacobean manor about four miles up Woodstock Road, toward Blenheim Palace. There I lived with other students in a Victorian cottage that had once housed the vicar of the manor's well-kept thirteenth-century church. Since we were both heavy smokers, I shared the cottage's ground floor with a Jewish Briton about my age, and we became friends as smokers will do. An Italian speaker of praiseworthy devotion to Dante, he adored his *shiksa* girlfriend from Wales. This tormented him.

For me it proved a year of unflagging scholarship. All three terms I studied the Church Fathers, especially Jerome, and I learned the first seven books of Pushkin's *Eugene Onegin* by heart in Russian. For one of my aged professors, I wrote my term papers in Latin. Nonplussed though he was at first, he surprised me in turn by correcting many grammatical mistakes. In addition to studies of Latin and of Hebrew, I plunged myself yet more deeply into eighteenth-century feminine French literature. I had recently developed this dangerous vice after combing through Vladimir Nabokoff's commentaries on *Eugene Onegin* and using its references to understand Tatiana's cultural and literary upbringing. Before I knew it, I found myself lapping up books such as Madame de Genlis' *Les Voeux Temeraires* and Madame Cottin's *Claire d'Albe*.

The manor's grounds were always open to us. Moreover, I had keys to the manor itself, so at my leisure I could walk into its wainscoted drawing room, sit down in its great leather chairs with books, and read until the morning. On Sundays I strolled through adjacent fields to the Oxford Oratory, where I sang in its respectable amateur choir.

During all this academic and cultural bustle, I fretted about what to do after Oxford. As the year passed, I grew ever more unnerved as the prospect of beginning doctoral studies in English history at Princeton loomed before me.

Toward the end of Trinity term, an Australian man came to Yarnton Manor to visit one of its temporary Australian residents. At that point a newly minted captain in the Australian Army, this visitor had once served in the French Foreign Legion. His barrel-chested bearing spellbound me, offering an enlivening contrast to what I believed to be the whimsical scholars surrounding me. Here, I thought as we chatted with him in our cottage's bright kitchen, was a man who "walks as though he owned himself and hogs his bristles short."

That summer's day on Yarton Manor's grounds, the French Foreign Legion became something incarnate to me.

Slightly over two years after that first encounter with a real-life former *legionnaire*, I walked up to Aubagne's gates and asked to join the Legion.

III

April 2007–May 2008

Every vocation begins in error and in illusion.

By April 2007, I had taken the decision to join the Foreign Legion. This was not immediately possible since I was woefully out of shape owing to a decade of scant physical activity and uninterrupted chain-smoking of cigarettes.

My first impulses were to leave Princeton behind, to exercise my body as long as it took to get it up to the Legion's formidable snuff, and to fly to France at the earliest possible date. During a dreary party at a Princeton dormitory in summer 2007, however, I learned from a colleague about the possibility of earning a terminal master's degree from Princeton without finishing the burdensome "general examinations" usually required of graduate students in the history faculty at the end of their second year. Since I had already finished almost all requirements for the degree, I decided to take advantage of subsidized digs on University Place near the house where F. Scott Fitzgerald once lived, the well-stocked bar in the basement of Princeton's Graduate School—the "Debasement Bar"—and the campus's many athletic facilities wherewith to whip my body back into shape.

The first step toward physical fitness was to quit smoking. This halting process began that summer of 2007. I locked myself up in my room and steeled myself for trials to come. Throughout the days of physical withdrawal, I slept as much as possible. Whenever cravings to smoke became too great to bear, either I went for a run or made myself a powerful alcoholic drink. Before long, I had spent my first week without cigarettes in almost a decade. Hitherto many former smokers had told me that upon quitting, everything would start tasting and smelling better. They were lying. To this day, I miss and prize the smell and texture of tobacco smoke.

For the rest of that summer, I rediscovered my body's potential for athletic activity. Running, lifting weights, eating regular meals—these were all new and remarkable changes to my wonted lifestyle. For my goals I set the physical standards outlined in Evan McGorman's *Life in the French Foreign Legion*—which still remains the most accurate and honest book about the Foreign Legion that I have ever read. Such goals comprised running eight kilometres in under thirty-five minutes, conducting twelve pull-ups with ease, and climbing a rope without using one's legs. By the long summer's end, I could approach some of these goals, and I was looking forward to nine months of healthy routine throughout the new academic year.

These nine months confirmed me in my decision to join the Foreign Legion. I got to know better old faces from the prior year at Princeton and to meet many more new students. They made for a miserable lot, victims of blithe entitlement only possible in a bubble such as Princeton's, bankrolled by a financial endowment unmatched in the Western Hemisphere. Among such new acquaintances that year, one was an engineering officer in the US Army. To my eyes, this officer was an outstanding contrast to other graduate students in that he was physically fit, confident, grateful for his opportunities at Princeton, and humble about his abilities and prospects. Rather unfairly, I compared my peers with him, and in his example, I found more to convince myself that I was making the right decision to pursue his line of work.

This decision taken, I regained peace about and interest in my studies. I began to read through Dante's *Divine Comedy* in earnest under the expert tutelage of an Italian professor. With an esteemed professor of the Classics faculty, I undertook detailed study of Caesar's *Commentaries on the Gallic Wars*, thereby accomplishing a lifelong dream to read and to understand this work in the Latin. To those at Princeton who would hear me, I announced that I was steeling myself to join the French Foreign Legion. Few believed me.

With almost fourteen years of soldiering behind me, whenever I look back now to this time and to what inspired me to join the Legion, I see mostly error and illusion. However noble, natural, or just might have been some of my impulses at that age, I nursed unhinged admiration for military pomp and delusory ideas about the efficiency of military discipline. I held on to a consoling thought that by killing, by risking death, and perhaps by perishing in the world's far-flung reaches, I could snatch that "life of life" that Lord Byron described in the introduction to his *Corsair*, verses that long haunted me. I believed that by means of military swashbuckling—or idealized imaginations of it inspired largely by television series and Hollywood films—I could pursue honour in a world without it. To serve in the military would forge me into a man in a world increasingly made up of mere males, who lived meekly and in terror of their womenfolk.

Only years later did I come to understand that I had largely fallen into the disordered line of thinking that Evelyn Waugh described toward the end of his *Sword of Honour* trilogy. At the conclusion of *Unconditional Surrender*, a Jewish woman at a refugee camp in Yugoslavia voiced Waugh's telling insight:

> *Even good men thought their private honour would be satisfied by war. They could assert their manhood by killing and being killed. They would accept hardships in return for having been selfish and lazy.*

Over time I would uncover and understand how misled were many beliefs and thoughts that underlay my steps to leave Princeton and to ask to enlist into the Foreign Legion's ranks. Perhaps some priests looking back on their younger selves as they began seminary would have similar shudders of embarrassment at their motives and thinking at the start of their vocations. Perhaps not.

Yet, no matter how misleading and misplaced my thoughts, there was something true in my calling to military ranks, whose depths I could not unearth without taking those first steps, however much I erred as I took them.

IV

June–August 2008

Before leaving the United States, I had resolved not to go to France without first learning how to drive vehicles with manual transmissions. In the early twenty-first century, it was rare for citizens of the United States under the age of forty to know how to drive such vehicles, but most vehicles in Europe still used manual transmissions. I took seriously the need to address this grave failing of mine.

For this reason, during that academic year before my planned enlistment, I enlisted the help of a Hungarian graduate student in economics, a pious Catholic with a lovely new Brazilian bride and a Volkswagen Jetta with six gears. He taught me the basics of controlling them along the winding roads near Princeton's Graduate School and Institute for Advanced Study. After completing my third master of arts at Princeton in late spring 2008, I went back to my parents' house in Texas and promptly bought a 1981 manual-transmission BMW 320i in order to practice thoroughly before my planned departure for France in August 2008. Each day I drove countless miles in this vehicle in preparation for my upcoming trip. This proved to be time well spent.

Aside from driving rural roads of Hays County, Texas, that summer I worked changing motor oil and conducting basic vehicle maintenance at a corporate chain of oil-changing shops called Jiffy Lube. My first idea for that summer was to get a temporary job at a local mechanic's shop, even if unpaid. This proved impossible, however, since none of them would take me to work in his shop, even as a volunteer, without costly and time-consuming "certifications" from regional and national authorities. It disheartened me to learn that by the twenty-first century, the cancer of "credentialism" had infiltrated and all but taken over even the world of suburban automobile mechanics in the United States. One afternoon I tried explaining to a mechanic in northern Austin that I simply wanted to spend time getting hands-on experience with vehicles and that I would be willing to work for him without pay to gain such experience. This man told me, without any hint of irony, that in order to work on cars I "needed to go back to school." Having just completed a degree at Princeton with the intention not to undertake serious studies again for many years, I gave up on the quest to work at a mechanic's shop and settled for an entry-level job in one of the United States' large franchise corporations, Jiffy Lube.

This experience turned out to be useful for many reasons. In addition to gaining basic knowledge about vehicles and motors, at Jiffy Lube I experienced my first impactful interactions with the United States' *Lumpenproletariat*. It changed me to have to overcome the unavoidable challenges of working with men of vastly different educational and social backgrounds and to treat them as my peers. This was the first step of a long process of learning how not to think about "workers" or "the working classes" in romantic and fantastical ways.

Each Sunday, my family and I drove from our sequestered location to downtown Austin to assist at Mass in the extraordinary form at Saint Mary's Cathedral. In 2008, Father E. Roberts of the Society of Jesus still said this Mass on Sunday afternoons. For me, this well-built priest in his early eighties was the embodiment of twentieth-century Catholicism in the United States at its high point. Four of his eight siblings had joined religious orders. His own studies with the Society of Jesus had given him a tour of the world, with multiple stays in Rome and in Louvain. I especially envied him his doctoral studies at Louvain before the university's ruinous break into Dutch-speaking and French-speaking enclaves. He ended his academic career as the president of a small Jesuit university in Seattle before retiring to Texas, where he had never before lived. He chose it for retirement since his mother's family traced its origins to the state.

To Father Roberts I owe many conversations and thoughts that have since shaped my beliefs and my life. Morality's vanity but necessity, Freemasonry's beguiling evils, God's inscrutable nature and ways, the sensibility of Pascal's Wager—I much appreciated opportunities to discuss all these and more with this learned priest. By 2008 senility—amplified perhaps by many prescription drugs—was already affecting his mind's formidable powers. Nonetheless, I was able to bid him a proper farewell during these summer months.

Several months of the Texan summer passed before I undertook my long-announced trip to join the French Foreign Legion, knowing little of what would happen after my arrival in France. With my parents, I attended Mass at Saint Mary's Cathedral for the Feast of the Assumption on 15 August 2008. The next day, early in the morning before daybreak, I bid my mother farewell, unsure of when I would next see her. My father drove me from our house in the Texan Hill Country to Houston International Aeroport, whence I took a flight to Frankfurt, followed by a shorter one to Marseilles.

After taking leave of my father at the aeroport, I boarded my Lufthansa flight full of worry. Upon my arrival at Frankfurt's aeroport, I had to wait for about six hours before my connecting flight to Marseilles. In one of the aeroport's hallways, I crossed paths with an Italian graduate student from Princeton's faculty of economics. He was on his way back to Italy to vacation after *Ferragosto*. Hurriedly I told him that I was heading to the French Riviera for my own holiday. We chatted only briefly before parting ways.

On television screens throughout Frankfurt's aeroport, I saw repeated reports about ten or more French soldiers who had just died in combat that took place in Afghanistan. Such reports convinced me of the gravity and moment of the path that I had set out to pursue in the French Foreign Legion.

Early that morning of 17 August 2008, I boarded my flight to Marseilles.

V

August 2008

France had been the first country that I visited outside of the United States. The first city overseas in which I slept was Biarritz. Before that trip in the late 1990s, I had already conjured up many images of Biarritz from reading Vladimir Nabokoff's short stories. Its beaches were far different from those that I had foreseen, but soon I had replaced my past imaginings with Biarritz' graceful real presence. No doubt I hoped for an impassioned and impromptu tryst along the crags of Biarritz' beaches, or better yet inside a forlorn cave filled with dampened echoes of crashing waves. None happened.

After two weeks on the coast, I spent a third in Paris at a well-provisioned hostel in the *Marais* district. From my early adolescence, my thoughts about the French language and French culture mirrored those espoused by Cicero in his *Brutus* with reference to Latin: it was not praiseworthy to know them, but rather shameful not to do. Until 2007, however, my knowledge of France and of French still wanted substance, as my visits to the country had been limited to Paris and northern regions. Most of these visits took place in winter, so I associated France and Paris with rain, with cold, and with dark, short days.

It was therefore startling to come straight to Marseilles in high summer and to confront a France hitherto unknown to me. Disembarking my flight, I walked out of Marseilles' aeroport and into its sun-soaked late morning.

Before leaving the aeroport, I had telephoned my mother from a phone booth to let her know of my safe arrival. As would be reasonable for any mother whose son was in the process of joining the French Foreign Legion, she was rather worried about me. Her recommendation was that I spend the evening in Marseilles and join the Legion the next day. I did not wish to heed her advice, so I took a taxi to the city's main railway station. Upon arrival I asked one of the station's workers how to find the Foreign Legion's recruitment office located there. He ogled me with suspicion and pointed toward an area on the right side as one enters the station, at the farthest edge of its platforms.

My heart pounded in my chest as I drew near to the Legion's recruitment office, one of the few times in my life that it has done so. It pounded far more powerfully than it ever did for any matter of love or hatred before or since then.

Crestfallen, perhaps, is the best word to describe how I felt when I found out that the Legion's office had already closed for the day.

Not having foreseen this possibility, I walked to a nearby tourist office and asked what one could do for a day in Marseilles. Two kindly, elderly ladies working at the office were shocked that I had never heard of *La Canebière*, which, as they explained to me, was known to everyone, all over the world. I took a room at the Ibis hotel near the station and walked down to this fabled *Canebière*. By the time I made it to the city's old port it was late afternoon, but the sun remained high on the horizon. I did not spend too much time touring the city, as I was rather edgy about what the next day might hold. All nerves notwithstanding, I was delighted to find myself in France's Mediterranean regions, and for the first time I thought to myself that I could love the country.

Months and years later I came to know the city better, but its bustle and its colour enchanted me from that first evening in the middle of August. As I caught glimpses of the *Château d'If* and of the broad sea behind it, episodes and facts from books of history sported in my mind. I tried to imagine Herod Antipas and Herodias arriving to their land of exile, stopping briefly on their way to other regions of Gaul. Could they have frequented the same establishments in Marseilles' port as Herod Archelaus did before them? With wine or other drinks in hand, ruefully looking out at the harbour's splendid views, which probably had not changed much since their day, did they scheme about ways to recover their lost regions? Without doubt they remained oblivious to the fact that the fame and power of obscure preachers whose execution they had made possible before their exile would far eclipse those of even the Roman emperors who had banished them to the Gallic sticks.

For all its elegance and sophistication, I still think of Paris as a Germanic city, and therefore as indelibly tinged with northern barbarities. In Marseilles, however, I perceived the mixing of Gaul's ancient peoples with the cultures and civilizations whose memories awed and inspired me.

After a long stroll through Marseilles' central promenades, I went to bed early in my hotel's narrow bed, probably less sterile in fact than in appearance. The next morning, I took a sizeable hotel breakfast and thereafter walked back to the Legion's recruitment office inside Saint Charles Station.

That morning an enlisted man from Hungary was staffing this small, tidy office. It bewildered him that any citizen of the United States would wish to join the Foreign Legion. Whereas I thought that my country was in terminal decline and decadence, in the summer of 2008 many foreigners could still believe that the land of my birth was an untouchable "superpower." His misgivings about my decision notwithstanding, he spoke well of the Legion and of its opportunities. He reassured me that the Legion "was not a prison." Since he could only give information at this office, he recommended that I take the train to Aubagne and then enjoy lunch at the local McDonald's restaurant before walking to the Legion's headquarters.

I took the train that he recommended but forewent McDonald's. Within an hour I was walking from Aubagne's station toward the Legion's *maison mère.*

VI

August 2008

To reach the Legion's *maison mère* from Aubagne's train station by foot, one dutifully trudges along a major thoroughfare dubbed the A501. I had already spent my store of emotions at the train station the prior afternoon, so as I walked toward the headquarters' gates my heart was still, my spirits quiet. At its entrance I buzzed the ringer on an austere-looking metalled gate. To answer a terse and incomprehensible greeting over a speakerphone, I uttered words that I had rehearsed many times up until that day, mustering for them all the resolve that I could for the occasion: "*Je veux m'engager à la Légion Étrangère.*"*

"Are your teeth rotten?" These were the first words that met my fateful entreaty. A stocky young soldier with black hair, who had come out to look at me, bared his own teeth and pointed at them. He eyed me with suspicion until I opened my mouth and showed him my teeth. Once he could inspect them and confirm their basic structural integrity, matter-of-factly and silently he ushered me to a small and barren room with a window that overlooked Aubagne and

---

* "I want to enlist in the Foreign Legion."

its surrounding hills. I was the first recruit to arrive that day, so the corporal bade me wait.

Not long after my arrival, a young Frenchman joined me. He was short, thin, and athletic looking after the wiry French way. Halting though my spoken French was at the time, we chatted. He was nineteen years old, and he had not told anyone in his family about his decision to join the Legion. Having grown up in the suburbs of Paris, he sought to escape the blandness of his lower middle-class existence and unwanted university studies. Within a few hours a sanguine Irishman joined us. He spoke no French whatsoever.

By about five o'clock in the afternoon there were six recruits in our waiting room. The black-haired corporal walked us into the First Foreign Regiment's grounds and led us to a small office where all of us, one-by-one and privately, surrendered our passports and other personal items and completed basic administrative procedures. None of us knew exactly what would happen once we had crossed the Legion's thresholds, so each step was fraught with physical and mental tensions.

In that small office a black man of African origin greeted me, looked briefly at my passport and other papers, searched through my belongings, and took record of the currencies and books that I had with me. He was surprised that I had brought American Express traveller's cheques worth many thousands of euros, and he paged with close attention through a leather-bound notebook that I had brought with me. We had a pleasant conversation, and he could not understand why any citizen of the United States would ever join the Legion.

This young African held a crucial perquisite—to assign pseudonyms or *noms de guerre* to all incoming recruits. His whims could haunt legionnaires throughout their tenure in the organization. At the very least his fanciful names would stick with incoming volunteers until they had completed the challenging and yearslong process of recovering their passports and true names. His most infamous misdeeds included naming a North American recruit "Chuck Norris" and a Chinese recruit "King Kong." To me he assigned the name "Christoph" and an irksome surname that sounded Anglo-Saxon enough to francophone ears. My new birthplace was Chicago. He confiscated most of my belongings, had me sign a few papers that I did not have time to read, and handed me over to the care of a senior corporal, or *caporal-chef*. Months later I recovered everything that I had surrendered this day, including the notebook given to me by my godfather, at whose beginning I had transcribed words in Hebrew from Ecclesiastes: "All things are full of labour; Man cannot utter it: the eye is not satisfied with seeing, nor the ear filled with hearing."*

The plump *caporal-chef* now in charge of us wore a black kepi, to which legionnaires of his rank with over fifteen years of service are entitled. He led us to a barrack room. He likewise searched our belongings to ensure that none of us had weapons, leaving us only the barest essentials for showering and for shaving. We did not eat that evening. Days were still long in August, so it was light outside as we six lay down to sleep on bunk beds. Our group included the teenage Frenchman, the Irishman, and three other French residents: the first a Frenchman from France's south, the second an enormous black man from Mali, and the third an Arab from the Maghreb. Already that evening the bravado of barrack talk began, and we began setting up a provisory pecking order. The *caporal-chef* gave the southern Frenchman the responsibility of keeping accountability of us and reporting any problems to him.

That evening as we lay down to sleep, with indirect sunlight still shining through the windows, I kept silence and listened while the southern Frenchman, the Malian, and the Maghrebian talked for hours. As I gazed out a window toward Aubagne's maritime pine trees and the horizon's softening light, the young men's conversation evolved to treat some of life's more appropriate questions. The Frenchman doubted the existence of God. The Malian discussed experiences with his country's largely unknown native religions and insisted on the reality of the spiritual realm. He decried organized religion's hypocrisy but reckoned it important to be a "spiritual person." The chubby Arab disagreed with such world-weary scepticism. He believed in God and in religion. As proof

* Ecclesiastes 1:8: ל הַדְּבָרִים יְגֵעִים לֹא יוּכַל אִישׁ לְדַבֵּר לֹא תִשְׂבַּע עַיִן לִרְאוֹת וְלֹא תִמָּלֵא אֹזֶן מִשׁ

of God's existence, he lustily spoke of the experience of sexual union between man and woman.

I do remember thinking with surprise and with melancholy that their ideas and conversation about such weighty questions were not noticeably less intelligent or informed than those of most of my former colleagues at Princeton. At least these three aspiring legionnaires had the good sense to lie awake at night and to ponder God's existence and nature.

VII

August 2008

At about 0530, we six newest recruits woke up, showered, shaved, dressed in our civilian clothes, and then stood outside in a straight row that seemed military-like to us *amateurs*. Soon the black-hatted *caporal-chef* came out of his office, told us to follow him, and took off running in a sprint. We trailed him with ease for about forty seconds until he stopped outside a nearby building. He had us line up and wait for several minutes before ushering us into the base's ordinary.

Coming as I did from a country whose cultural roots are Anglo-Saxon, this first Foreign Legion breakfast's sparse offerings rattled me. Daily breakfast was the same at any of the Legion's bases on French territory. It comprised a small roll of bread, jam, pieces of butter, and a bowl of one of three possible warm liquids, from which we recruits were not free to choose—these were milk, hot chocolate, or instant coffee. Tables were sparse. Murals depicting various episodes of the Legion's history and of its deployments overseas covered the ordinary's walls. Alone in this room that could fit at least 200 legionnaires at a time at table, we ate quickly and in silence. Afterward we formed up again in a row outside the building. Dawn had already begun during our hurried meal.

Breakfast is something about which I had given little thought before joining the Legion. After over two decades of travelling and living in France or in other countries whose cultures we might plausibly call "Latin," I have, however, come to rue that few pronouncements of folk wisdom could be more misleading and harmful than one commonly heard in English about the way to take one's meals: "Breakfast fit for a king, lunch fit for a prince, and dinner fit for a pauper." This statement's underlying idea is that to achieve greater physical health, one should eat large breakfasts, modest lunches, and sparing dinners.

Yet, as we survey countries and populations where large breakfasts are customary—the United Kingdom, Australia, the United States, and Germanic lands—it is precisely in these countries that one finds the greatest incidence of overweight and obese people. True, most of these countries' overweight probably eat large portions at all meals and therefore do not adhere to the foregoing folk wisdom. Whatever the case, the Legion's breakfasts slowly grew on me, and later bred in me a disdain for elaborate breakfast arrays. To this day, instinctively I judge a man negatively should he take large breakfasts, and I recoil inside myself at the ghoulish spectacle of hotel breakfast buffets.

At some point that morning the *caporal-chef* took us to a building near the headquarters' museum, which, among other treasures from the Legion's past, houses the famed wooden hand of Captain Jean Danjou, whose last stand at Camerone during France's colonial adventures in Mexico has become part of the Legion's mythology. In that building adjoining and overlooking Aubagne's expansive regimental assembly area—or *place d'armes*—we waited outside of a mysterious office. One-by-one we entered it to sign more enlistment papers as an officer watched us wordlessly from behind his desk. For the "francophones" in our group, it must have been challenging enough to parse out any sense from the formal language of these cumbersome legal documents. The rest of us signed papers of whose import we understood nothing.

All this transition from the civilian to the military took place with surprising suddenness. We were still in civilian clothes when we formed up again for lunch at the ordinary where we had earlier enjoyed our first Legion breakfast. From our position at the ordinary we could look directly down over the regiment's *place d'armes*, and for the first time we remarked that all its flags were flown at half-mast. At some point that afternoon we heard the bugles' mournful cry from a short ceremony that commemorated the Legion's most recent fallen in combat. We learned that the flags were being flown at half-mast in their honour.

A few days before, while I was wandering through the busyness of Frankfurt Aeroport, a Russian medic assigned to the Foreign Legion's Second Parachute Regiment breathed his last in Sper Kunday, Afghanistan. Sterile European media on televisions affixed to walls of Frankfurt Aeroport's terminals had reported that several French soldiers had died in significant engagements in Afghanistan. Such reports became fleshier to me as we looked down at all the regiment's flags fluttering to the wind at half-mast. Rumours raced about the Legion's newest dead in battle, and all of us took in these rumours with gravity.

That day we gave away our last civilian clothing and finished the transition to the isolated holding area for new recruits, where *engagés volontaires* wear colour-coded uniforms in accordance with their individual progress through various stages of selection. We were left with only the barest of goods for hygiene. Within a few days the southern Frenchman, the man from Mali, and the Arab had quit the Legion's recruitment process for different reasons.

In all these blurred moments of abrupt change, perhaps I was shocked most at the length of the shorts given to us to wear. These extended to at most ten to twelve inches below the waist, and on each side there was a slit that exposed yet more leg. At first, I thought that my discomfort at wearing such skimpy clothing was owing to my North American prurience, but soon I noted that Africans and almost all nationalities were scandalized at our shorts' scantness.

The Legion gave me the matriculation number of 200856. This number represented my place among the many men who had undertaken official steps to join the Legion since it began keeping track of such numbers in the 1930s. It was humbling to think of that long trail of so many souls who had walked through the Legion's doors with vastly different ideas and interests, and of the various forms of death that had already undone so many of the matriculated.

VIII

August–September 2008

All things military were new to me at this time, and my knowledge of what might happen once I had crossed the thresholds of the First Foreign Regiment came mostly from Evan McGorman's book, *Life in the French Foreign Legion.*

It was not without worry, then, that I walked into the gates of the small compound where the Legion corralled its newest volunteers. There was a two-story barracks where we slept six or more to a room. Adjoining the barracks was a small yard enclosed by chain-link fencing. As I walked into this yard, I remarked numerous raised bars for pull-ups, inclined boards for sit-ups, and a small running trail beaten into the ground by thousands of recruits. Broken up into different groups that thronged in this small space, we recruits wore distinctive black shirts, green shirts, or new military uniforms based on our progression through three distinct phases of selection. Caged though we were, we could enjoy memorable views of the hills surrounding Aubagne. Often as we sat or stood, we looked out with longing toward this rather dull Provençal town, each thinking of his own favourite civilian pleasures, now forbidden.

Throughout the day we stayed locked up in this fenced pen until called for meals at the ordinary, for interviews, for tests, or for work details, the latter of which we quickly learned to name *corvée*. This whole process was a skilfully designed trial of one's resolve and determination that quickly sifted out those whose personalities and motivations were not enough to weather the Legion's hardships. Citizens from almost every nation in the world peopled that small yard at Aubagne. Quickly we segregated ourselves into groups based on our preferred languages and grew accustomed to a daily rhythm.

After waking up about 0530 and getting into formation in front of a *caporal-chef* in charge of us for that day, he would ask who wanted to quit the selection process, reminding us that we were free to leave at any time. Each morning dozens of men at various stages of recruitment raised their hands to quit. They always left Aubagne before the day's end. Thereafter we moved to have our breakfast at the base's ordinary, after which we walked back to our pen, unable to leave it unless called for interviews or tests. To answer natural needs, we had to ask the permission of a *caporal-chef* and then to do whatever was necessary under supervision. Throughout the day we talked, exercised, and waited. For any infractions against prevailing discipline, we would be compelled to wear a rucksack (called "Bertha" or "Bernadette"—I do not remember which) with a large stone in it and metal wires for straps, and to carry it about the open area in front of the barracks for an appointed time.

Our small English-speaking group included the Irishman whom I encountered our first day. Here I also met "Lawrence," a bartender from North Carolina, a tall light-skinned black man with whom I later completed basic training. In this group we also had a bespectacled young Texan to whom the Legion ascribed the fanciful name "McCloud." We had a Mexican American from El Paso, Texas, several people who claimed to be former soldiers in the United States Marine Corps, and numerous British volunteers. Few *anglophones*, however, made it through the assessment and selection process.

One day a gallant man in his late thirties joined our group. He claimed to be a restaurant manager from Manhattan. He confessed to me that he was trying to reclaim the sense of adventure that he had once felt as a soldier in the United States Army during the First Gulf War. He told everyone that he had wearied of his regular and exhausting sexual activity with employees of the restaurant that he managed. "You just get tired of banging a different hostess every night, you know?" he informed me. I nodded, implying that I believed his tales and his protestations of *Weltschmertz* after years of supposed rakish dalliance, plundering attractive and nubile women at leisure. A few days later he failed the Legion's basic fitness test, whereupon the Legion sent him back to civilian life. Rumour had it that he had lain with the wife of a leader of organized crime in New York and therefore had fled to the Legion to escape his ordained execution. I would like to believe this far-fetched report.

Since I wished to maintain and to improve my Russian, in our pen I often joined the Russophone groups. At this time my familiarity with Russian profanity was limited, so when I first sat with Russian speakers, I could hardly understand what they were saying. In short order I learned that their conversations' vocabulary was limited and not much more sophisticated than that of Ellochka the Cannibal. Once I had established a basic vocabulary of Russian swear words, soon enough I was talking at ease with this group's raucous and irreverent participants. Countless Slavs showed up claiming to be former Russian special operations soldiers, or *spetsnaz*. Such boasts were so common that mocking references to other recruits' non-existent exploits in the *spetsnaz* became a running joke. Russian-speaking Moldovans, a polyglot bunch, seemed to make up most of this group. One of these Moldovans, whose incisors were almost as pointed as one sees in films about vampires, interrogated me in Italian about how many languages I spoke (at the time, I could communicate in five). Within a few days, this supposed former *spetsnaz* was removed from our ranks and returned to civilian life for unknown reasons.

Our tests and interviews were mostly in line with Evan McGorman's predictions. Our physical fitness test comprised pull-ups, a run, abdominal "crunches," and climbing a rope. After the physical test we had mental tests, medical tests, and interviews with specialized personnel for recruitment. If there were no tests for us on any given day, we simply waited in the pen, or we would be assigned to various work details in Aubagne or elsewhere.

IX

September 2008

One morning after breakfast, after we had formed up in front of our barracks under the colours of the breaking dawn, the *caporal-chef* in charge of our large assembly called out several roster numbers, including mine. We had been chosen for a detail, or *corvée*. However much we might welcome a break from our pen's monotony, we had already learned to dread *corvée*, which almost always included picking up cigarette butts (which legionnaires toss with abandon for the express purpose of contributing to their subordinates' *corvée*), sweeping, mopping, and cleaning bathing rooms, called *chiottes* in the Legion.

Soon a different *caporal-chef* came to collect us. He wore the distinctive white kepi with a golden band that all *caporaux-chef* wear until they earn the black kepi after fifteen years of service. We hopped into his small official van, whereupon he drove the five of us out from Aubagne's gates and toward Marseilles. After several weeks of confinement, as we approached the great city, I found its movement and noisiness jarring. I took careful notice of what I had once taken for granted—buzzing shops and restaurants that I might wish to visit, women's laughter, the city's ramshackle architecture and Mediterranean hubbub. None of us had any idea about our destination. After skirting the city's splendid *corniche*, we drove into a military compound and the gates closed behind us. We had come to Malmousque.

Before many Foreign Legion units supported the *putsch* against the French President Charles de Gaulle in 1961, thereby spelling the end of the Legion's presence in Algeria, its basic training facilities were located in Sidi Bel Abbès, Algeria—the Legion's original *maison mère*. For decades prior to the 1960s, all recruits for the Legion came to the military enclosure called Malmousque for final screening before they boarded regular vessels bound for Algeria. With the transfer of the Legion's facilities to Corsica and to the south of France in the 1970s, Malmousque lost its former importance. It has since become a holiday resort for legionnaires on leave, who in my days in the Legion could take a room at Malmousque for as little as ten euros a night—a pittance even for the lowliest of us. Most rooms were dreary and functional in their construction and in their decoration, but some of them opened up to balconies with spectacular views of the Mediterranean. Malmousque's location was hard to best.

For us members of this small detail, our tasks were simple enough—to clean several recently occupied rooms, to help the manager of this base's modest bar with various tasks, and to work as scullions in its ordinary. I spent most of the first day working at Malmousque's bar. Its offerings were typical for the Legion and included the Foreign Legion's official wines, the Legion's unofficial beer, *Kronenbourg*, bottles of pastis, and a few national liquors. It had an espresso machine and several snacks and sandwiches for sale. A portly, red-haired *caporal-chef* staffed the bar and treated us with relative kindness throughout the day. Sliding glass doors separated the bar, soaked all day in the August sunlight, from a large cement terrace that commanded arresting sea views. Below this terrace, small groups peopled diverse formations of rocks, and many women were sunbathing with their breasts bared for the sun's comprehensive tanning effects. For recruits unaccustomed to this habit, these topless women of all ages became the foremost topic of conversation.

Throughout the day, diverse and interesting men came into the bar. Some were legionnaires on leave, others former legionnaires who stopped by out of nostalgia or for practical reasons. One of these was an Australian who had completed his five-year contract and was now working somewhere in Europe. He strongly recommended that we finish our five-year contract and then leave the Legion for other adventures. It was worth the five-year experience to him, but no more. He had mostly positive things to say about the Legion, and he commended us for our adventure that was only just beginning.

After a day of random tasks and exercising on the pull-up bars that one finds at every Foreign Legion outpost, no matter how small, we ate dinner at Malmousque's ordinary. The facility's quiet and the leisurely pace of our meal contrasted with our experiences at Aubagne. For the first time, we recruits were able to hold conversations over our meals, and I spoke mostly with a young man from Moldova, whose French was already excellent. For years he had been working in Italy as a cook, and by serving in the Legion he was angling to gain French citizenship and to save enough money to start his own restaurant back in Italy. He never made it to basic training. After dinner we spent more time at work and cleaning before we were allowed to go to sleep in a large room with stone walls. Windows near its ceiling opened unto adjoining beaches.

As we lay down to sleep, the voices of women—voices that sounded young and fertile to our imaginations—wafted through these open windows. To no avail, one French recruit tried to climb up the stone walls to peer outside of the windows. This failure notwithstanding, he raved about all the bare-breasted *gonzesses* that he had supposedly ogled throughout the day.

In the middle of the night, I woke up to go to the *chiottes*, which were wretchedly equipped but, as is the Legion's wont, remarkably clean. All were sleeping, so I took this chance to walk outside our room and to climb up onto the fort's walls. It was past midnight, but voices from the beaches below still beckoned. Back then I knew nothing of local winds, but a warm one, probably the *sirocco*, blew in force. I must have spent half an hour alone on the walls, overlooking the sea, held in place by a *volupté* unique to Mediterranean nights. It swelled within me as I walked back to my cot in the stone-walled room and fell asleep.

X

September 2008

The work detail at Malmousque was the plummiest of them all. At Aubagne, aside from our most common details of cleaning up the ordinary and its kitchen after each meal, sweeping and mopping offices and *chiottes* throughout the regiment, and picking up cigarette butts (or *mégots*) everywhere, other regular *corvée* took place at a large nineteenth-century residence that overlooked the highway next to the base and housed the regimental officers' club. Here we often prepared the dining room and other areas for formal events. Keen as I was on matters of etiquette, some corporals' exacting standards for proper table settings impressed me.

During my five or more weeks at Aubagne, I was also taken for a detail at Puyloubier, a rural town to the east of Aix-en-Provence that hosts the Legion's facility for wounded veterans, or *invalides*. This establishment rests on the foundations of a former Roman villa and spans over 200 hectares. Founded in the 1950s, the Legion's home for wounded veterans has lived up to its charter to house and to take care of all legionnaires who had faithfully served the institution, but with nowhere else to turn. As I surveyed the entrance to the estate and its idyllic surroundings in the perfect weather of early September in Provence, I mused that this location might be a swell place to hole up for a few years should I ever fall on hard times.

The *caporal-chef* who drove us four legionnaires to Puyloubier did not have anything for us to do upon arrival, so he left us to wait on the terrace of the bar near the estate's entrance. There a man in his mid-thirties—short, thin, and with black hair—came out to greet us. Of Russian origins, for some reason this man had come to live at Puyloubier after serving his customary five-year contract. He seemed annoyed at his overall situation, but nonetheless voiced appreciation for Puyloubier's tranquillity. He served us coffee, and I think that he even gave us iced cream. During our wait, I explored as much of the estate as I could while staying within eyeshot and earshot of the bar. Puyloubier's buildings had clearly been refashioned in the nineteenth century, but some of their architectural elements betrayed more ancient provenance.

We ended up loitering at that bar for about two hours. At some point the Hungarian *caporal-chef* in charge of us came back to fetch and to lead us to the estate's ordinary. It was remarkably clean. After lunch, during which we discussed the Legion and its possibilities with this kindly *caporal-chef*, he assigned us to clean the ordinary and several surrounding buildings. Thereafter he brought me to the room of a former legionnaire who had just died. My task was to sort through his personal belongings, to box them up, and to clean the room in preparation for an incoming occupant.

The recently deceased man was German. Looking through his photographs and his medals, it became clear that he had served in the Legion's campaigns in Algeria in the late 1950s and early 1960s, where he had seen combat. He had probably joined the Legion in the early 1950s. It is often believed that most German legionnaires of that generation had previously served in the *Wehrmacht* or the *Schutzstaffel*, but among his personal belongings there was no evidence of this. It was more inspiring to me than it was tragic to rummage through this dead legionnaire's few artefacts remaining from a lifetime whose adventure and daring exceeded that of most humans on our planet. There was no correspondence with family or friends, no photographs of loved ones, and nothing to indicate that he had any connections outside of Puyloubier. During this task I thought of Pushkin's words from *Eugene Onegin*:

> *Sometimes we like to listen / To the tumultuous language of the passions / Of others, and it stirs our heart; / Exactly thus an old disabled soldier / Does willingly bend an assiduous ear / To the yarns of young moustached braves / while he remains forgotten in his shack.**

What would this German have thought about young legionnaires coming back from Afghanistan or from Africa in 2008? Would he have listened with eagerness or with disdain to tales about our age's own "savage wars of peace"?

As I stood on the cusp of years of intense soldiering, I could not help but reflect on my own future as I sifted through this German's effects. What I gleaned from them, but could not clearly express at the time, was that disappointed ambition and dashed hopes usually await young men who join militaries not for spoils, for pillage, and for rapine, but for what they believe to be patriotic ideas, just ambitions, and glory. The former's animalistic appetency is tumultuous but often sated, whereas among the more idealistic latter, only few slowly uncover:

> [the] rending pain of re-enactment / of all that you have done, and been; the shame / of motives late revealed, and the awareness / of things ill done and done to others' harm / which once you took for exercise of virtue / Then fools' approval stings and honour stains.†

* A.S. Pushkin, Eugene Onegin, Chapter I, Stanza XLVI:
Мы любим слушать иногда / Страстей чужих язык мятежный / И нам он сердце шевелит. / Так точно старый инвалид / Охотно клонит слух прилежный / Рассказам юных усачей / Забытый в хижине своей.

† T.S. Eliot, Little Gidding, Part II

Many self-critical former soldiers probably remain suspended between bitterness at their thwarted hopes and disappointments and some awareness of their wrong-headed motives. The more blissful cannot acknowledge these things and instead nurse lies and falsehoods until death.

The aged German probably had set out to meet his Maker without any sacramental consolations or succour. There was no one to grieve him and no one to remember him save for the few workers and colleagues at Puyloubier and for me, who looked carefully through his few photographs before storing them away in a cardboard box bound for a dustbin in due time.

That legionnaire had suffered more than most, he had fought in the desert, and he had weathered his fill of adventure's boredom. These things are not vanity.

Even now I wish that voyager a heartful "fare forward."

XI

September 2008

About two weeks had passed since my arrival at Aubagne on 17 August 2008. To that point I had not found any of the Legion's tests or activities overly trying. The work details at Malmousque and Puyloubier had proven to be interesting, and I enjoyed aspects of my new community of prospective legionnaires.

Rumours swirled about our pending summons to speak with the Legion's internal security service, which we called "the Gestapo." This was usually the last interview at Aubagne for *engagés volontaires*. Already we were familiar with the Gestapo's unremarkable building, whose yard we had cleared of cigarette butts many times during *corvée*. The wiry young Mexican American spoke with the Gestapo before anyone else in the Anglophone group. He warned us that somehow, probably through Interpol, the Gestapo knew about assault and battery charges brought against him over a decade earlier in a small town near El Paso, Texas. I did not remember much that I wished to hide from the Gestapo, but nonetheless the thought of the interview fazed me.

One morning a corporal from the Legion's recruitment staff brought me and several other recruits from our barrack compound to the Gestapo's redoubtable three-storied headquarters. Our escorts accompanied us upstairs to a long hallway where each of us awaited his turn for an interview with Gestapo personnel. Since many recruits spoke no French whatsoever, the Gestapo employed non-commissioned officers who were native speakers of the world's major languages to conduct these interviews. My French was sufficient for this matter, so I was pooled with the French-speaking group.

At first a Romanian non-commissioned officer with excellent French and good English asked me basic questions about my past. He was especially curious about the outstanding debt from my university years in the United States. Indeed, he seemed to believe that I was running away from this debt, because otherwise he could not imagine why I was leaving the United States. After finishing our discussion, he mentioned that his supervisor wished to speak with me and sent me back into the hallway to wait.

Before long this Romanian ushered me into a large and brightly lit office and left me alone with his supervisor, who was sitting behind a desk and looking at files. I stood awkwardly at attention, relaxing only at the instructions of this lieutenant-colonel in his early forties. Dark-haired, he was slightly overweight, and he wore the typical summer dress uniform that the Legion used in those years. He smoked cigarettes throughout our discussion, a classic touch that I appreciated. Few details of his office come to mind other than engraved artillery shells near his desk. Before all else, he asked me if I was able to shower in the barracks, since my body's odour somehow penetrated the thick cigarette smoke that wafted about the whole room. I answered that we showered every night, but that I had been wearing the same shirt and shorts for over seven days.

A few weeks before I would have been fearful of the prospect of having a conversation and interview in French, but even the short time locked up in the Legion's pen had given me a confidence with French that I hitherto could not have mustered. He first asked me about the notebook that I had brought with me. Perhaps owing to my transcription in Hebrew from Ecclesiastes, he asked me if I had ever maintained associations with any Israeli intelligence services and eyed me with suspicion. In his pupils I imagined *soupçons* of discreet *anti-Dreyfusard* sentiments that he never would have acknowledged beyond his own trusted circles. He accepted my answers to the negative and then asked about my family history, financial background, and motivations for joining the Legion. He concluded that I must indeed have a "fire in my arse."

To his queries, I answered that I was interested in pursuing a long-term military career, but that, in any event, serving out a five-year contract in the Foreign Legion would be an extraordinary experience, and I would be glad to set out on different adventures after its conclusion should things not turn out to my liking. I did make known to him my interest in becoming an officer in the Foreign Legion, should all the necessary stars align.

All this made sense enough to him. What began as an interrogation evolved into banter more philosophical in nature. He noted that it would be exceedingly challenging for me to take orders from the mostly uneducated and violent young men who would be my superiors for the next few years. To this I answered that I had already experienced some of this and that there is much for a man to learn through such humiliation. He gave his assent with a thoughtful nod. At length, he sat back in his chair. Waving a lit cigarette in one hand, he spoke words that filled me with motivation for this new enterprise.

"Remember," said the lieutenant-colonel, "when others see someone like you, many will dislike you and instead of being inspired to follow your example, they will want to drag you down to their level." He elaborated on this theme for about a minute. His comments on this occasion flattered me, inspired me, and left me with the belief that I was destined for great military feats in the Legion. Perhaps he was sincere in his comments, which were skilfully put to influence a young man drenched in the Classics and obsessed with Caesar's *Commentaries on the Gallic Wars* and Cicero's *The Dream of Scipio*, facts whose broad outlines he could have understood from paging through my notebook.

Five months later, after finishing the Legion's selection and basic training, while taking my first holiday at Malmousque in Marseilles, I saw this lieutenant-colonel among a group of officers in winter uniforms, sitting at a table in the bar overlooking the ocean with obligatory Kronenbourg beers at hand.

I wanted to thank him for his encouragement, but to do so would have been untoward.

XII

September 2008

In the months before travelling to Marseilles to join the Legion, I was worried that deficient eyesight might disqualify me from serving in the organization. Years of reading in dimly lit libraries and countless hours of staring into computer screens had taken a toll on my vision, leaving me nearsighted to such an extent that soon after finishing university I needed to wear prescription glasses to drive an automobile. In the year prior to my planned enlistment in the Legion, I bought a book of eye exercises that promised to restore vision to normal military standards, what we called "twenty-twenty vision" in the United States. These exercises worked, and my vision improved.

Not knowing how exacting the Legion's medical standards would be, I had many doubts as I went through the Legion's medical tests and examinations, which took place during my first weeks at Aubagne. As it turned out, there were no problems during my vision examinations. The dentist who looked at my teeth found nothing of concern. My blood and urine tests all came back satisfactory. The only hitch, to my knowledge, was a hearing test, which they asked me to repeat with a professional audiologist. Such repeated hearing tests were quite normal for aspiring legionnaires, so I thought little of this.

A few days after the initial hearing tests at Aubagne, several of us *engagés volontaires* went to Marseilles one morning to take more precise hearing tests at the Laveran military training hospital. This outing was a treat for us, since in this public setting the corporal in charge of us treated us civilly and let us buy coffee and snacks from vending machines. After several weeks of deprivation, by this time I appreciated even freeze-dried coffee, so I had several cups while awaiting my appointment. At length the corporal brought us to an audiology clinic, where a middle-aged Asian man carried out tests in a sound-resistant booth. Several of us went through this booth in turn. For all the other recruits the tests' results came back positive, so I had few concerns. When my turn came, I walked into the booth fully expecting the tests to go well, since before this I had no awareness of any hearing loss.

As the Asian man looked at my test results, he shook his head with unmistakable disappointment to communicate that these results were not acceptable. I asked him to take the test again and he obliged, so I took especial care to listen for the faintest sounds. Once again, according to the tests, my hearing did not meet the Foreign Legion's minimal standards for admission to its ranks, but I did not understand this at the time. The technician simply told me that the tests were not satisfactory and that I would probably not be able to serve in the Legion. The corporal in charge drove us back to Aubagne. During this drive and subsequent days, my mind swirled in foreboding and dread that I would not, after all, be admitted to the Legion. All this came as a shock to me.

Days went by after these tests, and I was still in Aubagne. Having completed all of the requirements to move on to basic training, I was given a few military uniforms and basic equipment, thereby becoming part of the group called *rouges*, which took its name from the red bands that we wore around one shoulder. In becoming *rouges* we had begun the last progression from civilian life before our departure for initial training at Castelnaudary, and therefore sat atop our pen's pecking order. Instead of newcomers who wore physical fitness clothing and running shoes, we wore military uniforms and sported black leather

French Army boots, which we polished with exaggerated enthusiasm at least ten times a day. Having more experience with Aubagne's unique circumstances than most other *engagés volontaires* at this point, we were also responsible for additional tasks and for the reception and incorporation of new recruits. I knew that my hearing tests had caused some problems, since I had not progressed to Castelnaudary with a group of *rouges* that left us one morning. Instead, I stayed behind for additional testing or decisions. The only hint about my status came when a lieutenant who had recently interviewed me stopped me and asked about my hearing. Yet, as the days passed and I remained in the selection process, I assumed that some solution had been found and that my hearing could not possibly be that problematic.

To this day I do not know how or when my hearing was damaged, but one possibility comes to mind. Although I did shoot large rifles and shotguns without adequate hearing protection in my youth, this was not frequent enough to make me think that such rare blasts had damaged the hearing exclusively in my left ear. In the aftermath of these tests with the Legion, I thought back to various episodes in my life. At length I remembered a night when I was about six years old, when my family lived in an early-twentieth-century house on the border between Louisiana and Texas. That night in winter I had a painful ear infection that kept me awake. Panicked and not knowing how to assuage the throbbing pain in my left ear, throughout the night I used a cup to pour tap water into my ear, the only action that seemed to calm the pain momentarily. Early in the morning, relief of this pain came when my left eardrum ruptured. My mother hurried me to a doctor as soon as possible, but at that point options for further treatment were few and the worst had passed. Perhaps my eardrum would have ruptured no matter what, but putting water in my ear all night probably did not help matters.

Whatever had caused the hearing loss in my left ear, this loss had a lasting impact on my career in the Legion and determined several broad outlines of my life's subsequent course.

XIII

September 2008

Over five weeks had passed since I had come to Aubagne. It became clear that our group of *rouges* would soon be heading to basic training. At an office in our compound, we hurriedly signed additional papers that few of us could read. In a spirited and virile uproar, we prepared our newly acquired military possessions for the journey to Castelnaudary, headquarters of the Foreign Legion's Fourth Foreign Regiment, where all new recruits undergo the Legion's unique "integration" for about four months before heading to their first assigned units.

The night before our departure a man with a black kepi and a Polish-sounding surname arrived to meet us and to let us know that he was escorting us to Castelnaudary. He was one of the sergeants who would be responsible for our training over the coming months. Blond, stocky, and well-built, to us he looked to be in fearsome physical shape. His most distinguishing features were his large, bulging blue eyes that displayed a rare intensity and seemed to promise unknown tortures and hardships. He spoke French confidently, peppered though it was with standard phrases from the Legion's demotic idiom that are not at all common to modern French. His thick accent and deep, staccato voice quickly became distinctive to us. His demeanour and bearing switched unpredictably between joviality and intensity. Most of us liked and feared him.

Later a tall, lanky, and angry-looking sergeant from the Ukraine's western regions joined him. He spoke French with a pronounced and almost violent Eastern European accent. I could not place his native language, to which he almost always reverted when speaking to legionnaires of Slavic origins, but it seemed to comprise some mix of Russian, Ukrainian, and Polish. Most of us *rouges* still did not understand how to read the uniforms of legionnaires, non-commissioned, and commissioned officers—an essential skill for any soldier —so we spent quite a bit of time speculating about the various decorations and badges on these sergeants' uniforms. Their speech was usually direct and short, and they took every occasion to remind us that we were about to begin in earnest our formation as legionnaires. Sometimes with intense stares and sometimes to menacing laughter, they repeated the words, "*Vous allez voir*."

We awoke very early the next morning for travel to Marseilles' Saint Charles Station. It was about half past five in the morning when we formed up outside the station's main entrance, on the large square from which I had walked down to stroll to *La Canebière* a few weeks earlier. As we stood together in silence and in rigid formation, lingering evidence of the night's recreational activities in the station's seedy surroundings faded as the sky lightened above us. Although the square was empty at our arrival, before long commuters and workers trickled through it with varied trajectories either heading for trains or for the city. Most of them took a moment in passing to gaze at us. For my part, I was thrilled to have made it out of Aubagne, and I took especial note of the sky's colours in the early morning, as seagulls flew and cried above us and workers swept and sprayed the begrimed pavements with soapy water from pressure washers.

At length, the sergeants in charge of us gave us tickets and we boarded a slow, four-hour regional train from Marseilles to Carcassonne. We sat mainly with each other, but the occasional civilian sat near or among us. Most of them looked at us with concern. When a young lady in the national train service's employ walked through our cabin and offered to sell us drinks, I asked for a coffee.

As I was paying, the Polish sergeant looked at me with admonishment in his eyes while simultaneously shaking his head and index finger. More fearful than disappointed, I put away my money. That morning I did not have any coffee.

As we alighted at Castelnaudary's small station, the overcast skies and cooler temperatures, taken together with the station's dreariness, did little to encourage us. Military buses awaited us in front of the station, and we boarded them not knowing what to expect or where we were going.

The trip to the Fourth Foreign Regiment was quick enough, as within a few minutes we were driving beside a chain-link fence that surrounded much of the base. Posted at regular intervals on this fence were signs that read: *terrain militaire, défense d'entrer.** When reading them it occurred to me that this was, to my memory, the first time in my life that I would enter a military base.

Legionnaires in full-dress uniform greeted our buses as we arrived at the base's gates. As they did for every passing vehicle, they saluted us as we left the outside world and crossed into the Fourth Foreign Regiment. Before us stood its large, empty *place d'armes*. The buses turned left, then right.

It was still morning when we arrived at our company. Its concrete buildings' drab construction, dating from the 1960s, promised Spartan living. The military state's utter foreignness to me, combined with the Legion's unique culture and this new environment in rural France, filled me with feelings and sensations that I could not label with words. Never before had I experienced such a concentrated combination of opposite and conflicting ideas, thoughts, feelings, and spiritual reactions, and I have never felt this combination since that day. I have spoken about this experience with other legionnaires. No matter their backgrounds, many of them have seconded my idea that entering the Fourth Foreign Regiment was the most bizarre and unsettling moment of their lives.

We were assigned to the regiment's second company, which wore red arm bands. Its company song was based on a popular German paratrooper anthem from the last great war, "*Die Sonne Scheint*." It was a weekend, and the company

---

* Military area, entry is forbidden.

building was quiet. We settled into our rooms and began learning the company song. Our Korean corporal's pedagogical battery took place that evening.

XIV

September 2008

The most bizarre moments of my life so far quickly became the stuff of habit, thus confirming one of those truths for humankind that Pushkin so artfully corralled into two lines of iambic tetrameter:

> Habit is a gift of God / It is the substitute for happiness.*

During the first few days at the Fourth Foreign Regiment—which we already abbreviated to "Castel" among ourselves—we took standard physical fitness tests. At the time these tests comprised pull-ups with palms facing away from the body, abdominal crunches, a rope-climb, and a timed run. To be considered a *bon sportif* in the Foreign Legion, one had to perform at least twelve to fifteen pull-ups, to run 3,200 metres in twelve minutes, and to climb six metres of rope without using one's legs.

Of all these, the truest metric in the Legion was the *teste Cooper*, named

* A.S. Pushkin, *Eugene Onegin*, Chapter II, Stanza XXXI: Привычка свыше нам дана: замена счастию она.

after the man who first developed it for the United States Army. This test's goal was to run as far as possible in twelve minutes on a four-hundred metre track. In our initial *testes Cooper*, a recruit from Senegal ran over 3,600 metres in twelve minutes. A bald forty-year-old German, whom the Legion had baptized as Müller, beat this impressive feat with a run that surpassed 3,800 metres. For my part, I ran about 3,000 metres, which was good enough for me given the lingering consequences of ten years of smoking cigarettes and forswearing any deliberate physical activity or sport.

During these tests I was unable to climb a rope at all owing to the injury from the Korean corporal's repeated punches to my sternum. This angered me since I had spent over a year building the strength needed to climb ropes skilfully and without using my legs. Instead, I came away looking like a pathetic weakling. I squeaked out ten or so pull-ups since, for some reason, performing this exercise did not strain my sternum as much as the rope-climb.

After these fitness tests, several of us wounded by the Korean corporal asked to see the Legion's medics, since the effects of his discipline had clearly undermined our physical capabilities. A chubby Belorussian corporal took us to the medical office. We explained our injuries to the chief medic, a middle-aged Romanian who, to judge by his many exasperated outbreaks and scowls, probably should have penned his own *Journal of a Disappointed Man*. After hearing our complaints, he threatened us, screamed, and made it clear that if we came back with similar gripes, we would leave the clinic with greater injuries still. When this medic learned that I was from the United States, he decried the land of my birth's evil influence on the world, and especially on France. "With Chirac we still had a French president," he shouted in the clinic's hallway, "but Sarkozy is Jewish!" After ranting about the baleful dealings of World Jewry and the United States, he booted us out of the clinic.

Over the few remaining days in Castelnaudary, we learned the basic ways of life in garrison at the Fourth Foreign Regiment. These included how to line up and to march in formation toward the dining hall, how to sing the company's song in a reasonably sonorous way, and how to file through the dining hall in silence during appointed mealtimes. Three times daily we cleaned our rooms and hallways and circled about the company area, picking up any rubbish and ubiquitous *mégots*. On the whole, our food was plentiful and of decent quality. We new arrivals formed one platoon in our assigned company. Interactions with the company's other two platoons were limited, but already gossip and rumours abounded. A few times we caught glimpses of our platoon leader, a non-commissioned officer (*adjudant* in the Legion) from French Polynesia with an English last name. During this time, we were given a basic issue of military gear, to include rucksacks and sleeping bags. Also, we visited the company armoury to be assigned our individual FAMAS rifles, whose serial numbers we put to memory.

In the evenings we began our first all-night guard shifts, both in the hallways allotted to our platoon and elsewhere on the base. One of these evenings I was assigned to guard the place where the regiment kept its vehicles and petrol fuelling points—what is called a "motor pool" in the US Army. To a new recruit like me, even such a mundane task was full of interest and intrigue, and I would guess that most of us approached this and similar tasks with surfeits of motivation. Armed with a baton to which the key to the petrol fuelling point was attached, in pairs we patrolled the area throughout the night.

After midnight, as I fulfilled my two-hour shift with eagerness, peering out into the darkness beyond the regiment's fences for unknown enemies, our platoon sergeant—a *sergeant-chef* in the Legion—walked out to inspect us. He was a haughty and fat-cheeked Frenchman whose every word oozed contempt for us, which he often amplified by taking the time to contort his face into actual sneers—perhaps the first time in my life that I had seen such facial expressions in the flesh. He said a few words to us, sneered, sniffed loudly, and made his way back to the company.

During lunches and dinners, as we lined up for our meals, all the ordinary's eyes were upon us as the newest recruits who had not yet made it through "the farm." One platoon from a different company had just come back from the farm, and most of its members were haggard in appearance and gazed upon the ordinary's food with ravenous eyes. Prevailing verdicts and rumours about their experience at the farm were mixed. For some it was the worst thing that one could ever go through in life, whereas for others it was not that bad, or something that, albeit challenging, had many positive aspects.

We had not long to find out for ourselves.

XV

September 2008

We had only a few days at Castel before moving out to "the farm," the crucible of the Foreign Legion's basic-training experience. Positioned on the departmental road D119 that winds southwest from Fanjeaux to Mirepoix, *La Ferme du Cuin* was the second company's rustic and newly renovated retreat, mostly used for training aspiring legionnaires. Each of the Fourth Foreign Regiment's four main training companies had its own farm, sequestered from the world's prying eyes and without the many distractions of garrison life.

The ride from Castelnaudary to our new lodging lasted about twenty-five minutes. Along the route there were numerous signs welcoming tourists to the *pays cathare*. To me, it seemed that local tourist offices must have been trying to profit from heresy's chic among a recently Catholic, but now religiously indifferent, society. I doubt that *pays cathare* promotions yielded great tourist harvests, since even heresy's tang was fading at that time. I knew more about the Cathars than most contemporary young men, since Hilaire Belloc's treatment of them in his *The Great Heresies* had intrigued me and led me to read quite a few articles and monographs about Saint Dominic's struggles against Cathar enthusiasms.

On this first ride I remember seeing the monastery *Sainte Marie de Prouille*, where Saint Dominic himself had spent some years in the thirteenth century.

Stately plane trees commonly found along France's departmental roads—or *platanes*—were thick with late summer's mature blooms as we sped through various townships. Before long we entered a stretch of open fields and turned left off the departmental road and onto a barely paved trail. Here the buses stopped. Our sergeants ordered us out of the buses and promptly had us do push-ups and other martial exercises. Then we sprinted the rest of the way from the gate to the farm buildings, led by one sergeant and spurred by others. Once there, more push-ups and stock forms of physical activity awaited us.

After such physical performances, the platoon leadership—our *cadres* or cadre, to use the English borrowing—introduced us to the layout of the farm, to its expectations, and to its rhythms. On the farm's northernmost side two buildings lay parallel to each other—the farm's combined ordinary and all-purpose ("polyvalent") room and our sleeping areas. Both buildings must have dated from the nineteenth century, but perhaps they were nineteenth-century reconstructions of older buildings. In the dormitories to the northeast, we recruits slept upstairs, while our cadre dwelt downstairs in better accommodations. We walked through our sleeping areas, grabbed cots, and stood where corporals told us to stand. About fifteen of us shared one of the upstairs rooms, and we began setting up our living spaces according to the Legion's meticulous standards. It took hours to do so.

In a small room above the ordinary lived a Polish *caporal-chef*. His job was to take care of the farm during the absence of cadre and soldiers. His life here must have been truly anchoretic. I only spoke a few words to him throughout our stay at the farm, but I remember his introductory speech when we arrived, the respect that our cadre showed him, and his passion for "his farm," whose grounds we would damage and sully at our peril. To the southeast lay the farm's obstacle course, or *parcours du combattant*, comprising twenty obstacles standard throughout the French military. On the farm's southern side stood the training "classroom" where we spent most of our time. This classroom was a large, uninsulated structure paved in concrete, walled-in on three sides with painted cinderblocks, and roofed with sheet metal. Its unwalled side overlooked a well-kept field with a large rendering of the Foreign Legion's symbol, the seven-flamed grenade, assembled from painted rocks.

Most of the farm's rules would not rattle anyone with sound military experience, but one did bewilder me. Recruits were allowed to smoke cigarettes throughout basic training at appointed hours. Our cadre—who otherwise showed brutality probably unmatched in contemporary Western European militaries, and who withheld from us basic items for hygiene such as toilet paper for weeks at a time—nonetheless took great pains to ensure, almost delicately so, that recruits who smoked had time, space, and special areas to indulge their habit. Odder still, despite such extravagant accommodations for smokers, they were not allowed to buy cigarettes or otherwise to resource them from outside the farm. These circumstances made for a lively black-market trade.

At some point that first day, we formed up in front of the ordinary for dinner. Before filing in for our meal, we aligned our metal canteen cups in rows whose symmetry the *caporal du jour*—or corporal in charge for the day—had to approve before we could enter the ordinary. This ordeal sometimes took as much as half an hour. As I took my first tray of food, a boyish-looking young corporal from the Maghreb looked at me and remarked that I would be losing a lot of weight. He was right. I entered the Legion as strong as I have ever been, weighing approximately eighty-five kilogrammes. I left the farm weighing about seventy kilogrammes.

Before we could eat any meal, it was required to enact an established ritual—the singing of the Legion's anthem, "*Tiens, voilà du boudin*." I already knew this song by heart, but I did not know the anticlerical tune that legionnaires used to set our collective pitch. Before beginning "*Tiens, voilà du boudin*," a designated legionnaire chimed in clear tones: "*Encore un giron d'enculé, sous la guitoune de l'aumônier!*"* After this introductory chant, we sang. If the corporals judged

* "Look here, another catamite hiding under the chaplain's tent!"

our singing poor, we repeated the song until it passed muster. Then we drank an entire canteen cup filled with water before sitting down for our meals.

Unlike in other armed forces, whose training cadre often force new recruits to stuff down their food with hurried desperation, we had leisure to eat. This was the French Army, and it brooked no affronts to principles of sound digestion.

XVI

September 2008

The next day, the regimental commander came to visit us. Once we had finished our first morning run through the surrounding countryside, our cadre herded us through preparations for the colonel's visit. To those recruits new to the military life, the prospect of welcoming this tall, lanky colonel with distinctively large ears was daunting. After driving up in his white official Renault sedan, he carried out a quick but engaged review of our formation. With befitting gravity, he surveyed us gathered before him. Then, in a brief elocution, he promised us that life in the Legion would be hard and challenging and congratulated us for making *la choix d'un homme*—"a manly choice." He was correct. No matter what our shortcomings, our illusions, and our individual reasons for joining, to make it thus far each of us had made manly choices.

This same day acquainted us with the farm's enduring rhythms. After waking up about four o'clock in the morning, we dressed in the Legion's skimpy sports clothing and, as every morning in the Legion, began the day with *corvée*. For about thirty minutes we cleaned various areas in our encampment and completed any other tasks that our *caporal du jour* assigned us. Once these details were finished, we formed up in the dissipating darkness and began conducting exercises in marching and drill and ceremony, for which the Legion's standards were high. Legionnaires march at the pace of eighty-eight steps per minute, an inheritance from its many Swiss members in the late nineteenth century. Learning to march at this unnaturally halting pace posed more challenges than the layman might think.

After this marching practice, we took our Legion breakfast that never changed—a small piece of bread and some jam and butter with coffee or hot chocolate. Afterward we carried out more cleaning chores and then assembled in front of the farm's small ceremonial area. About seven o'clock every morning, we stood together before the flagpole, raised the French tricolour along with the Legion's green-and-red flag, and listened to some words from our platoon leader. Following this we broke up into separate running categories based on our recent performance on the Cooper test. I found myself in the middling group.

Once in these groups, one of our three sergeants led us on runs through the surrounding countryside that lasted from one to three hours. I believe that our shortest run was eight kilometres, and the longest twenty-five to thirty. The average morning run was probably between fifteen to twenty kilometres. However much our platoon leader boasted about the purportedly "scientific" planning behind these runs, in retrospect there seemed to be little science to them. Corporals enforced our speed and endurance throughout these runs through various means of verbal and physical motivation. The Polish sergeant was, perhaps, the easiest leader of these runs, followed by the lanky Ukrainian sergeant. The most dreaded sergeant for such runs was Sergeant Park, a stout and muscular Korean from the Second Foreign Parachute Regiment. Once back from our runs, our sergeants led us through sessions of push-ups, pull-ups, abdominal crunches, and rope-climbs that usually lasted no longer than half an hour. After these we showered and changed into our combat uniforms.

These frigid showers represented a noteworthy chance to defecate in a relatively clean way since we rarely had hygienic paper. Many of us tried to hold our bowel movements until this time of the day. Deliberately deprived of hygienic paper, we saw these daily showers as our best opportunity to wash ourselves thoroughly. At any other time, there were few means for normal hygiene. In this case, as in so many others, the Legion expected and taught us "to make do," a phrase more colourfully rendered in French as *démerdez-vous*. The sense of this phrase is indeed "to make do," but its literal translation is "to de-shit oneself." It was in the most extreme and literal of ways, therefore, that the Legion taught its recruits new and compelling meanings of *se démerder*.

After these showers we had lessons on topics related to soldiering—such as assembling and disassembling our FAMAS rifles, moving in tactical formations, learning how to tie knots, and operating radio systems. In general, this training's quality was high. Before long came lunch, after which we once again cleaned areas in the camp and fulfilled other assigned *corvée*. In the afternoon we returned to our varied instruction. At some point before forming up for dinner we again practiced marching in formation. Once dinner ended, we moved to the classroom where we learned and practiced Legion songs for hours.

Throughout our stay at the farm, we learned about twenty Legion songs by heart. Since I had years of classical training in singing and the best baritone voice in the group, I emerged as a leader for our chants, along with a young tenor from Madagascar who seemed to have perfect pitch. All my favorite songs were inherited from German legionnaires, including "*Westerwald*," which we sang in the original German, and "the wild geese." The latter was originally entitled "*Wildgänse rauschen durch die Nacht*," but we learned it as *Les oies sauvages* and sang it in a French translation. We were released to shower and to go to sleep at some point after midnight. Often, we stayed up singing until well past two o'clock in the morning before our corporals ended our chorus.

This rhythm was typical from Monday through Thursday every week at the farm. It changed only toward the end of our stay, as we hurried to finish training requirements and conducted evaluations and events that marked the end of this trying sojourn. There we received a sound basic military formation coupled with sizeable, skilful doses of instruction in the French language. Many recruits in my platoon with little or no French upon their initial entry left the farm with functional fluency in the Legion's peculiar jargon, which relied on evocative phrases and images to convey meaning, intent, and emotion.

XVII

September–October 2008

Friday was upon us. All that week our corporals forewarned us about the forced march on Friday evening. That morning we ran as usual, but a shorter distance. After lunch we began preparations for the march, packing our rucksacks with assigned items and ensuring that they fit properly on our backs. I estimate that our "packing list" weighed about twenty kilogrammes. At this time, the Legion had just fielded a new rucksack and we legionnaires benefited from this, since older models were infamous for rubbing the skin off legionnaires' backs.

In the early afternoon the Polish sergeant formed up our platoon and threatened us with the prescribed words—"*vous allez voir*!" We stepped off on a march that wound through the open lands to the farm's south, along roads already familiar to us from our morning runs. In the end this march continued until about 2100 and lasted for what must have been six hours. It reduced many participants to limping back to the base, and we left behind ten or so members of our platoon as they straggled and became lost. For over two hours we waited in our open-air classroom while cadre went to look for our lost *engagés volontaires*.

At long last they all came back in a military truck.

It was almost midnight by the time we filed into the ordinary and ate one of the most enjoyable meals of our time at the farm, since we were starving and quite cold. We did not sing after this dinner but instead were allowed to go to sleep relatively early. During this whole time, I dealt with the consequences of the Korean corporal's punches to my chest. Although I could complete most tasks and exercises, I still could not climb a rope. Whenever I lay down sharp pains radiated throughout my upper chest. Whereas it merely hurt to breathe that first night after the corporal's punches, by this time the act of breathing while lying down on a cot brought sharp and regular pain. However tired I was, these pains kept me awake until exhaustion overcame them.

The next day we did not go for a morning run, which surprised us. It was well enough that we did not run since most of us were nursing painful wounds on our feet. For my part, that Saturday I treated the first and only blister from a ruck march of my whole military career, caused mainly by the hard black leather of our standard-issue boots. Some recruits' feet, however, looked like minced meat. Several corporals stayed with us that morning and helped us to tend to our wounds, since few of us knew how properly to treat them. While dressing these wounds we also used electronic clippers to cut our hair to the shortest possible length that did not actually leave us bald. After lunch we held well-structured French classes with the platoon leader.

Several hours before dinner, we began clearing out the normal tables from the ordinary's main room and setting up taller tables at which one could stand. On these tables our cadre placed peanuts, crisps, and various snacks, all arranged with a mind for aesthetics. It was about seven o'clock in the evening when our platoon filed into the ordinary for our first Foreign Legion *pot*—a social event to build unit cohesion. The platoon leader watched closely as recruits rushed into the *pot*, many desperately scrambling for peanuts and pretzels. A few of us stood away from this frenzy, and on this account the platoon leader called us over to him and gave us pieces of sausage to reward us for our continence. To our surprise, that evening the cadre gave us all several bottles of Kronenbourg beer to drink, and we ate plates of cooked meats while mingling and singing Legion songs for a few hours. A timorous Muslim recruit from Tunisia protested that he did not drink alcohol, but the platoon leader shoved a bottle of beer in his face and decreed: "You do today." After this *pot* we went back to singing in our classroom, our voices cheerier than usual owing to the alcohol's effects.

The next morning was our first Sunday at the farm. Once again, we undertook *corvée*, hygiene, and French lessons after waking up noticeably later than usual. By late morning we were finishing various activities when the cadre took those of us in better physical condition and supervised us as we set up our classroom for a large communal meal. Two of the corporals had begun to barbecue meats and other items on open pits, and we gathered bottles of beer and the Foreign Legion's red wine, a *Côtes de Provence* that turned out to be perfectly respectable plonk. By noon, the meats were cooked, and the tables set with glasses, utensils, and tablecloths. We formed up, moved to the classroom, and gathered behind places at table.

The platoon leader sat at the centre table with cadre to his left and to his right, as one would imagine kings of old at banquet. We legionnaires sat behind rows of tables perpendicular to this centre table, making a shape like the letter "u." As usual, we began this feast with "*Tiens, voilà du boudin*," and the platoon leader had various legionnaires present themselves before the centre table and perform skits or sing songs particular to their nations. Our platoon's five citizens of the United States, for example, sang "The Star-Spangled Banner." Three Italians, two of whom would later desert in dramatic fashion, sang "*Bella Ciao*." Skits and singing continued for several hours, during which we all drank quantities of wine that left us tipsy. It was already past four o'clock in the afternoon when we wrapped up these festivities and cleaned the classroom. After a normal dinner, we began the usual weekly routine on the following Monday morning.

As our stay at the farm progressed, our weekends were as regular as our weeks, and usually included the above activities.

XVIII

October 2008

Today I no longer remember many of the farm's trials. As days passed, our platoon began to form its own identity as its members' abilities to speak in French improved, thereby allowing recruits without a prior common language to communicate. One day our platoon leader called me aside to talk with a teacher from a nearby university who was at the farm to observe the Legion's unique manner of teaching the French language to recruits, called the *méthode Képi Blanc*. This method mainly comprised singing and memorizing songs in French, endless repetition of words and phrases and the goading threat of physical punishment for any mistakes. It worked better than most.

When I joined the Foreign Legion, I spoke no foreign language fluently, despite my having studied several of them for years at university. Plunged into life at the farm, quickly I gained fluency in French. My Russian also improved markedly, as I often associated with our platoon's Russian speakers, who, all told, numbered about ten. Their perspectives, histories, and goals were fascinating to me. One Belorussian, who was almost an albino, often talked to me about his post-Legion plans. He had recently left behind his life as an officer in the

Belorussian Army to join the Legion. To be sure, he wished to improve his material situation, but he had the rather odd goal of becoming a detective in France after his initial five-year contract. A short, black-haired, and chain-smoking Ukrainian with the *nom de guerre* "Boris" confessed to me how happy he was to be in the Legion and that life at the farm was a kind of paradise when compared to his bleak former existence in the Ukraine.

The Foreign Legion's ethnic and national composition usually reflects world events. To this day, when one looks at registries of all legionnaires since the institution's foundation in 1831, the historical majority of them has come from Switzerland and Germany. Contrary to common banter, the influx of Germans to the Foreign Legion in the years immediately after 1945 was not exceptional. Of many factors contributing to the diminishing numbers of Germans and Swiss legionnaires throughout the twentieth century's latter half, increasing prosperity in both countries most likely played a role.

In the 1920s Russians came to the Legion in substantial numbers, but this Slavic influx was short-lived once it became harder to leave the Soviet Union. Again in the 1990s, Russians rushed into the Legion in droves, given the generalized chaos following the Soviet Union's collapse. By 2008, however, the situation in Russia had improved such that recruits from Russia itself were few and far between. Indeed, we had more United States citizens than Russians in our basic training platoon. That said, the situation in most of the Soviet Union's former satellite states had worsened since its collapse in 1991, and I would estimate that about 30 percent of our recruits were from ex-Soviet states. Their *lingua franca* was an amorphous version of Russian—simple, grammatically loose, and characterized by needless swear words.

During the five or so weeks that we spent at the farm, there was only one time when I regretted my decision to join the Foreign Legion. Sergeant Park had taken us out for a run that exceeded twenty-five kilometres. It had been raining all morning, and the autumn air was frigid, but we were only allowed to wear our skimpy shorts and tee-shirts. As we continued our run that morning the rain's intensity increased. At some point we were trudging, I think, the paved roads between Escueillens-et-Saint-Just-de-Bélengard and Mazerolles-du-Razès. We had just climbed and run down a long hill, and we looked up with dread at a larger hill that stretched before us. We were freezing and our wet polyester tee-shirts clung to our bodies. As our pace slackened along with our motivation, Sergeant Park screamed at us with terrifying intensity: "*En avant!*"

For some reason it was at the bottom of the hill that I thought of Yulia, a blonde Russian girl who was a graduate student at Princeton. I doubt that I had ever spoken to her on more than three occasions. One spring evening at Princeton we held a Russian poetry reading, which Yulia attended along with many other Russian graduate students. We dressed up smartly for the event, which my Ukrainian friend Olya and I hosted in a well-equipped room at the dormitories of Princeton's Graduate School. To wine, vodka, and Russian snacks—*zakuski*—we read poems for almost two hours. For my part, I read Nikolai Gumiloff's "The Tramway That Lost Its Way" and concluded the evening with Mikhail Lermontoff's "Demon." Afterward we descended to the Graduate School's *Debasement Bar* and drank vodka until its closure.

Yulia's role in that evening was marginal, but at the bottom of that hill I thought of her pleasant face, of her lithe young body, and of her soft voice when speaking Russian. That rainy morning on a hill in the Aude, for some unknown reason the image of Yulia reading poetry in the wainscoted rooms at Princeton University's Graduate College, warmed by fireplaces, overpowered me and made me ask myself: "What on earth am I doing here?" With this question in mind, I looked up at the hill before us, my legs aching, my body freezing.

These regrets lasted only a few moments, but it is the one time throughout my Legion career when I truly questioned my decision to join.

After this especially memorable and difficult run, Sergeant Park took us behind the open bays at the farm and gave what remains one of the most amusing motivational speeches that I have ever heard:

> "Being a legionnaire hurts sometimes. If you have pain in your knee, drink water. If you have pain in your back, stretch. *Si tu as*

mal à la tête, taper une branlette et en avant!"*

I would be surprised if many of us under the farm's training conditions could have managed enough sexual arousal to consummate Sergeant Park's advice.

---

* This latter phrase is hard to translate, but perhaps best rendered as: "If you have something messed-up in your head, beat one off and move out!"

XIX

October 2008

"Every knight-errant needs his Dulcinea." So remarked one of my colleagues at Princeton a month before I left the university in 2008. For he knew that I still desired a young lady from France who had left Princeton in spring 2007.

My enchantment with her beauty was constructive, as it helped me to overcome what I would still label the most formative passion of my life. In his review of Somerset Maugham's *Christmas Holiday*, Evelyn Waugh wryly remarked:

> "Mr. Maugham has elsewhere, more than once, given evidence of the belief that association with a Russian is a necessary part of an Englishman's adult education."

I second this idea for all men. My association began on Rome's *Via dell'Umiltà*, where in August 2005 I saw two girls busking, playing Bach's double violin concerto in D-minor. I congratulated them on their skilful performance and chatted with them that evening, thus beginning a shattering passion for one of these students from Saint Petersburg State Conservatory. When I matriculated at Princeton's Graduate School in autumn 2006, I had not overcome my obsession.

This passion calmed only as a *Versaillaise*'s charms overpowered it. I first saw her while I was working an odd job as a porter at Princeton's Graduate College, where she lived in a faux-gothic tower. Her hyphenated given names bespoke tradition notwithstanding their combination's rarity. They became familiar to me since I sorted students' mail and helped them with problems of daily life at these dormitories. In this job, I ended up seeing her and speaking with her frequently. Before long I found myself smitten and compelled to woo.

With twelve or thirteen years of perspective, what I told her in a well-written letter, accompanied by flowers, was not untrue—she was an exceptionally beautiful woman. Her features were mostly Latin, to include her thick, dark hair, her darker eyes, and the thin figure that betrayed both discipline and fortunate genetics. Her complexion was more Celtic or Germanic, however, as was, I think, her smile. It was a smile that overwhelmed her face, and it did not quite sit well with her other features.

The courtship that ensued was filled with charming coincidences. For example, at one point, when she was in a phase of responding to my attentions with cruel remarks and avoidance, she walked in late to the Mass which we both attended at Princeton. The usher sat her right in front of me. For the first time in my life, as someone fond of older liturgical norms, I was grateful for the customary handshaking during the "kiss of peace," typical of modernized Roman Catholic services. As she turned to face me that Sunday, I saw what usually happened whenever our gazes met—as soon as possible she forced her unorthodox smile and thrilled eyes into scowls and glares.

Today I find it remarkable that I had only courted her in earnest for two months before she let me know, with a clever and literary gesture, that she found my attentions interesting. For a woman so lovely, of good taste, responsible, and, as it turned out by coincidence, a faithful Catholic, my efforts were indeed paltry. Yet, when she finally did make known to me her cautious but serious interest in an unmistakable way, I, still smarting from the unwarranted testiness of her previous rejections, was unable to respond with grace. As she smiled purposefully and showed her willingness to discuss conditions of some budding attachment, I responded wordlessly with an angry stare. Thus, my wooing foundered. She left Princeton a month later to work at a bank in New York City.

About a year after I had answered so coldly her *disïato riso*, I was sitting on the steps of New York's Saint Patrick's Cathedral one Sunday afternoon prior to Mass. Given past coincidences, it barely surprised me when she and an older couple, clearly her parents, walked right by me. I gathered my aplomb and walked up to her in the nave, whereupon she scurried away to her mother's side. Her mother, visibly shocked at this public scene, asked who I was, and this young lady answered with a familiar smile on her face, "Someone from Princeton." Our eyes locked and we both managed to assume hardened facial expressions. We wished each other good luck from a distance and turned away, she to her parents to leave the cathedral and I to my pew for the afternoon Mass. It was all too fiery an episode for two privileged adults who had never even touched each other aside from a handshake at a Sunday liturgy.

The next week I wrote her a valedictory letter in polished French on Pineider *Vaticano* paper and gave the sealed envelope to one of her friends at Princeton for delivery. I have never seen her or heard from her since. Many months later, when already in the Legion, I came across a document that listed a colonel with her unusual surname as a director of studies at Saint-Cyr Military Academy. From what I glimpsed of her elderly father during that encounter at Saint Patrick's, he fit the bill for a French colonel.

I did not mind encouraging the thought that I might have joined the Foreign Legion for this *Versaillaise*. I was already determined to stake out radical change before I met her, however, so I believe that she was the last being who could have persuaded me to accept an academic or otherwise bourgeois career. It is undeniable that my inability to approach her confidently in French utterly enraged me. I resolved never again to be unable to speak the language.

Pasolini remarked: "*La passione non ottiene mai il perdono.*"* Chaste as my passion for her was, it was real and lasting. It was also unmanly stuff. I hope that I am no longer capable of such sentiments, but heed Petrarch's warning:

> *Quel foco ch'i' pensai che fosse spento*
> *dal freddo tempo et da l'età men fresca,*
> *fiamma et martir ne l'anima rinfresca.*†

* "Passion is never forgiven."

† Petrarch, *Canzoniere*, 55: "That fire that I thought had been quenched / by chill time and declining years / rekindles flame and suffering in the soul."

XX

October 2008

I joined the Legion in August intentionally to avoid training in the hot summers of southern France. Such was my innocence at the time that never had I considered the effects of cold weather on soldiers. By the time we finished our five weeks at the farm in November 2008, I had learnt that cold is probably the infantryman's worst foe. There began my lasting hatred for it.

At the farm we had little time indoors. The closest thing to it were the few hours of sleep that we had in our unheated barrack rooms without insulation. The only heated and insulated space that we ever entered was the ordinary, and this only for limited stints during meals. Our bodies became used to the weather, but with each passing day the misery of our tenure grew greater.

The lengths of our Friday marches increased. To take the place of customary *pots* on Saturday nights, sometimes we bivouacked in the expanses of unpeopled land surrounding the farm. At these overnight campsites we built fires, drank mulled wine, performed skits, and sang songs late into the evening.

Our weekly routines changed little from what I have described earlier, save that we occasionally performed obstacle courses, learned how to dig fighting positions, and worked at bettering our camping techniques. We also began to spend more time ironing, such that we passed entire nights—or *nuits blanches*—pressing and preparing our combat and dress uniforms. The Legion maintained exacting standards for both uniforms, and at the Fourth Foreign Regiment we became far more proficient with our irons than with our weapons.

As we reached the last days of training and preparations for the farm's culminating event, the *marche du képi blanc*, we undertook evaluations of our skills as budding infantrymen, or *fantassins*. These included assembling and disassembling our weapons to time, operating basic military equipment, executing drill and ceremony, and reacting to various contingencies during simulated patrols. The day of the march, which we both longed for and dreaded, came upon us at last. We spent most of the night before the march adjusting our gear, ironing our one combat uniform reserved for ceremonies, and scrubbing our kepis with soap and toothbrushes to ensure their iconic whiteness on the forthcoming day, when we would don them for the first time.

Crisp, cold, and open skies greeted us in the early morning as we stepped off on the march that took us fifty or sixty kilometres through the surrounding countryside over the next thirty-six hours. I do not remember our route save that it passed through Fanjeaux. The countryside was lovely, as was the weather for most of our march. For this event our platoon separated into smaller groups, or squads, and the platoon leader led mine. At one point he gave me his map and compass and let me try to point out where we were on the map. This was still an arcane concept to me, so I held the map as I would a tome in unknown cuneiform, trying to unravel its secrets. Later, in the US Army, it took me years as well as significant and embarrassing trial and error to become proficient in the art of orienteering.

The Aude is a region full of colour and of beauty. In the summertime its hilly northwest could almost be compared to Tuscany, and its southeast stretches all the way to Narbonne, that Roman city whose Mediterranean flare is markedly different from the combative stoniness of Languedoc. Throughout this march we had an enviable walking tour of the Aude's northwest, the increasingly heavy loads on our backs notwithstanding. Well into the night we stopped to camp, resting for a few hours before the next morning. Even then we took the time to start a fire, to warm ourselves, and to sing a few Legion songs before retiring to our sleeping bags and fending off the cold to the best of our abilities.

It was on the afternoon of its first day that the march's most enchanting moment for me took place. Our squad was passing through what seemed to be a wholly isolated draw, walking along an unpaved trail. To our left the wooded terrain sloped upward, whereas to the right thick woods limited our visibility to perhaps one hundred metres. For several kilometres we had seen no signs of human life or dwellings, nor did any appear before us.

Out of nowhere, a lady of remarkable beauty approached us on horseback.

Her presence commanded our attention. She appeared to be in her late teens or early twenties, and her black hair was drawn up in lengthy braids. To my memory, she wore a white long-sleeved shirt, denim jeans, and riding boots. The horse that she rode seemed enormous for her stature. Intrigued and making no attempt to hide it, she smiled bemusedly at us. Her fleeting glances penetrated our formation in some way—chemical, electrical, spiritual, or otherwise. Whatever the means by which she affected us, we gained springs in our step, lost our weariness, and tried to comport ourselves as soldiers and as men, not as muttering peons waiting for our next pause to snack on military rations. Quickly she passed us and rode away, but within our squad there was no need to speak of her to know that she had captivated us, dominating our thoughts as we trudged no longer, but now really marched.

I would need several months of dedicated study of psychology, of philosophy, and of history to contrive a more robust theory about how soldiering and soldiers could not exist without women, and how so much of what soldiers do is with a mind to prove to them our worth as men. Yet I know from experience that this is true and that the mere passing glimpse of a lovely woman on horseback, whom we would never see again, strengthened us for the remainder of our journey that day as substantially as any rations or drink.

XXI

October 2008

The last hours of the *marche du képi blanc* proved the most physically painful. The packs weighed heavily on our backs. Our weariness from marching and from poor and little sleep was taking a greater toll on us. Clouds gathered above us and darkened the late-morning skies. It began to drizzle.

Yet, the sight of towns familiar to us from the farm's running routes raised our spirits, even as our rucksacks' straps dug more deeply into our shoulders. At last, we walked onto a trail leading to the farm, visible to us in the distance.

To take off one's rucksack after a long march brings sensual pleasures known only to infantrymen. We luxuriated in its consolations as we set down our rucksacks in the farm's open-air classroom. While awaiting the arrival of other squads separated from us on the march, we laughed and joked, celebrating our completion of the *marche de képi blanc*. Those with cigarettes pulled them out and smoked them to mark the occasion. I smoked one offered to me.

This march marks a crucial point of transition in the life of every legionnaire. Its completion entitles one to wear the fabled *képi blanc*. Until the march, our cadre referred to us only as new recruits, or *engagés volontaires*. Having completed it, we had earned the right to be called *legionnaires de deuxième classe*. The Legion formalizes most landmarks in its soldiers' careers with elaborate ceremonies followed by boozy meals, as it did for us that evening.

Once we had all come back from the march, we undertook preparations for the ceremony scheduled for that evening. We showered, shaved, and put on the pristine camouflage duty uniforms that we had carefully ironed and set aside for this occasion. We polished our boots with special care. Given the cold temperatures, our cadre even gave us permission to wear a long-sleeved cotton garment below our duty uniforms for extra warmth—something permitted in French Army uniform regulations, but a treat hitherto unknown to us. We marched out to the field behind our open-air classroom. Behind us was the representation in painted stones of the Legion's seven-flamed grenade.

Hours before the evening's official events, we began a Legion tradition still new to us—lengthy rehearsals for ceremonies. Painful and repetitive rehearsals are common to militaries worldwide, but the Legion's were tiresome to an extent that I never again experienced until I finished the Colombian Army's Lancero School in 2019. For hours we practiced so that when the speaker read the meaningful words—"*Coiffez vos képis blancs*," or "Don your kepi blancs"—we would all don them in a specifically prescribed three-part motion, followed by a vigorous slap to the right thigh in unison and the simultaneous shouting of one of the Legion's informal mottos: "*Legio Patria Nostra*," or "the Legion is our Fatherland." The lion's share of these ceremonial trappings was the work of one man, or at least inspired by his example—General Paul-Frédéric Rollet. This visionary Foreign Legion commander created most of its current historical narratives and cultural traditions. Had he been there to see us that evening in 2008, I doubt that our ceremony would have been much different from those which he had created for his own legionnaires in the 1930s.

After rehearsing until the last possible moment, our platoon leader deemed us ready for the ceremony. We drew up in formation, with him at the head, and awaited the regimental commander's arrival, which was expected any minute. By this time significant rainfall had begun and temperatures were dropping quickly, so already we had become quite frozen. We stood rigidly in formation for what must have been half an hour before our platoon leader finally relented and let us rest in place. Still, the colonel had not arrived. It was perhaps an hour later when the colonel's vehicle approached. He walked up to his place as our ceremony's guest of honour. Accompanying him was a tall, well-fed, and balding man wearing spectacles and a black woollen coat. By the time the ceremony began, we were all shivering uncontrollably. Even our platoon leader barely seemed to hold himself together in these conditions. For many of us, this was probably one of the coldest and most miserable moments in our lives so far.

All the same, as we donned our kepis, to a man we were proud to have reached a significant milestone in our Legion careers. Afterward we moved into the open-air classroom where tables decorated in green and red colours awaited us. To begin dinner, we sang a rousing "*Tiens, voilà du boudin*" and quaffed glasses of the Legion's *Côtes de Provence*. We then sat down to table, some of us eating, some serving other tables in unformalized shifts. The barbecued meat was of adequate quality, and there was plenty to eat and to drink. A contracted photographer snapped photos of us with our cadre and with our peers. Most of us grew tipsy, if not outright drunk. As the dinner progressed, the colonel sought me out and introduced me to the large man who accompanied him. It turned out that he was from the United States and currently worked as a lawyer for an aviation company in Toulouse. This gentleman gave me his calling card and asked me to get in touch with him when I could.

The rest of the night was a blur. I remember that the celebrations abruptly ended, and our joviality became panicked hurriedness as our cadre commanded us to clean up the classroom areas quickly. They then corralled us into French Army trucks and brought us back to the barracks in Castelnaudary. Most of us were still intoxicated when the platoon sergeant forced us to stand in formation and to empty all our bags in the rain until we found a missing piece of equipment. This item was in the rucksack of a French legionnaire who had heatedly denied possessing it.

We did not go to sleep until about 0400.

XXII

October 2008

To shoot live ammunition from our FAMAS rifles was not allowed throughout our time at the farm, where we only carried blank ammunition on rare occasions. With our graduation to the rank of legionnaire, however, we had earned enough trust to train at the Fourth Foreign Regiment's indoor firing range. With little sleep, some of us still shaking off effects of overindulgence in drink, we drew our FAMAS rifles from the company's armoury and marched to the range.

There we spent the whole day shooting at various targets from distances of twenty-five to two hundred metres in a small but well-equipped indoor range, using both nine-millimetre PA MAC 50 pistols and FAMAS rifles. Since arriving at Castelnaudary, most of us claimed and believed that we could hardly wait to be done with the trifles of marching, singing, and bivouacking and to get to the real business of soldiering—shooting our rifles and growing proficient with them, thereby becoming lethal "killers." Yet, when at last the time came to spend a whole day shooting, most of us seemed bored and vexed. Surely, we had more concerns about how tired we were, about what we would eat in the ordinary, and about when we would go to sleep that night.

Training at the range was not of high quality or intensity, since its purpose at this stage was mainly to ensure that we had basic familiarity with these weapons. Some members of our platoon had military backgrounds, but even many of these had little conversance with firearms. Only a few of us, like me, had ample experience in civilian life shooting rifles, and at least one legionnaire in our platoon, a Swede, was supposedly on the run from the law as a former weapons smuggler. For this small minority, handling weapons was nothing new, but for half or more of our platoon this day marked the first occasion that they shot live ammunition from actual rifles. Therefore, one could understand the jitters of our sergeants, who watched us like hawks, as many greenhorn riflemen brandished their arms in unsafe ways. The sergeants' attention was certainly necessary, as there were several accidental discharges on the range.

Little boys—and not a few little girls—play soldier almost as if by instinct. They brandish swords, pistols, and rifles, feign battles, and orchestrate elaborate combats. Those who grow up never experiencing soldierly life seem to cherish idealized visions of the military experience. I have even seen professors at Princeton University advertise and host "dissertation boot camps," meant to project visions of tight groups of graduate students going through gruelling experiences of book reading and draft writing together, formative experiences that would bond them into tighter-knit cohorts and forge better scholars.

The few of us in modern Western nations who do undertake today's versions of military service quickly lose relish for playing war, as the martial existence's realities become clear. How often as a child did I lie camouflaged and hidden in the woods, waiting to ambush a sibling or a playmate and hardly able to contain my enthusiasm! Yet, to my surprise, the first time that my Legion cadre taught me to dig a fighting position and to hold watch for the enemy, I, like everyone else in my platoon, almost immediately began nodding off to sleep.

There is worthwhile accuracy in suggesting that most infantrymen perform and muster enthusiasm for military tasks for much the same reason that many women yearn for and agree to sexual relations—not so much for the experience and its pleasures, but for their memory. Rarely do infantrymen enjoy their duties even in ideal circumstances. It is much harder to do so in the far less than ideal circumstances in which modern soldiers march, shoot, jump out of airplanes, and much more. Yet, we look back to the memory of these military tasks duly performed, and they bring us great satisfaction. They put a stamp of approval on our manhood and on our prowess as military professionals, giving lasting material for stories and tall tales to friends, family, and prospective mates.

With years of experience, I have slowly grown indifferent to the infantry's pains and hardships, and I know how to wait for the satisfaction of a task well completed. At Castelnaudary, my idealized visions of soldiering were still crashing up against the day-to-day realities of life devoted to demanding infantry training, as was the case for many legionnaires.

I first sensed the disconnect between my fantasies about soldiering and its realities during our second or third night in Castelnaudary, before we had even left for the farm. That night a Polish corporal slept in our room. A trained sniper in the Foreign Legion, he spent the entire night playing loud video games about snipers. At the time I could not possibly imagine how such a game could be interesting to a real Foreign Legion sniper. Now I understand that the electronic fantasy was much more enjoyable to him than the painful reality of training to become a sniper and of performing one's duties as such, even in mere training.

One North American corporal in the Legion—a man who claimed to be a former Navy Seal but almost surely was no such thing—months later told me during a booze-fuelled Christmas party that he hated to see heady enthusiasm and spunk in soldiers, and that the true legionnaire has totally lost his motivation, but stoically carries out his tasks at a high level. I have come to agree with him to some measure. I had already seen that few recruits who joined with boyish excitement lasted more than a week in Aubagne, before voluntarily giving up and going home. To reach a more stoic state, most of us had to pass through bitter disillusionment with legionary realities and then to discover and to create within ourselves the motivation to perform tasks to high standards. Some of us never overcame the disillusion, and others only with partial success.

XXIII

October–December 2008

Before long we settled into the routines of garrison life at the Fourth Foreign Regiment. Each week at *Quartier Capitaine Danjou* began with the colonel's review of the entire regiment. This event took place no matter what the weather. After formally reviewing all his troops to traditional martial music blared over loudspeakers, the colonel shared a few comments before releasing us to our companies. For the most part the colonel's remarks were bland and predictable, but I do remember that he once caused quite a stir by his use of the outmoded adjective *idoine* (or "perfectly suitable") to describe the winter weather.

At Castelnaudary we usually woke up about five in the morning. After shaving and brushing our teeth, we cleaned our rooms and common areas and undertook the loathed *corvée quartier*—that is, circling the company area and picking up rubbish and cigarette butts. Thereafter we went to breakfast at the ordinary. We formed up as a company at about seven, and shortly thereafter we went running as a platoon or in smaller groups. The only variables were the distances, the routes, and the speeds.

Most days we ran down the nearby *Canal du Midi*, one of UNESCO's world heritage sites. Sometimes we ran into Castelnaudary itself, and at others through the open fields south of our base. In these same fields we also undertook the Legion's rucksack running event, which we had to pass as part of basic training. This comprised running eight kilometres with a rucksack, helmet, and weapon. For this event a good time was under forty-five minutes, but all were expected to make it in about fifty minutes. The first time that we finished this event about ten in the morning, we crowded into the company club and shared celebratory beers. Sometimes we practiced the Legion's twenty-event obstacle course, and on regular occasions we went swimming in the regiment's excellent pool. Unlike the US Army, the Legion insisted that recruits learn how to swim and painstakingly ensured that all graduates of basic training could do so. About ten recruits in our platoon could not swim at all when they joined the Legion, but they had become passable swimmers when they left Castelnaudary. Whenever we finished our running, rucking, or obstacle navigating, we went back to the company and performed numerous repetitions of sit-ups and push-ups, followed by at least one rope-climb.

It was usually about ten o'clock when we finished physical training. After showering, there was limited time to do anything until lunch, so we usually held short classes with our cadre, learned a new Legion song, or finished basic administrative tasks. While our cadre and leaders had two hours to enjoy leisurely and sometimes boozy lunches, followed by siestas, we legionnaires moved immediately from the ordinary after lunch to clean our barracks' spaces and common areas and to perform *corvée quartier* for the second time in the day. With any remaining time, we were assigned the task of *maintenance d'équipage*, or upkeep of our equipment. We were not allowed to take siestas. Corporals routinely patrolled our rooms, so napping in these hours was a risk, but one which most of us took sooner or later.

In the afternoons we followed prescribed programmes of instruction that ensured our basic proficiency as infantrymen and legionnaires. At Castelnaudary, the primary focus was to form our corporate identity and to integrate us into the Legion's distinctive culture. Many legionnaires desert within the first two years of their contract, so giving much beyond rudimentary training before they reach the rank of corporal does not make for good returns on investment. Dinner was at five o'clock, and was preceded, of course, by *corvée quartier*. After this we continued training and other planned events with our corporals until about nine in the evening, when we got ready for bed. At this time, we cleaned our rooms for the third time each day, showered for the second time, and went to sleep. The showers were usually cold or even frigid, but occasionally there were random streams of heated water. For the most part, these only served to tease us about the possibility of hot water.

One noteworthy aspect of our life in garrison was singing our company song before lunch and dinner. After assembling near the company, one of our non-commissioned officers or corporals would release us to form up again in the middle of the *place d'armes*. We would then march to the ordinary while singing our company or platoon song. Each mealtime made for a colourful pageant, as platoons from different companies angled to get to the ordinary first, singing their distinct songs and all brandishing bands of distinct colours on their left shoulders that designated their company. It was normal to hear the cacophonous collision of multiple company or unit songs as formations simultaneously belted them out as they marched toward the ordinary.

On weekends the pace of life grew calmer. In the Foreign Legion, cadre usually worked Saturday mornings. Saturday afternoons, however, they left for home and did not come back until Monday, leaving us in the hands of designated corporals. It was during these times that all bets were off depending on the corporals in charge, their whims, and their moods. Once, two French corporals in charge of us over the weekend consumed drugs on Saturday evening and kept us up with inspired hazing events until the wee hours of the morning, but this was an extreme. Corporals' lives were, if anything, more taxing than ours, and they also wanted to rest and left us alone for the most part on weekends. Usually, the company commander authorized us to spend a few euros from our monthly pay at the company bar or "club," where beers, sodas, and various snacks were for sale. As we progressed in training, sometimes we were even permitted to go to the regimental *foyer*, where we could buy food, watch football matches, drink beers, and mingle. Then came our day of rest, Sunday.

XXIV

October–December 2008

Each Sunday we began the day as late as half past seven in the morning with a leisurely breakfast, before going back to our barracks room. All Sunday morning, we were usually given our favourite task—*maintenance d'équipage*. In these relaxed conditions it was possible to nap for much of the morning, even if in theory this was not allowed. Legionnaires were always given the opportunity to go to Catholic Mass in Castelnaudary, since there was no chaplain at the regiment. To facilitate our religious practice, the regiment devoted a bus and driver to take us to Mass and assigned a corporal to escort us.

Until asking to join the Legion in August 2008, I had not missed Sunday Mass or any Roman Catholic Holy Day of Obligation for over four years. Therefore, it came as welcome relief to be able to attend Mass at Castelnaudary's *Collégiale Saint-Michel*. This was a stately Romanesque church whose construction was mostly finished in the thirteenth century. Some battle scars from the Black Prince's violent passage through Castelnaudary in the fourteenth century remained visible. A few cosmetic details aside, the *collégiale* kept much of its thirteenth-century flare, and I appreciated that the various priests and bishops in charge of the *collégiale* had never installed pews in the church's nave. Temporary chairs instead accommodated modern worshipers, thereby preserving the structure's integrity. As one would expect from any self-respecting French church, the organ, installed in the eighteenth century, was formidable.

Whenever at Mass I always took time at the statue of Saint Theresa of Lisieux, found in a bleak chapel on the right side of the *collégiale*'s nave. The coats of paint on this poorly wrought and tastelessly decorated statue were peeling. For reasons still unclear to me, during this time at Castelnaudary I commended myself to this saint's intercession more earnestly than ever before, as almost every day brought unexpected and vexing challenges to face and to overcome.

On most Sundays, I was one of only a handful of legionnaires to attend Mass. From what I could gather, few of the other occasional volunteers for Mass were Roman Catholics, much less practicing ones. Perhaps they simply wished to leave the base and to see the outside world. Corporals often accused us of this whenever we volunteered to attend Mass, hurling charges that we only wished to gawk at *gonzesses*. But *gonzesses* were few and far between at Sunday Mass, and corporals kept us on tight leashes throughout our excursion. Whatever their complaints, our enlisted cadre hardly ever kept us from going to Mass since the Foreign Legion's officer corps is solidly Catholic. Moreover, it was hard for our corporals to doubt the sincerity of those who volunteered for Mass, since doing so entailed the additional tasks of ironing and of preparing our dress uniforms, not to mention foregoing what is probably dearer to legionnaires than anything else—the siesta. To give up a coveted siesta in order to attend a rather drowsily executed liturgy in a dreary town showed commitment to the unworldly that even the most cynical corporals acknowledged.

After Mass, the few participants returned to base in time for Sunday lunch, which was usually of better quality than what we ate during the week, and which we could enjoy at a more leisurely pace. Afterward we were occasionally given permission to buy items at the company club or at the *foyer*. By and large, nothing of importance happened on Sundays, and many of us would grow so bored by the day's end that we almost desired the next day's charged activity.

One Sunday the non-commissioned officer left in charge of the company was an Italian who had previously served at the Second Foreign Infantry Regiment in Nîmes. He was of stocky build, far larger than I. That day I was the only volunteer to go to Mass, which meant that he would have to inconvenience his corporal to accompany one lowly legionnaire. He told me that I was not allowed to go to Mass that Sunday, to which I answered that I had the right to attend Mass. He said many things to intimidate me and to make me back down, but I insisted that I should be able to attend. At last, he ordered me away and told me to come back to his office at my peril. I decided not to push the envelope, and I missed Sunday Mass that week owing to the sergeant's testy refusal to honour his superiors' orders and established custom at the Fourth Foreign Regiment.

Several weeks later this Italian sergeant deliberately took me aside and told me, in excellent English, that he respected me for how I had stood my ground that Sunday. He sat me down and shared with me many of his observations from Nîmes and from his time in the Legion's Third Foreign Regiment in French Guyana. He stressed that no matter how many pleasures the Legion had offered him—his personal favourites being Brazilian women and cocaine—the Legion had also taught him to live peaceably alone and without chemical or sexual consolations, something that had changed his life entirely. To me, this sounded like the realization of Blaise Cendrar's summary of his time in the Legion in *La Main Coupée*, so it inspired me to see such a thing embodied, perhaps, in this cantankerous and iconoclastic non-commissioned officer.

Later, once I had left basic training and I could venture out to different liturgies, I would sometimes go to the sparsely attended "Tridentine Mass" offered each Sunday about eleven o'clock at a small chapel in Castelnaudary, whose name I do not remember. The first time that I attended this Mass there, I saw the regimental commander with his five children and stately wife. He seemed rather startled to see me at this Mass, if pleasantly so. Many Foreign Legion officers persisted in their belief that all North Americans are Protestants, repeatedly showing surprise and perplexity at every evidence of my Catholicism.

XXV

October–December 2008

In the winter of 2003, I spent the Christmas holidays with a class-conscious acquaintance from The Johns Hopkins University. Scion of a *blésois* family ennobled by Charles X, he set great store by his family's Bourbon-derived title and ancestral estate where, he proudly claimed, his family's "peasants" still worked the fields. At the time, I was living in Saint Petersburg and running short on money, and I was just as curious to pry into the truth of his claims as I was in need of a place to stay over Christmas while waiting to renew my Russian visa. So, I took a bus from Saint Petersburg to Paris, which involved a two-day trek by way of Warsaw. My friend's parents kindly hosted me for a week in their flat near Paris' Montparnasse station, after which we drove out to spend Christmas at the family's late-fifteenth-century country home near Angers.

This friend's father was an incorrigible Anglophile and enjoyed flaunting rarefied English words in my presence. However much I found distasteful his old-fashioned *illuminisme*, to this modest baron I owe much. Before all else, he taught me how properly to eat rice. Today I still strictly adhere to techniques that he patiently demonstrated to me. Moreover, he was my first in-the-flesh guide to many aspects of French civilization. Under his tutelage I experienced for the first time Muscadet and oysters, nightly *apéritifs* and *digestifs*, Breton seafood at a restaurant near Paris' Montsouris Park, his towered *châtelet* completed in 1492, rustic dinners cooked by his ravishing sister-in-law, and poets such as Joachim du Bellay, who wrote of *la douceur angevine*. For my part I still much prefer Roman palaces and "marine air" to anything in Anjou, but I remember du Bellay's poem as choice praise of the French countryside's charms.

As a small nook in the deep southern French countryside, Castelnaudary and its surrounding regions boasted their own *douceurs*, and we legionnaires experienced many of them. Perhaps the most remarkable charms of life at *Quartier Capitaine Danjou* were the mornings. Before joining the Foreign Legion, the rare occasions when I witnessed the dawn's lights were after prolonged festivities at Princeton or, far more frequently, when I studied until I fell asleep. Given the radically different schedules of soldierly life, for the first time I had the chance to see the dawn each morning. At our regiment, east lay directly in front of our ordinary. Thence one's line of sight stretched across the regiment's *place d'Armes* and ended in trees scattered throughout the park where the regimental officer's club—or *cercle des officiers*—was housed in a Second Empire *château*. As we formed up each morning for breakfast, we caught daily glimpses of the sky's varying colours above this *château* and its surrounding deer park (more precisely a "doe park," since in French we called it a "*parc à biches*"). Before breakfast many legionnaires waxed almost lyrical about the morning skies, captivated by its colours. These marvellous dawns were one of so many natural beauties that would have remained largely unknown to me had I spent my life in our age's tamed and hermetic offices.

For at least three weeks during our basic training, it was our platoon's responsibility to fill most of the regiment's work details. Such menial tasks were not so much an interruption to our military training but rather an integral part of it, especially in the Legion. Work details comprised supporting operations at any number of the regiment's moving parts, to include its ordinary, its shooting range, its guard-posts, its prison, and its headquarters. One of my favourite details during these weeks was to work at the *cercle des officiers*. Here we performed various tasks such as picking up leaves, trimming flower beds, tending lawns, cleaning out gutters, scrubbing water closets, sweeping and mopping floors, and setting tables. Usually assigned to an aloof *caporal-chef* for such details, we had time to walk about the grounds and inside the *château* with little, if any, supervision.

To tarry in the *château*'s wainscoted dining room and bar brought me great enjoyment. I envied the officers their *cercle des officiers* in the middle of nowhere in southern France, decidedly ho-hum by French military standards but which would surpass the most spectacular officers' clubs in the US Army, and rival even Washington, DC's *Army and Navy Club*.

Not all garrison details were so glitzy, but most of them gave us the chance to learn more about the Legion, about its workings, and about its people. Some of the most interesting and meaningful conversations that I ever had in the Legion were during such details, whether at Castelnaudary, later at my regiment in Nîmes, or on deployment in Afghanistan. I especially remember one conversation with a Russian sergeant at Castelnaudary who, from all reports, had previously been a conductor for a significant orchestra within the Russian military. His French was as delicate as his demeanour, so it was jarring to me when he made a pronouncement that comes to my mind with great frequency even over a decade later. "The hardest thing in life to learn how to do," he affirmed solemnly, "is to know how to shut up (*comment fermer sa gueule*)."

Each evening the regiment's flags lowered at six in the evening. Two legionnaires and a corporal were always present in full dress uniform for the flags' rising and falling. The bugler was a special position in the Legion, and officers scoured their formations for suitable candidates. It is quite challenging to play a bugle well, but a Frenchman in our platoon (an incorrigible troublemaker who stole cigarettes from cadre at the farm and whose peers in his regiment later viciously stabbed him in the thigh in some act of reprisal) had a remarkable talent for the instrument and played many nights of the week.

Most armies have long since adopted loudspeakers and recordings for such traditional garrison music. The Legion's continued investment in buglers and bugling speaks volumes about its nature.

XXVI

October–December 2008

Bowel movements rarely commanded my attention before 2008. To find reasonably clean toilets was never much of a challenge in the United States or in Europe, and hitherto it had not crossed my mind that one might have to purge bodily waste under duress.

During my time at the farm, I had somehow managed to avoid defecating in the woods. It was only seven weeks later, during a miserable field exercise, that I woke up in the middle of the night to answer nature's unmistakable call. Owing to the event's novelty I still remember reluctantly leaving the warmth of my sleeping bag and walking off from our bivouac site to a secluded location. To follow our established protocol, I brought along a metal shovel, called the "*pelle US*" in French since these were duplicates of US Army field shovels introduced to the French military in the 1940s. As light drizzle came down, I dug a suitable hole and executed my first bowel movement under field conditions.

It was not until such experiences in the Legion that much of my past education came to life. For until one has shared the soldier's lot, even if only as an enlisted man or an officer in training, it is hard to understand many things in our literary canon and history books. Several years before joining the Legion, I had read Evelyn Waugh's *Sword of Honour*. In this trilogy's first book, *Men at Arms*, Waugh devoted a long section to describing British Army Halberdiers in training. For this training an enterprising young officer brings and stashes away a magnificent antique field chemical toilet, or "thunder-box," that had once belonged to a duke on campaign in some eighteenth-century continental war. It soon became an object of envy and of intrigue. This section finishes with the spiteful destruction of the "thunder-box" by a planted explosive device, which ended internecine infighting and wrangling over its possession.

When I read this passage as a civilian, I found its lengthy treatment of struggles over the "thunder-box" uninteresting and perplexing. After a few months of military service, however, I understood that this episode, far from being fanciful, is probably one of the more realistic passages in the trilogy, with universal relevance to the military experience. It gave, moreover, some noteworthy insights into a fundamental aspect of sound soldiering and of military leadership—namely, the prudent management of human waste.

Since my time in the Legion, whenever I survey sites of past great battles, invariably I think of the smells of accumulated human urine and feces and of where and how leaders would have disposed of waste. Whether it be at Alesia's site or near Italy's Rapido river—where an enormous Allied force gathered under the watchful eye of German Paratroopers at Montecasino and dumped untold amounts of human waste into local fields and rivers—when I envision the military "operational art" in practice, I think of skilful waste management as a fundamental part of successfully manoeuvring one's forces and of optimizing its performance, thereby simultaneously staving off disease and preserving unit morale. A military truism in the English language states that whereas amateur military leaders think about tactics, professionals think about logistics. I would take this logic one step further by positing that whereas professionals think about logistics, the visionary thinks about waste management in the field.

Learning the hard way is sometimes the only way. For my part, I did not understand why many legionnaires saved large plastic bottles and brought empty ones with them on our trips in the back of military trucks. It was only during a long, bouncy voyage to a rural location during basic training that I finally understood this practice, as my urge to urinate after three hours in the truck grew excruciating. Rather than soil myself, I held on to the rails on the back of the moving truck, opened my trousers, and let my urine flow onto the moving highway below me, making for a memorable scene, no doubt, for the civilians driving in vehicles behind us. From that day, I never travel in a military vehicle or aircraft without first securing an empty plastic bottle.

Also, having grown up in the United States, I retained a curious aspect of the nation's dietary habits—a dogged and generalized refusal to change one's eating and drinking practices based on their likely effects on the urinary tract and digestive system. On this matter, sometimes it seems that what every other people in the world recognizes to be logical and necessary—namely, that we should understand the effects of various foods and drink and change our diet in light of upcoming events in one's life—is deemed pseudoscience and quackery by large swaths of the United States' population. Once, as we sat for breakfast, a recruit from Ukraine warned me about drinking too much coffee, making the reasonable suggestion that coffee's diuretic and laxative properties are potentially dangerous prior to long-distance runs through the countryside. I did not pay heed to his comments and drank three bowls of coffee. When I subsequently had to stop three times to urinate during our morning run, his comments made sense.

"A legionnaire always has toilet paper with him." Thus declared our Korean corporal once as he pulled out a portable, folded supply from one of his trousers' pockets. To this day I would never set out on even the shortest military exercise or event without an adequate supply of toilet paper in my rucksack, and at least enough on my person to be able to address one bowel event. Proper sanitation and field hygiene is essential to soldier morale and readiness, as the corporal rightly understood.

The fact that there are so few realistic and detailed discussions of defecation—not to mention its associated logistical and hygienic concerns—in existing literature about war experiences shows how much such recounts are stylized and artificial. Defecation remains a sempiternal preoccupation of the soldier deployed in training or in combat.

XXVII

October–December 2008

Well into the twenty-first century, France's conquest of and later adventures in Algeria loomed large in the Foreign Legion's sequestered and unique culture. Until my service as a legionnaire, I had only vague ideas about France's past and present involvements in the Maghreb. Undergraduate history and French literature courses had exposed me to the writings of Albert Camus and of other *pieds-noirs* as well as to films such as the *Battle of Algiers*, which boasts one of the twentieth century's best popular songs ("*Hasta Mañana*" performed by the Belgian group of musicians named the Chakachas). France's history in Northern Africa was therefore not altogether unknown to me when I joined the Foreign Legion, but it was still something mysterious.

During a sojourn in Paris in 2004, I was taken aback at seeing an altar that celebrated the glories of French Algeria at the "traditionalist" Catholic church Saint-Nicolas-du-Chardonnet. This altar, at which the Republican French tricolour and Roman Catholic images were intermingled, radiated assertions of worldviews and convictions quite different from those prisms through which I had been trained to understand my own civilization and others.

Before joining the Foreign Legion, I had not read Carroll Quigley's *Tragedy and Hope* or *The Anglo-American Establishment*, but I espoused most of these works' underlying beliefs without necessarily understanding their origins and their import. As a dutiful stepchild of Anglo-Saxon hegemony dating back to the Congress of Vienna, I had no inkling that any truly respectable civilization existed aside from those espoused by the British, by those in various British dominions, or in the United States, which look back to the sceptered isle for their inspiration. In this respect, my attitudes largely conformed to those that Leo Tolstoy outlined over a century before my time:

> An Englishman is self-assured, as being a citizen of the best organized state in the world, and therefore as an Englishman always knows what he should do and knows that all he does as an Englishman is undoubtedly correct.*

Throughout my youth, countless films, books, and lectures reinforced the moral and ideological supremacy of the Anglo-Saxon legacy. Thus, the Foreign Legion and its culture came as a shock to my intellectual and cultural systems.

Many of the Legion's songs celebrated French Algeria. One outstanding example of these is *Soldats de la Légion Étrangère*, whose melodies were, predictably, based on a traditional German folksong named "*Jenseits des Tales*," which became popular with the Hitler Youth in the 1930s. The lyrics of the Foreign Legion's adaptation of this song are worth repeating since they pithily capture so much of the cultural baggage that underlies the Legion's traditions and unique *esprit de corps* that I learned to take in and to cherish during my service within the organization. At some point, I simply took for granted marching with my peers and singing at full kilter such lyrics as:

---

* Leo Tolstoy, Anna Karenina, Part III, Chapter 1: "Англичанин самоуверен на том основании, что он есть гражданин благоустроеннейшего в мире государства, и потому, как англичанин, знает всегда, что ему делать нужно, и знает, что все, что он делает как англичанин, несомненно хорошо."

Soldats de la Légion Étrangère,
Se sont battus partout en Algérie,
Beaucoup sont tombés, de braves légionnaires,
Pour la Légion, qui est notre Patrie.
Comme nos anciens, Nous défendrons l'Algérie,
Contre le Diable, et cotre les fellaghas,
Avec nos drapeaux, Honneur, Fidélité,
*Nous tomberons ou nous vaincrons au combat.**

I had recently left behind Princeton's posh surroundings where, before the onslaught of a financial crisis about which I heard little until 2009, very few would have imagined any future aside from that dominated by financial institutions and banks in New York and in London, whose calculating whims determined the fates of peoples and of nations. Thrust into an environment where forgotten battles and campaigns in Algeria were far more prominent than the latest movements and exchanges of stocks, of commodities, and of other ethereal and nebulous financial products, I learned to speak, to think, and to believe with new vocabulary. Arrogant self-sacrifice, fights against "the devil," honour, loyalty—such concepts would have seemed foreign and even absurd to my former peers and superiors if not presented to them as mere abstractions and anachronisms to contemplate with the condescending benevolence of conquerors.

My studies of history served me well as a legionnaire. With basic knowledge of European history and a capacity to undertake research, I was able to understand my environment more quickly than most. My company commander's occasional, guarded comments about his family piqued my curiosity. As it turned out, his grandfather ranked among those generals who spearheaded

* "Soldiers of the Foreign Legion / have fought everywhere in Algeria / So many have fallen, such brave legionnaires / For the Foreign Legion, our Fatherland / As did our ancestors, we shall defend Algeria / Against the devil, and against the fellaghas [anti-French bandits] / Brandishing our flags, Honor and Loyalty / We shall die or emerge victorious in combat."

the attempted *putsch* against Charles de Gaulle as the president ordered the withdrawal of French forces from Algeria in 1961. But for some of the plotters' mistakes, my company commander's grandfather would have provided aircraft for transporting Foreign Legion paratroopers to occupy Paris. Once, in conversation with this commander, he casually mentioned that his grandfather had been in the military, but that his father had chosen not to pursue military service. It stood to reason!

Later I discovered that my company's *adjudant d'unité* (its senior non-commissioned officer, or "first sergeant" in the US Army) also stemmed from a military family involved in the attempt to stay the Legion's withdrawal from French Algeria. Having risen from the ranks of a lowly legionnaire to command one of the Legion's cavalry regiments that supported the *putsch*, my first sergeant's father had some ten children. Almost all my first sergeant's brothers were officers, and many of them had served in Foreign Legion regiments. My first sergeant, however, was trying to follow his father's footsteps as he strove to rise from simple legionnaire to the highest ranks of tactical and operational command. Whatever his oddities, I could not help but to admire his ambition as well as his extraordinary physique and stamina.

Later I found out that many of my peers and even accomplished faculty of the English-speaking academy were unaware that the French had ever left Algeria, as they asked me for my thoughts about our training and operations in this former French colony. Such questions surprised me and made me understand that immersion in the Foreign Legion's collective and personal histories had progressively upended foundational assumptions of my prior education.

XXVIII

November 2008

In mid-November we took a week-long journey into the Pyrenees, where the Legion owns a recreational facility not far from Foix. As we formed up before our company at Castelnaudary and prepared to board open-backed Renault military transport vehicles, our Belorussian corporal—the most loathed of them all—called out for a volunteer to ride in the vehicle's passenger seat with him. For about half a minute no one answered, but at last I raised my hand, wagering that it would be better to ride alongside this abusive corporal than to brave the elements in the truck's rear. My wager was sound.

This corporal was biding his time until the end of his five-year contract. Not yet in his thirties, already he was plump and bald, and his face unmistakably resembled a pig's. He held most conversations with legionnaires at various pitches of screaming, and he was prone to using physical violence with us. As often proved to be the case in the Legion, notwithstanding his out-of-shape appearance, he showed surprising physical stamina and prowess. His demonstrations on the French Army obstacle course, including his effortless passing over the *table irlandaise*—a two-metre-tall board suspended on two poles which one must climb over, preferably in one fluid motion—astounded us. His skills on the ironing board were no less masterful, and throughout our time at the farm it was he who spent most of his time in the kitchen cooking for us.

I foresaw an unpleasant ride with this corporal, but once we were alone, he struck up conversation with me, curious about North America. He was convinced that he could make a fortune by importing and exporting various used vehicles between the United States and Eastern Europe, and he already had Belorussian contacts in Chicago ready for business upon the end of his contract. It was a warm and comfortable ride for three hours as we climbed into the snowy Pyrenees. Once we disembarked, my fellow legionnaires in the back of the truck were frozen stiff, almost frostbitten.

This week in the mountains was meant to serve both as a confidence-building and cohesion event in the middle of basic training. Here, we began each day with runs of relatively modest distances, usually eight to twelve kilometres, before breaking up into small groups for specific events. The first day we climbed nearby mountains, making use of a carefully installed *via ferrata*, and then performed several obstacles in the mountains that were not too challenging, but nonetheless terrifying for anyone remotely afraid of heights. The second day we took snowshoes out into the mountains for a long march, which was exhausting and ended in such a steep descent that many of us tumbled head over heels in the snow until we reached the bottom of a large hill. The third day we went orienteering. Our last activity was to spend the day negotiating nearby caves, where we climbed through a variety of tight spaces and even went rappelling in deep caverns. As we prepared to leave the caves one legionnaire fell off a large rock and became temporarily paralyzed. Most of our group went back to the surface, but several legionnaires and I stayed behind with our Ukrainian sergeant to wait for civilian rescue personnel. After several hours rough Frenchmen of the mountains, wearing gaslit lanterns on their foreheads, made their way to us. Skilfully they stabilized the young man's body and slid him through the cave's tight creases and up to the surface. This stalwart legionnaire from South America recovered within a week.

However boozy the Legion is, there is usually a prohibition against serving any spirits at unit events, and for good reason. Whereas the legionnaire's usual alcoholic fare of wine and weak beer does little to threaten good order and discipline unless consumed to outrageous excess, the introduction of spirits may quickly turn tame "cohesion events" into dangerous brawls. The only time that I ever consumed liquor with fellow legionnaires was during this week in the Pyrenees. For unknown reasons, our platoon leader took us in military trucks to a nearby bar and allowed us to buy any drink of our choosing. As whiskey and other spirits flowed, the night grew increasingly hazy.

At one point a boyish-looking legionnaire from Madagascar came up to me crying in dismay. He was holding a tooth in his hand. As he opened his mouth to speak, I saw that he was missing one of his top incisors. He told me that a legionnaire named Bailey had just sucker punched him, thereby dislodging the now missing tooth. I cannot remember if we did anything to treat this Malagasy. In any event, he remained without a front tooth for the rest of basic training.

Bailey was a quiet Briton with curly dark hair. Wiry and of sullen disposition, he kept to himself, but he always proved a good sport and dependable comrade. His French remained hopeless, however, which led to numerous misunderstandings and mistakes on his part, whose outcomes were sometimes humorous and often humiliating. He hailed from Yorkshire, where he had worked in forestry. As had I, Bailey had spent time in Cornwall's countryside, so I enjoyed asking him about his experiences and about Old Blighty's rustic charms. He had a green thumb and knew his way around the woods, both assets for any infantryman. Bailey had also served in some British "territorial" unit before coming to the Legion. He was an excellent shot with his FAMAS.

Bailey's violent outbreak that evening under the influence of spirits shocked us. For anyone else such assault would have led to significant punishment, but we knew Bailey as someone so docile and mild-mannered that I do not think that he suffered any consequences at all. He and the young Malagasy were quickly reconciled, and the source of Bailey's rage in that evening's blurry revelry remained a mystery to us. Perhaps when sozzled and uninhibited he simply felt a need to live up to national stereotypes.

XXIX

November 2008

Since the beginning of our basic training, the nearby town of Castelnaudary piqued our curiosity and our longing. In any normal situation, I would reckon that none of us, not even those from the poorest recesses of Mongolia or of the Ukraine, would have cared about this small town in the Aude. Known mainly for its cassoulet, a robust dish whose meatiness is excessive even by carnivorous French standards, Castelnaudary is one of countless settlements in southern France whose local populations are probably smaller now than in the centuries of their mediaeval primes. Castelnaudary's glum and forlorn aspects notwithstanding, we were thrilled at the prospect of our first *permission*—a supervised four-hour trip to Castelnaudary that was part of our basic training experience.

For days we worked zealously to make sure that our dress uniforms were ready for this coveted outing. We scrubbed our kepis with Marseilles soap and toothbrushes until they were as speckless as possible. We fought over irons and ironing boards to press out the required fourteen creases on our dress shirts to near perfection and to leave no suspicion of a wrinkle on our grey jackets made from an uninspiring blend of polyester and wool.

The day came when we embarked in two of the regiment's civilian buses and drove to a parking place near Castelnaudary's *course de la République*, whence our cadre released us for four hours with warnings that we should behave ourselves and come back on time. Throughout our *permission*, they roved the city looking out for patent misdeeds. Alcohol was on almost everyone's mind. There was a small bar close to our bus, and half of my platoon soon peopled it. Locals seemed used to such occasions and barely noticed us.

Transitions from cloistered military environments to civilian ones make for curious sensations. This was my first taste of such abrupt shifts in life that persisted throughout my military career. Things that we had once taken for granted became possible again after months of confinement. We could walk into shops, buy and drink coffee and alcohol, telephone family, read newspapers and watch television, and eat whatever we chose to buy. Since until this *permission* we had not been allowed to spend almost anything from the salaries that we had earned since our enlistment, money was not a question. For us this was a short burst of possibility, a respite from months of pressure and hardship. Many stayed at that first available bar the entire four hours, drinking as much as was possible. A surprising number of us, however, ventured out into the town to enjoy the sites and to learn more about it.

For my part, I was starved for reading material. My first deed after ordering a *Picon bière* at our platoon's new bar was to buy a copy of that day's *Le Figaro*. I only glanced at it during these hours of freedom, saving it for later consumption. Thereafter I made my way to a bakery, where I ordered typical French pastries. Next, I visited a bookshop. Determined to improve my French and to have literary companionship for the next months in training, I bought portable editions of several of Molière's plays. I did not have enough time to try what was reputed to be one of Castelnaudary's best cassoulets, offered at the *Hôtel du Centre et du Lauragais*. Later I would come to prefer the cassoulets at the rustic *Hôtel de France* and at specialized purveyors in the nearby village of Bram, but the *Hôtel du Centre et du Lauragais* remains an obligatory stop—or *incontournable*—for any connoisseur of this hearty dish. Soon our four hours of freedom came to an end, and we hurried back to the appointed assembly area. There our sergeants were waiting for us.

As it happens during any regimented *permission*, a few legionnaires did not arrive back on time. Our sergeants had foreseen this and had punishments at the ready. Even though we had all spent hours preparing our dress uniforms, they made us perform push-ups and other exercises on the ground until the late legionnaires made it back to the bus. Two legionnaires were dispatched to seek out the stragglers as the rest of us created countless new wrinkles in our uniforms. Jeers and taunts greeted the latecomers. Before long we were back at the company. This would be our last taste of civilian life for several months.

Once we had returned to base, our sergeants searched us and our bags for any contraband, especially mobile phones. Despite the relative thoroughness of these searches, some legionnaires managed to sneak mobile telephones into the barracks. Thereafter we developed procedures such that most of us had the ability to phone friends and family almost weekly. Strictly speaking, recreational books and reading material were not allowed, but the Polish sergeant searched my bags and seemed nonplussed at my newspaper and the volumes of Molière. I justified these items by claiming that I was using them to better my French, something expected of all legionnaires. At this explanation the sergeant laughed and let me keep them.

That evening we reminisced together about our episodes of freedom. For some of us it was the first occasion to speak with family and friends at home since stepping inside Aubagne's gates. Depending on the news, there was the warm contentment of good tidings, expressions of longing and anxiety, or outright gnashing of teeth. As I opened *Le Figaro*, I was able to glean something about an ongoing crisis in worldwide financial markets. Since something significant had clearly happened months before the paper's publication, I tried to piece out details from articles that mentioned past financial shocks as they related to newer events, political measures, or fiscal policies.

From one article it became clear that a second major bank in New York had failed and that a worldwide financial crisis had ensued. In vain I struggled to learn more about what had happened from that one copy of *Le Figaro*.

XXX

October–December 2008

To desert from military formations is usually an extreme step. In the United States, soldiers who desert are described with the legalistic term "Absent Without Leave," commonly abbreviated in writing and in speech as "AWOL." "To go AWOL" in the United States military has serious repercussions and often leads to the arrest and prosecution of offending soldiers, to say nothing of lifelong blemishes on one's employment history. My experience with deserting soldiers in other militaries is limited, but to my understanding significant legal and social consequences await "deserters" in most nation-states in the twenty-first century, provided that these malcontents do not take the next logical step and flee the country whose military they have deserted.

In this respect the Foreign Legion is aberrant. Desertion is not only commonplace in the ranks, but sometimes implicitly encouraged by leadership weary of problematic soldiers. True consequences for desertion are downright laughable. In large part this is owing to the Legion's international composition and to the non-existent border controls within most of Europe's so-called Schengen Area since its establishment in the 1990s. Although I am merely guessing, I believe that desertions prior to France's entrance into the Schengen Area would have been rather challenging, since legionnaires are stripped of their passports and national identity papers upon enlistment. For a Pole, Slovak, or Russian to cross several borders on the way back to his homeland without any identity papers must have strained one's resources before the establishment of the Schengen Area. In 2008, however, there were few border controls within Europe. Desertion had therefore become something as simple as escaping from a base and travelling discreetly to the nearest border.

During my experience in basic training at Castelnaudary, we had at least six desertions from our platoon of fifty or so legionnaires. One was a Russian who had lived in Germany for several years prior to his joining the Legion. He once confessed to me that he had a substantial criminal past in Germany and that going back to civilian life was not an option for him, so his disappearance surprised me. Two departures that did not surprise us were our platoon's two German *engagés volontaires*. One of these was the gregarious "Blum" who, as it turned out, had left his girlfriend impregnated in Germany. He explained this situation to our chain of command, and our company commander let him leave the Legion without much fanfare. The second German was a troublemaker, baptized "Hauptmann," a dark, short, and wiry young man with excellent English and an enduring criminal glint in his eyes. Unlike Blum, Hauptmann had the raw material to make a fine soldier—he was hard-working, able to shift deftly from honesty to dishonesty and back again according to the demands of circumstance, talented with his weapons, a skilled thief, and incapable of behaving as a braggart. It was close to the end of basic training that he slipped away in the night—to almost universal regret.

The simultaneous flights of two of our platoon's three Italians made for our platoon's most dramatic episode of desertion. The one Italian who finished training and went to his regiment was a postman from Lombardy, an exemplary soldier and comrade. The other two Italians were scrawny and melancholic university students. I do not remember anything about their origins, but one of them gave us our platoon's informal marching song, "*Bella Ciao*." Our Polish sergeant enjoyed its fetching melody and its refrain's words so much that he always had these young Italians sing this song during our marches with him. One night these two brooding, pouty countrymen left our barracks and were never seen again. Our corporals woke us up about four in the morning to alert us to their desertion. We waited in the hallways until we could begin established protocols for such cases.

Most outstanding of all was the desertion of a young citizen of the United States, whose legionary name I do not remember. He was tall, lanky, balding and, like me, from Texas. He could not have been more than twenty-four years old. After having caused unusually disruptive troubles in a different training company, he had been assigned to our platoon. One of our sergeants asked me to take him under my wing, since this young man was already deemed a lost cause. He must have spent a month in our platoon since we underwent several training events together, but finally he tried to desert.

This young Texan was, to my knowledge, the only legionnaire during my time at Castelnaudary who was actually caught in the course of the regiment's decidedly *pro forma* search for deserters. I believe that he must have climbed over the regiment's fence, walked straight to Castelnaudary's train station, and tried to catch a train from there to Paris. This course of action was probably the only way that a potential deserter could get caught by our regiment's search parties. Caught he was, and according to the rules for legionnaires in basic training he was thrown into the regimental prison—*en taule*—for several weeks before he was packed off to Aubagne to be processed out of the Legion.

Our unit's protocols for desertion were uniform and desultory. Our leadership would alert the entire formation and then designate several of us in the deserter's platoon to go out on a "search party." I never served on such a party, but it was welcome to those chosen for it, since it gave them opportunities to buy cigarettes and snacks. Our efforts to find and to catch deserters comprised little more than setting up posts at Castelnaudary's train station and driving down a few streets and country roads of nearby townships before calling it quits after three to five hours. For the most part, desertions came to our platoon's tense social environment as welcome comic relief. The general feeling about those who left was "good riddance," and we would forget them quickly after a few jokes, comments, and reflections about their wobbly character.

XXXI

October–December 2008

Until my four months of basic training in the Foreign Legion, not breaking the seventh and tenth commandments, at least in their explicit directions, had never greatly challenged me. Only once had I committed laughably petty theft in my teenage years in a rash, unthinking episode, and this event filled me with unquenchable shame. Covetousness makes for snakier misdeeds, and I must stand guilty of many of these. Still, I would say that in my youth I had an abhorrence for the very idea of theft. Then I joined the French Foreign Legion.

Almost immediately upon walking through Aubagne's gates, I found myself in a regimented world whose moral complexity was radically new to me. We never went hungry in Aubagne, but trips to the mess hall were strictly regulated. No snacking was allowed between meals, and anyone caught in such acts would have been unceremoniously booted out of the selection process. During in-processing all our possessions save for the barest necessities for hygiene were locked away in storage. In this environment, theft became rampant, but even under the duress of recruitment I was never tempted to steal.

My outlook changed during basic training at Castelnaudary, where our cadre discreetly taught us—largely by deed rather than by word—that learning to steal without detection is important to soldiering and necessary for larger acts of warfare. I would go so far as to suggest that few men can be good enlisted soldiers without becoming passable thieves. A thief conducts reconnaissance before his robberies, much as any soldier worth his salt reconnoitres enemy positions and determines patterns of activity before launching attacks. In any military manoeuvre, just as in thieving, to avoid detection by the enemy altogether, or until the last possible moment, is of utmost importance. To the victors, of course, go the spoils, and few soldiers have scruples about taking and using their vanquished enemy's goods. In these and in many other respects, the trades of the soldier and the thief share common ground.

Many conditions set in place from our first days at the farm encouraged thievery. Most outstanding of these was the bizarre policy of allowing *engagés volontaires* to smoke but not to buy cigarettes. Soon this led desperate smokers to commit brazen acts such as stealing cigarettes from one of our corporals, which led to a night of reprisals for the whole platoon. In the end, enterprising legionnaires managed to procure cigarettes by parlaying with the men who delivered bread each morning to the farm or by sneaking out under cover of darkness to get cigarettes at local farmsteads. Perhaps some of them bribed our corporals. By hook or by crook, they kept cigarettes coming throughout our six weeks in isolation at the farm, thereby showing resourcefulness critical to the legionnaire's identity. A second aspect of this training was the deliberate refusal to supply us with any toilet paper or other means to clean ourselves after using the latrines. In such settings, to acquire and to hoard any available and suitable scrap of paper became an hygienic imperative.

To survive in reasonable conditions at the farm one almost had to pilfer. Sometimes it was absconding with extra food during kitchen duty, hiding it for later, or slipping it to other legionnaires. At other times it was supplying or taking part in the farm's robust black market. Yet at others it was stealing or somehow "finding" an item necessary for training but which had been misplaced, lost, or damaged beyond repair. Most commonly, it was the accepted fact that any item of equipment left unattended for too long would change hands. Not keeping close watch over one's assigned items was *de facto* abdication of ownership. Such actions of questionable honesty would have been largely unnecessary in our prior civilian lives, even for many legionnaires from troubled countries or familial poverty. At the farm, however, even the most scrupulous among us soon learned to connive, if not to steal outright, and to view such acts as the natural order of things. This was excellent training for the occupation of soldiering.

As training at Castelnaudary progressed, often we were told to prepare for field exercises and to bring items which we had either never received or which we had lost or damaged during prior training. The only way to get these items was to buy them at Castelnaudary's *foyer*. Going to the *foyer* without authorization was forbidden, and being caught at the *foyer* without authorization led to punishment for individuals and for our platoon. Yet often our leadership left us absolutely in need of items at the *foyer* while also strictly prohibiting our going to it. On one such occasion, when we protested the absurdity of the situation to our Belorussian corporal, he laughed and repeated a common phrase of the Legion: "*Pas vu, pas pris.*" Translated literally this means, "Not seen, not caught." Its true meaning is that if no appropriate authority witnesses your crime and chooses to apprehend you for it, then you enjoy immunity from its customary consequences. *Pas vu, pas pris* became a guiding moral principle in basic training, and before long we learned to conduct carefully planned "raids" on the *foyer*. Thus, we also rehearsed and refined many basic tactics.

Legionnaires have a reputation for being thieves. Yet I was only robbed of cash once in the Legion—probably by a Bulgarian corporal who had the tact to leave untouched my credit cards and identity documents. Overt theft in the ranks is rare. I do believe, however, that legionnaires are taught to develop a moral code specific to their condition, according to which "theft" in the eyes of many would appear to the legionnaire as "repurposing." As my military career has progressed, I have come to think that lying and stealing within careful limits are foundational skills for soldiers, especially when serving under large and unresponsive bureaucracies. Missions cannot fail owing to moral scruples about property, and the latter's importance fades before the former's.

XXXII

October–December 2008

Rites of passage are not wanting in the Foreign Legion. Indeed, its distinctive culture forged over decades—mostly in far-flung parts of the world such as Algeria or French Indochina—puts exaggerated emphasis on corporate mythology and rites of passage. Such rites incorporate almost every known tool of arcane ceremony, including torchlit ceremonies at night. Of these established and customary rites, one of the most common was to be sent to the Legion's regimental prisons for relatively minor misdeeds and mistakes.

In the Legion's often archaic terminology, to be sent to the regimental prison was to go *en taule*. Introduced to these words in the Legion, I thought them part of normal French parlance until I used "*en taule*" in conversation with a friend in Paris, whereupon he burst out laughing at this old-fashioned word. Therefore, I would translate *en taule* not as "in prison," but rather with the Wodehousian phrase "in chokey," since *en taule* probably sounds about as quirky to the modern French ear as Edwardian slang would to today's English speakers.

To spend time *en taule* became an obligatory and formative part of the legionnaire's experience. Commissioned and senior non-commissioned officers tended to view with suspicion legionnaires without a few stints *en taule*, as though such bizarrely well-behaved and careful legionnaires might harbour dangerous ambitions. Such suspicions were perhaps warranted. In my case, they were.

Officers meted out punishment for infractions summarily. If memory serves, company commanders had the authority to send legionnaires *en taule* for a limited period. For heavier punishments, the guilty party would have to appear before the regimental commander, who could ordain longer sentences likewise limited by regulation and custom. Offending legionnaires would report to their commanders in full dress uniform according to a strictly prescribed formula. Poor ironing and preparation of one's uniform or a botched presentation—not uncommon for junior legionnaires whose command of French was shaky and whose nerves were rattled on such occasions—could be grounds for lengthier sentences *en taule*. Toward the end of my Legion career, I happened to be in the room when one Foreign Legion commander heard the case of a Polynesian legionnaire who had been in my basic training platoon. This intelligent and judicious man—whose father was a noted functionary in France's provinces—gave short shrift to the evidence, and assigned the legionnaire a week *en taule* for what I thought a minor misunderstanding.

The *taules* themselves were usually located near the closely controlled regimental gates, one of few points where legionnaires and the wider public could enter and exit the regiment. Once *en taule*, legionnaires were assigned a variety of menial tasks throughout the day and slept and ate in isolation. Prized luxuries such as *la sieste* were stripped from the incarcerated. Life *en taule* was anything but pleasant, and prison quarters were often cramped and dreary. In some respects, however, this time could be a respite from the pace of life at one's assigned company. Throughout any given day in a Foreign Legion regiment, one would see groups of legionnaires *en taule* working at various projects such as caring for lawns and gardens and cleaning areas and facilities. It was almost always customary for legionnaires to offer shouts of encouragement and cheers for these groups of their brothers-in-arms *en taule*.

This system may appear as arbitrary to some in the more pampered militaries of the early twenty-first century, but one of its many benefits was that once the legionnaire's time *en taule* ended, he was absolved of his crime. To be sure, legionnaires with a record of repeated trips *en taule* tended to develop bad reputations that would eventually affect their potential in the organization, but for relatively few trips *en taule* legionnaires suffered no additional consequences aside from their sentences. For the most part, fellow legionnaires and superiors chummily welcomed and reintegrated legionnaires returning from *taule*, and often the warmest greetings would come from the very commander who had punished the legionnaire. In this respect, the Legion maintained an effective means of enforcing discipline that also bolstered its cohesion and corporate identity.

Years later, when I served as an officer in the United States Army, I grew increasingly frustrated at how challenging it was to enforce physical restraints and discipline on soldiers, and I came to appreciate the Legion's more freewheeling and heavy-handed approach to these matters. Few soldiers are saints, but many are quite intelligent. In the Legion I learned that physical punishment and its threat are extremely effective means of enforcing conformity and discipline no matter what one's background. A blow to the chest, a firm slap on the back of one's neck, or harsher measures—all distinct possibilities in the Legion—held in check legionnaires' baser instincts, in moments where "administrative" punishments would have proven to be objects of scorn. Even the Legion's methods of French instruction were enhanced by resort to physical correction for grammatical mistakes or for general inability to communicate.

In my later career as an officer, to put a soldier in the US Army into military prison involved tangled procedures that consumed weeks of officers' lives. It took many months from the time of starting these legal procedures to be able to enforce the appropriate prison sentence, so few officers even bothered to start them save for in the most heinous cases. I always found it challenging to enforce discipline in regular and even "special" US Army units, and I deemed their discipline rather slipshod in comparison with that of Foreign Legion units.

I believe that the remarkably different disciplinary measures of these two armed forces in which I have served reflect the substantial divergences of

Latin and Anglo-Saxon legal cultures. However august the law may seem in the former, in practice its limits are considerable. Good order and discipline require that most action and consensus be governed by extra-legal means. In contrast, militaries of Anglo-Saxon origin rely more on explicit laws, such as the US armed forces' "Uniform Code of Military Justice."

XXXIII

December 2008

Two great festivals dominate the calendars of Foreign Legion regiments: Christmas and Camerone, which takes place on 30 April. In 2008, my platoon celebrated our first Christmas *à la Légion* toward the end of basic training.

Weeks before Christmas, our preparations for the holiday came to the forefront, taking precedence over other activities. The two great legionary feasts usually include a regimental *crosse* (a running competition of various distances and under different conditions), a regimental march, seasonal festivities at company clubs, sporting competitions, and an official Mass. One Christmas tradition was to hold a competition to create the best company nativity scene, or *crèche*. To support this effort at our company, platoon leaders specially chose and assigned legionnaires to work several hours a day—sometimes all day—under the direction of the company's first sergeant.

I happened to be one of the company's better singers, so the commander assigned me and a few other legionnaires to the regimental choir to sing for the Christmas Mass. For weeks we spent every evening under the supervision of a knowledgeable Russian choirmaster. Thanks to his guidance our amateur voices made for a respectable choir. During our last rehearsal at a church in Castelnaudary, the regimental commander himself came to observe us singing. After we had finished one of the season's traditional French hymns, he spoke to us earnestly about how good choirs are fundamental to the Legion's identity.

One day we left for our first company march in celebration of Christmas. This was a march of about thirty-five kilometres through the hills of the Aude, led by our company commander. The most memorable moment of this whole march for me was when one legionnaire from our platoon—a large and loud Frenchman with an indelible shiftiness in his eyes and smiles—self-assuredly broadcast to our marching column that our company commander was lost. "*Officiers de merde*!" he cried out with bombast. This legionnaire had no clue how to read a map and spoke utter nonsense. The whole route was very familiar to our commander, who knew exactly where we were. In later years, I still recall this moment when I hear enlisted men decry their officers for shortcomings in areas where they themselves lack any competence whatsoever. This is a poison that must be checked, and ruthlessly if necessary.

Later, we held our regimental run, or *crosse de Noël*. It took place at a park to the north of Castelnaudary, where we ran eight kilometres in combat trousers, combat boots, and our brightly coloured company sweaters. To take more than forty minutes to complete this run was considered bad form. Our company's executive officer won the race, and a non-commissioned officer from our company came in third. The executive officer was a Swiss national of wiry build. He spoke with a thoughtful, almost feminine expression and a quiet voice, and he chain-smoked cigarettes in his office and everywhere else. He completed this run in about twenty-eight minutes. Our company's winner of third place, who was on the executive officer's heels the whole race, was likewise a heavy smoker. So, on this occasion I truly began to question my efforts to quit smoking in order to become a better runner.

For months we had also been preparing for the Christmas sporting competition, which included events such as water polo, cross-country biking, and a two-mile run. Our company won this sporting competition, which redounded greatly to the commander's credit. By Christmas Eve the regiment was abuzz. The regimental commander carefully inspected and rated each company's *crèche*. Ours did not win, but it would have cut a respectable figure on Naples' *via San Gregorio Armeno*. Christmas Mass took place at six in the evening, and almost every officer in the regiment attended in full dress uniform. After we had returned to the regiment, we prepared for our company Christmas celebration, which for us would take place in the regimental *foyer* across from our company building.

In our dress uniforms we filed into the *foyer* and sat at our assigned tables, which were carefully decorated with plates, cups, and cutlery. This Christmas dinner was catered by civilians from outside the regiment and the food was of better quality than usual. It comprised at least seven courses, and wine and beer flowed abundantly. Throughout the dinner legionnaires performed skits in front of the company commander and his assembled cadre. Legionnaires were encouraged to mock their leaders and even the commander in these skits, and the chosen legionnaires did a fairly good job at their task, much to the assembled company's merriment. For many legionnaires from poorer parts of the world, our Christmas celebration must have been a remarkable feast.

After dinner we repaired to the company club and continued to share beers with those in our company and even to mix with legionnaires from other companies who, exceptionally, were allowed to leave their respective buildings that evening to visit the decorated bars of other companies and to admire their *crèches*. Carousing lasted well past midnight and a jolly anarchy reigned throughout the regiment. Our commander himself—normally a reserved character—drank more than his fill and prudently slipped away from the merriment to sleep in his dedicated room at the company. This made us think better of him, since it was the first time that any of us had witnessed his human side.

On Christmas Day itself, the company commander and first sergeant walked through the hallways and served "breakfast in bed" to all legionnaires. We had been told about this tradition, but it still surprised us to see it. This breakfast was far more ample than the Legion's usual fare. Later that day we received Christmas gifts from the platoon and the company, which were customarily useful and costly items. To this day I keep with me a fine bespoke Laguiole knife that we received as our gift that Christmas. In true Foreign Legion style, this knife's only accessory aside from its main blade is a corkscrew.

XXXIV

January 2009

Our platoon leader often stretched the truth. Whatever his experience and however many his good qualities, he could not hide this fact even from his greenhorn legionnaires. He was also an unabashed bibber and, unlike other cadre at the Fourth Foreign Regiment, he would occasionally drink to oblivion in the presence of officers, senior enlisted, and legionnaires.

The Epiphany is known to legionnaires as the *Fête des Rois*, and from what I have seen this holiday was a chance for the Legion's commissioned and non-commissioned officers to throw celebratory lunches in their respective clubs that were riotously boozy even by the Legion's standards. Our platoon leader stumbled back from this event in a state of utter incoherence and seemed to threaten bodily harm to all those in his way.

Many legionnaires from his platoon saw this behaviour and immediately, and perhaps irrecoverably, lost some of our respect for him. In this way we instinctively responded as I would now expect soldiers to do after years of experience. Leaders should use chemicals such as alcohol and nicotine strategically, as subordinates will judge them poorly and lose respect for them on account of any embarrassing exhibition of excess. The supreme role of alcoholic drinks in the Legion's daily life and corporate rituals notwithstanding, along with this embedded culture came real expectations of temperance and of prudence. Commanders and even many experienced non-commissioned officers frowned upon overindulgence in drink, something reckoned a particular and lamentable vice of Anglo-Saxons and of Slavs. Indeed, in the regular evaluation form for legionnaires there is a section in which leaders officially and numerically rate each legionnaire's temperance with alcohol.

Shortly after the Epiphany, we should have carried out the culminating event of the Foreign Legion's challenging and unique basic training—a 120-kilometre march over four days, with numerous tactical and academic evaluations conducted along the way. This long march was an accepted standard for training in the Foreign Legion. It would be a lie to state that any of us was looking forward to extended periods of marching outdoors subject to early January's whims and cruelties, but many of us were keen to face the challenge. One day we rode military trucks to the farm expecting to begin our march there.

To our great surprise, we never left the farm, and instead stayed there for four days conducting tactical and academic evaluations in its familiar fields and open-air classroom. None of us knew why this was happening. Surely none of us could or would complain about this. From later remarks of others in the company and from various clues, I gleaned that our platoon leader had simply decided not to do what was expected of him, probably because he himself did not wish to spend four days in such a challenging winter climate. So, in effect, we were "hiding" from our company leadership at the farm, while the platoon leader most probably reported that we were out conducting the required march.

It seems to me hardly possible that our commander did not figure out relatively soon what was happening with our platoon, and that we were not fulfilling his intent. And yet, we saw no intervention—at least at the legionnaire's level. Our platoon leader had a reputation of being a steely warrior and the physical presence to bolster such beliefs. Indeed, he looked like a stereotypical rugby player from the Pacific Islands. Most notably, he had served at Sarajevo during the conflict there in the 1990s—a rare "combat" experience for legionnaires before the regular deployments to Afghanistan began about 2008. So, it is quite possible that he assumed that owing to his clout at the company, our commander would never dare to confront him about his decision. For all I know, he may have been correct in this assumption. In any event, this did not reflect well on his character as a senior non-commissioned officer.

Like everyone in our platoon, I fell under the spell of the platoon leader's charisma during basic training. Later, as I saw repeated examples of his untoward dealings, these led me to question his reputed tactical wizardry. After many years of serving in infantry units of worldwide reputation, now I would consider ranking our platoon leader among the camp of schemers not uncommon in military formations. In the US Army, whenever I would hear non-commissioned officers boasting, protesting their superior expertise in all matters of importance, and solemnly professing exaggerated solidarity with their soldiers, I questioned their sincerity as I instinctively called to mind the bluster of my basic training platoon leader in the Legion. Perhaps my prejudice is unfair, but I cannot think of many professional and trustworthy commissioned or non-commissioned officers who are also inveterate braggarts.

Ceremonies to mark the conclusion of the Legion's basic training are at times solemn and magnificent affairs, but ours was quite simple. It took place on our regimental *place d'armes* on an overcast and frigid January afternoon. Before this we had finished a week of administrative paperwork and learned our future assignments, and most of us eagerly awaited arriving at our regiments and the "real" Legion. Together our platoon took the meandering train back to Aubagne to conduct final interviews and to sign our definitive contracts with the Legion. At this time a few more men, including the Irishman with whom I joined the Legion some five months before, chose to leave the Legion.

From Aubagne our platoon spread out to almost every regiment in the Legion, with the exception that no one was assigned to the thirteenth half-brigade in Djibouti—where posts were coveted since salaries for legionnaires there were three times more than the regular pay at other Foreign Legion units. For my part, I went back to Castelnaudary to continue service while trying to overcome the limitations of my diagnosed hearing loss. After discussions with my company commander, this seemed the best way to try to negotiate the medical and legal obstacles to my further progress within the organization.

XXXV

January 2009

After basic training, most legionnaires travel directly from Aubagne to their newly assigned regiments, and immediately begin weeks of further training tailored by each unit to meet its specific needs. At Calvi's Second Foreign Parachute Regiment, for example, incoming legionnaires join a *promotion* that includes airborne training, weapon qualifications, and fitness tests, not to mention the Foreign Legion's most extreme hazing. Other regiments integrate new soldiers in less harrowing ways, but in general new legionnaires are assigned the most menial tasks, experience regular hazing and even violence, and have few freedoms. Almost every regiment experiences a few desertions from its group of new arrivals from Castelnaudary's basic training.

Of course, there were exceptions to the above norms. One teenage legionnaire from Mongolia—who had paid Russian smugglers two thousand US dollars to bring him to France so that he could join the Legion—was a talented drummer. After basic training, the Legion immediately assigned him to its respectable ceremonial band at Aubagne, where he remained for his entire career. The Legion also recruited long-distance runners and boxers, and usually these recruits were assigned to special teams at Aubagne after basic training. Given my limiting medical diagnosis, I also found myself in an exceptional case and travelled right back to my company at Castelnaudary, where I would work as an assistant to my basic training platoon until further notice. Since my platoon's leadership was taking holiday for three weeks after completing our basic training class, I had the chance to take my first leave, or *permission*.

All this came as a surprise to me, so I had little time to plan this unforeseen holiday. First, I spent a few days walking about and discovering Castelnaudary. Ever since our supervised jaunt in the town, I had wished to try the cassoulet at the *Hôtel du Centre et Lauragais* and at the *Hôtel de France*. I had lunch at both. After a few days of this fattening cassoulet tour and of spending more unhurried time at the *Collégiale Saint-Michel*, I took the train to Carcassone, where I spent several days touring its new and old cities. The next leg of my journey took me to Marseilles, and I looked forward to proper leisure at the Legion's facility at Malmousque. As I emerged from Saint Charles Station, I reflected on my initial, heart-pounding attempt to join the Foreign Legion several months before, and to the morning when we first left for Castelnaudary. The ensuing months had changed me. Though I hardly understood this at the time, I had just received an exceptional introduction to the life of an infantryman. It prepared me well for the rest of my military career, and indeed set my lasting expectations, habits, and prejudices as a soldier.

In Marseilles, I made many occasions to sample *bouillabaisse marseillaise* at the source. One Frenchman in my platoon had raved about the food at *La Petite Nice* right next to Malmousque, and when I tried to eat there, I found out why. It was one of Marseilles' most famous restaurants, whose chef had boasted three Michelin stars for years. This discovery did leave me wondering if—and if so, how and when—this legionnaire had eaten there. I could not yet afford such indulgence on my legionnaire's salary, but I undertook thorough investigations of *bouillabaisse* and found a listing called the *Chartre de la Bouillabaisse Marseillaise*, of which the nearby restaurant *Le Rhul* was a founding member. So, after dressing up as well as I could with my few civilian clothes, I took lunch at

Le Rhul at one of its tables overlooking Marseilles' *corniche* and the *Château d'If*. This hotel and restaurant have since become an obligatory stop for me during any trip to Marseilles, which remains one of my favourite cities in France.

Thereafter I travelled in the *train de grande vitesse,* or TGV, from Marseilles to Paris, taking advantage of our military discount that made such comfortable and fast transportation all but free. Staying for several days at the Legion's *Fort de Nogent* in Paris' eastern reaches, I revisited many familiar places in Paris with new eyes and a true ability to speak passable French. At the Louvre I looked for one of my favourite paintings by Poussin, *Orphée et Eurydice*, but it must have been on loan or in conservation, for it was no longer with the other Poussin paintings where I remembered it.

In later years I have become careful to avoid Paris' wintertime dreariness, but in those weeks of liberation I was thankful to be back in the familiar city and thrilled to revisit favourite bakeries from years past. This holiday also saw the beginning of an important and enduring friendship. A fellow Princetonian had put me in touch with one of her former colleagues at Columbia University in New York, named Jean-Paul. After Jean-Paul and I had exchanged telephone numbers by means of electronic messages, we met one evening at a well-known café near the *Gare Montparnasse*—either *Le Dôme* or *Le Select*.

Little did I know that I would be meeting one of my foremost guides to French culture, a young man who consistently challenged me as few ever would, and of whose company I never tired. In this respect I would label him as one of my truest friends, since he ranks among the few people whose presence I would prefer to their absence in all but the most extreme circumstances. That evening we ended up speaking for hours about Paris' cultural life, art, and music. Jean-Paul found intriguing my own background combined with my new endeavours in the Foreign Legion. It was the first friendship that I cultivated wholly in the French language, for we never spoke any other despite Jean-Paul's superb English.

Before I knew it, my unforeseen holiday had finished, and I was back in Castelnaudary for new experiences in the Foreign Legion's basic training, but now as an observer and enforcer of its methods—a temporary *aide-moniteur.*

XXXVI

January 2009

My platoon's leadership trickled back from holiday, but we had little to do beyond the normal working day. For training cadre in our company at Castelnaudary, our first formation was about 0600 inside the company club. All cadre gathered here in the mornings, shook hands with everyone in the room, drank the club's grimace-making coffee, and began the day with casual discussion about its tasks and expectations. Later, as an officer in the US Army, I often looked back and appreciated this morning ritual reproduced at almost every Foreign Legion company, most of which have impressive clubs probably without peer in similar military organizations worldwide. During my first years in the US Army, it struck me as very odd that leaders did not shake hands every morning, such had the Legion ingrained into me this habit.

For the Fourth Foreign Regiment's cadre, life had predictable rhythms distinct from the chaotic changes at the Legion's operational regiments. With relatively unburdened evenings and free weekends, over the coming weeks I began to travel both within the region and back to Paris whenever possible. For the first of these weekend trips my port of call was Toulouse. By telephone I reached out to the trenchcoated United States citizen who, several months before, had given me his calling card at our *képi blanc* ceremony at the farm. He kindly invited me to stay at his apartment over the weekend.

One Friday evening in late winter I arrived at Toulouse's train station and walked to this man's apartment on the *Rue des Arts*. After considering the rules of decorum to which I had been exposed over the years—from intensive scouring of Emily Post's works to the Legion's own elaborate rituals—I thought it unwise to arrive without bearing a gift and therefore purchased a fine bottle of red Burgundy from a nearby vintner. When my host greeted me at his apartment, he acknowledged the wine and welcomed me.

From our initial conversation we found each other interesting. He worked as a lawyer for a multinational aviation company based in Toulouse. After his undergraduate education and serving as a non-commissioned officer in the artillery of the US Army, he had completed his training at a law school in Washington, DC, and done well for himself in several distinct industries. He was also Roman Catholic and frequented the local "Tridentine" Mass, so we shared a penchant for liturgical beauty and ecclesiastical continuity.

I remain forever thankful that my first months in the Legion began the longer process of curing me of that typical and destructive North American vice, Anglophilia. Yet, my previous and shameless indulgence in this vice also gave me something more in common with my new friend. For notwithstanding his Irish origins and Roman Catholicism, he was a confirmed Anglophile—to such extremes that he would even refer to his weight in "stone."

He had married a younger lady from the East Coast of the United States, and that evening he introduced me to her as she was making what turned out to be a well-presented and balanced dinner. Blessed with thick, curly red hair that handsomely framed her pleasant, if not striking, face, her body was well-proportioned and well-kept, even if it did already show a propensity to corpulence if her discipline in diet and exercise were to waver. Their two young boys were loud and bursting with energy. On a later occasion their mother confessed to me that as an only child herself, she had limited experience with children and had never imagined being a mother to male offspring. She seemed to find their mischief, their boundless energy, and their constant need for attention somewhat shocking. Their instinctive attraction to motor vehicles and to firearms before they could speak a word amazed her.

The next day for lunch my kind host took me to taste the many fruits of Toulouse's *marché des Carmes*, where we ate a variety of oysters washed down with Muscadet. Later we walked through the city and enjoyed one of the best wine bars that I have ever visited in France, whose skillful owner introduced me to red Lirac. Indeed, this and most of my later visits to Toulouse with this knowledgeable foreign resident tended to include indulgence in fine wines.

The next morning he and I went to Mass with his two sons at the nearby *Chapelle Saint-Jean-Baptiste*, which belonged to a French religious order that only said Mass according to the "Tridentine" or "extraordinary" form. His wife did not join us since she was not Catholic. I do not remember the Mass, but I do remember lingering outside the chapel after Mass as we chatted with the priest and with several parishioners. Nearby a gaggle of teenage girls—almost all thin, well-dressed, delicately groomed, and attractive owing to their land of birth, social origins, and education—chattered buoyantly as they crowded about the chapel's entrance immediately after Mass, many of them smoking cigarettes.

It occurred to me then that such a scene would be unthinkable in the United States, even among "traditionalist" Catholics who, for all their supposed reservations about the nation's larger Protestant culture, nonetheless ape the mores and morality of their more charismatic, Puritan-inspired Protestant countrymen. At a well-ordered parish in the United States in 2009, to smoke with fellow Catholics after Mass would have been socially unacceptable. Anyone indulging in such conspicuous displays of vice would have done so guiltily and probably with intentions to scandalize other parishioners.

That morning in Toulouse, it would not have surprised me to see the parish priest ask one of these girls for a cigarette. He probably did so at some point. If I were a painter, I would surely try to put this image to canvas, since it remains one of the most remarkable memories from my many trips to Toulouse over the years. If I ever were to achieve such a work, I could not resist entitling it: *À l'ombre des jeunes filles en fumes.*

XXXVII

January 2009

A few years after I had left the Foreign Legion, I was walking through a well-known room in Rome's Barberini Palace. There my eyes fell upon a comely sight. A middle-aged Italian father, dressed with enviable *sprezzatura*, held his daughter in his arms. She, too, was dressed stylishly in those ways by which only French and Italian parents manage to outfit their toddlers and young children. For a moment I lost my train of thought as I looked at the charming real-life scene that they offered. The girl pointed with glee at one of the large canvases in the room and cried out, "*Guarda Papa, Caravaggio*!"

She could not have been more than five years old, but her eyes had not misled her. I do not remember if she was pointing at *Narcissus*, *Judith Beheading Holofernes,* or *Saint John the Baptist*, but it was probably the last of these. It struck me how different was the upbringing that she had already known at that tender age to my own in the United States. Having attended respectable state-run and private schools and some of my country's better universities for much of my life, I could not have recognized a single painting by Caravaggio until well into my twenties. This episode was exemplary and humbling testimony to how different North American and European systems of education remained.

It was during my time in the Foreign Legion that I cultivated a true appreciation and love for the plastic arts. During those first weekends in Toulouse, I began to frequent not only the city's *Musée des Augustins*, but also a place that would become especially dear to me, the Bemberg Foundation, housed in one of Toulouse's Renaissance palaces, now called the Hôtel d'Assézat. This foundation and its well-chosen collection rekindled in me a love for the humanities that I had lost over the years prior to my enlistment, when the prospect of an academic career prematurely sapped my enthusiasm. Had I never experienced the Legion's basic training, most probably I would have walked through this collection with indifference or boredom, allowing distractions to rule over my thoughts. Instead, I spent hours in this foundation scouring the details of paintings, reading all that I could about them in the museum's guides and explanatory labels and posts.

In the years during and after my undergraduate education, I had travelled throughout Europe and often visited many of its best museums. While living in Saint Petersburg I frequented the Hermitage and the Russian Museum, thanks to a student pass that provided free entrance to all the city's museums. At the Hermitage I spent many dozens of days wandering through its halls and getting better acquainted with its unending collections. For some reason, along with Diego Velázquez, Jacob van Ruisdael, of all artists, stood out from the crowd for me at this time. A year later I had the chance to spend all day in the Louvre for three straight weeks. In addition to these major collections, I had been blessed to visit repeatedly Vienna's *Kunsthistorisches Museum* and many smaller collections. Moreover, there were single visits to major museums and churches throughout the continent. At least consciously, these visits had not made any major impact on my way of thinking. Far more interested in letters and in history than in art, I mainly visited such establishments out of a sense of obligation to good taste and for my own betterment during my *Lehrejahre.*

However little impact such visits seemed to have had, they had laid sound foundations for the appreciation of art that I began to cultivate in earnest that winter of 2009. Much as countless visits to museums had impressed on that

Italian girl in the Barberini Palace an ability to acknowledge Caravaggio's work at such a young age, my past visits, too, had shovelled into the waters of my own consciousness enough impressions and memories, even if usually unreachable to me in my waking state, to build sound foundations for understanding and admiring the plastic arts.

From this time onward my travels in France included a focus on improving my understanding of painting. Future trips to Paris revolved around the Louvre and the capital's other splendid museums, such as the *Petit-Palais*, the *Grand-Palais*, and the *Musée Jacquemart-André*. No matter where I travelled, I made the local art museum, no matter how small or seemingly inconsequential, an obligatory visit. Knowledge hitherto dormant within me came alive, and in no small part do I have the Foreign Legion to thank for this. In one fell swoop its basic training had done away with the chronic and debilitating bouts of Onegin-like "spleen" or *khandra* that had long plagued me, instilling in their stead a craving for and an abiding appreciation of human attempts to capture the beauty of the created world.

Toulouse's art also reminded me of recent disappointments in matters of affection. For as I visited the city's *Capitolium* and paid attention to its decorations, I saw in two of Paul Gervais' paintings what appeared to me the spitting image of the French woman who had recently commanded my botched attentions, and whose beauty and arrogance still vexed me whenever I thought about them. To me it seemed that it was she herself largely nude and reclining on a young man's breast in Gervais' *L'Amour à Cythère*. To be sure, the woman's figure in this painting was rather more muscular than that of the young lady of my acquaintance, but I thought their faces almost identical. In a second painting, *Amour source heureuse de vie à quarante ans*, it seemed that Gervais had used the same model, so again I thought to see that *Versaillaise*'s very face looking down at me. In actual fact she did, with local variations, only embody an archetype of French beauty that one encounters not infrequently. I imagine that Paul Gervais' model was one of thousands of women in France whose faces would have called to my mind the "Dulcinea" of my recent past.

XXXVIII

February 2009

I visited Mirepoix for the second time almost a year after leaving the Foreign Legion. On that occasion I was touring the region with a Foreign Legion chaplain who owned a house in nearby Montréal dans l'Aude. The two of us sat on Mirepoix' main square in high summer's sunshine, under whose benevolent rays this chaplain introduced me to the French liquor *Suze*. As we downed several portions of it, served in small glasses called *galopins*, our conversation mostly focused on Mirepoix' cathedral.

My first visit to Mirepoix took place several weeks after I had begun working at our company's farm as an *aide-moniteur*. Today I remember little of our new platoon of recruits and their training. Once back at the farm I had the obligation to repeat most of its events, and they were only slightly more tolerable since they held less mystery. In general, the corporals and I slept in the same areas as recruits in training and shared most of their hardships while bearing greater responsibilities, so this was no relaxing time. It was difficult for me to change from student to trainer so quickly, and for the most part I failed.

During one's first years in the Foreign Legion, learning to wield an iron and to crease shirts is given more attention than training to shoot assigned weapons. To press out flawless creases in several different versions of dress uniforms and to remove all visible wrinkles from them were essential tasks at which legionnaires could ill afford to fail. One night, all corporals and *engagés volontaires* stayed up until morning ironing the gathered recruits' shirts, dress uniforms, and combat uniforms. Never shall I forget a Malagasy corporal's words as he lashed out at one *engagé volontaire* in bilious shouts heard throughout the room: "You call yourself a man and you can't iron! Didn't your mother ever teach you how to iron?" This abashed young man did not have any answer, and he lowered his head in shame. We began this task shortly after dinner and ended only about half an hour before morning formation. After our morning run, we rushed headlong into the farm's obstacle course.

A much-appreciated comedic addition to our training was the arrival of a Russian *caporal-chef* to serve as one of our cadre. Heavily Frenchified after over fifteen years of service but nonetheless with a strong accent that betrayed his origins, this *caporal-chef* came to us after experiencing an operational career at the Legion's most renowned regiments. This was his first "training" assignment, and he found many aspects of Castelnaudary's lifestyle and management horrifying. More so than other cadre, he showed patience with potential legionnaires and tried to teach them as best he could. He spoke only two words of English, "chicky dance," which he repeated so often and used in so many contexts that it could have meant almost anything, from expressing extreme disappointment to utmost elation. I never could determine what "chicky dance" meant. A corporal implied that these words had something to do with cocaine in French Guyana, but I have never been able to figure out definitively the origins and the import of this mysterious phrase.

As the weeks in our rustic retreat progressed, at length I asked the platoon leader if I could attend Mass at the nearest town one Sunday, especially given our usual relaxed rituals of barbecues and drinking beer and wine on our day of rest. Since there truly was little for us to do on the Sabbath, he gave me permission to put on civilian clothes and to walk the several kilometres south to

Mirepoix, right across the border separating the *départements* Aude and Ariège. After several weeks of confinement on the farm, it was a breath of fresh air to walk along the open roads of these expansive territories.

Before long I found myself in Mirepoix' central square, admiring its many post-and-beam houses. The city's only Mass was held in the early afternoon, and I had arrived two hours before its beginning, so I took this occasion to browse through many small shops, to buy cigarettes for two corporals, and to visit the town's admirable mediaeval Cathedral of Saint-Maurice.

That winter's meagre sunlight meekly checked the darkness of the nave, but even in such gloomy illumination I could not help but to be cheered at the site of so much Christian chaos accumulated over centuries. Some of the cathedral's vaults were covered in stars typical of mediaeval churches, whereas elsewhere peeling layers of paint betrayed various religious images that had once covered these vaults—images long since painted over or worn away by centuries of exposure to the air and to the smoke of countless candles.

The Mass that evening was sparsely attended. To my memory, no more than twenty people came to Mirepoix' only Sunday liturgy. As soon as Mass ended, I walked back to the farm, cutting through various fields to quicken the return journey. All was quiet at the farm as I regained my room shared with our *engagés volontaires* and changed into my military uniform. Recruits who knew that I had ventured out to a nearby town asked me wide-eyed about my journey and what I had done back in the civilian world. Already these young men viewed a small village that would never have interested them before with an almost pained curiosity, as it beckoned with pleasures and possibilities now denied them. For many legionnaires and for my cadre, it was bizarre that I would go to such lengths to attend Mass, and I imagine that they suspected that I had spent the afternoon drinking and carousing in whatever fleshpots the sleepy town could muster.

For me, that Sunday afternoon walk to Mirepoix was my first glimpse of a quasi-mythical *France profonde*, a place far enough removed from train stations, settlements, and major highways that it seemed to broadcast its realities on entirely different frequencies from those of France's larger cities and more populous and well-connected regions.

XXXIX

February 2009

Four weeks at the farm passed quickly, and already we were preparing for the new recruits' *marche de Képi Blanc*. The day before the march, my company commander called me back to Castelnaudary. I had no idea what he wanted to discuss with me and why I would not continue training with our platoon at the farm. My instructions were to pack all my belongings. Clueless about the reasons behind such instructions, my mind raced with questions and worries, foreseeing a variety of possible emergencies or mishaps.

As I arrived back at the company, the first sergeant greeted me in his loud and jerky way and told me to report immediately to the commander. After knocking on the commander's door and presenting myself to him using the Legion's formula for junior enlisted, I stood before him and awaited his news or guidance. After some banter about my latest experiences at the farm, he explained to me that he was sending me to Paris to take part in a ceremony for the opening of a museum exhibition—a *vernissage*. Nonplussed, I asked for clarification about these instructions, but he referred me to the first sergeant and dismissed me.

This was my first chance to experience the direct supervision of this first sergeant, a man whom I did not like at first but who later turned out to be one of my favourite characters in the Legion. My initially negative impressions of him were one of many cases that taught me to distrust such instincts, or at least to believe that any understanding that they offer may prove deceptive. The first sergeant provided me with some administrative instructions and told me to be ready to depart for Paris on the overnight train leaving Castelnaudary about midnight.

By coincidence, my sister was travelling in southern France at that time, as she had a musical audition in Toulouse. This was the first opportunity to see any of my family since leaving my parents' house in Texas. We met briefly that evening in Castelnaudary and arranged to meet again in Paris after her audition, as I would be staying there for several days for the *vernissage*. Once back at the barracks, I packed my bags. A driver from the company brought me to Castelnaudary's train station. The overnight train journey took over eight hours, and the Legion did not pay for a sleeping berth. As best I could, I tried to sleep in a coach seat. The next morning, after alighting in Paris, I made my way to Fort de Nogent. I reported, occupied an assigned room, and joined a group comprising one legionnaire from each regiment based on the French mainland.

All day we legionnaires pressed our uniforms, polished our boots, used forks dipped in tap water to comb and to stiffen the red tassels of our epaulettes, and rehearsed ceremonial movements and protocols for that evening. A French corporal from one of the Legion's engineering regiments took me under his wing and taught me many things about ironing and uniform management.

That evening we went to represent the Legion of 2009 at the *vernissage* for an exhibition of Foreign Legion uniforms, past and present, located in a museum that was part of the *Val-de-Grâce* compound in Paris' fifth district. Turnout for the *vernissage* was rather star-studded for the Legion, including many former and present general officers. Although I imagine that most of the snacks offered by the uniformly dressed servants were *surgelés*, to my untrained eye and deprived senses they were redolent with forgotten flavours and textures. Wine flowed, and it would have been terrible form for legionnaires to abstain.

Drink we did, but with guardedness owing to many watchful eyes.

That evening I met one of the Legion's anglophone legends, Simon Murray. He had joined the Legion in 1960, served in its Second Parachute Regiment, and fought in campaigns against the Algerian *Front de Libération National*. After finishing his five-year contract, he moved on to begin a wildly successful career as a businessman in Hong Kong. At the time I knew neither of his posh origins back in England nor of his great personal wealth, and we spoke for over ten minutes about his experiences in the early 1960s, the last period of extended warfare for the Legion—and back when its ranks were supposedly filled with the hardest veterans from Germany's *Schutzstaffel* and *Wehrmacht*. I listened with fascination as he recounted his departure from Malmousque for basic training at and near Sidi-bel-Abbès. It was encouraging to learn that after the passage of so many decades, our basic training experiences were more alike than not.

This was hardly a sentimental old man coming to Paris to relive worn memories. Still a member of the boards of several well-known enterprises throughout the world, Mr. Murray had taken time out of his busy schedule and from any number of hobbies and passions that he might have pursued to be there that evening for this *vernissage* of a modest Foreign Legion exhibition. For him and for so many others present at the *vernissage*, the shadow of Algeria and of the *putsch* loomed large. For an hour I listened eagerly to an elderly French gentleman who had been part of the First Foreign Parachute Regiment during the *putsch* and faced demotion and imprisonment for his decisions as an officer to support this effort. He had known Hélie Denoix de Saint Marc, one of the men whose writings had inspired my enlistment. As we sat on a secluded bench in the exhibition halls, he patiently offered me sound observations about the legionnaire's condition.

Too soon the *vernissage* and our duties ended. After attending Sunday Mass in Fontenay-sous-Bois, I was on my way to visit the Louvre when the first sergeant telephoned me, accused me of prolonging an unlicensed holiday in Paris, and ordered me to return to the company. A few hours later I boarded the TGV for Toulouse, and then took the regional train to Castelnaudary.

XL

February 2009

Toward the end of my brief trip to Paris for the *vernissage*, I received an electronic message from an old friend from Princeton, named James. He had just taken up quarters on *Rue d'Ulm* as part of an exchange between Princeton and Paris' *École Normale Supérieure*, where he would study for the coming academic term. We settled on meeting during my next trip to Paris.

This was not long in coming, as cadre once again enjoyed weekends off from work after our platoon had returned from the farm to garrison life at Castelnaudary. A few weeks after the exhibition, James and I met in the Luxembourg Garden. It had only been eight months since we had last shared drinks together at Princeton's *Debasement Bar*. Already I felt happily cut off from that world. My friendship with James was one of few to outlive this rupture, for we shared a bond that remains with us to this day.

In the summer of 2005, James and I first met in Rome, where both of us attended summer courses offered by Father Reginald Foster. Father Foster was a cranky Discalced Capuchin who, almost alone among scholars of his generation, zealously kept up his ability to speak Latin. When not working as the chief

Latin translator at the Vatican's Secretariat of State, Father Foster taught at the Pontifical Gregorian University. Among his many efforts to appear iconoclastic, he always dressed like a plumber from the United States' Midwest and avowed himself a Maoist. Every summer, he hosted Latin courses for students from across the world. These courses took place in the humble cafeteria of a Catholic elementary school not far from Father Foster's monastery near the Basilica of Saint Pancras, and at no cost to students.

Many memories of my first arrival in the Eternal City remain vivid today. Until that time, I had never really cared to visit Rome, and I would have been much happier to spend a summer in London rather than in Italy. After arriving at Rome's Leonardo da Vinci Aeroport, I took a taxi that sped down the well-kept roads now so familiar to me. In the intensity of an early-June afternoon, I gazed out the taxi's open windows at the surrounding hills and their stone pines. Despite my relatively enthusiastic Catholic faith and love for the Classics, I was filled with scepticism about what awaited me in Rome. In my pitiable ignorance, I was inclined to look at modern Italy with unchecked contempt.

Taking advantage of the internet from my temporary location in Central Texas, I had found a room in a graceful pension near the Vatican run by a French-speaking religious order. After a night's rest, early the next morning I walked to the address for my Latin classes. To get there I crossed Saint Peter's Square and then got lost in the roads winding up the Janiculum Hill. In the late morning's accumulating heat, as I climbed cobbled streets with my Lewis and Short Dictionary in tow, cicadas' rhythmic humming, joined with the blinding sunshine, sparked within me an ill-defined foreboding that seemed to throb along with the cicadas' singing. Something inside me understood that I had come up against a force that would sweep away the comfortable platitudes that hitherto underlay my understanding of the world, overthrowing my prior beliefs, mocking cherished icons, and setting my life on a new and irrevocable course.

It was my first day in Italy.

Reginald Foster ranked among those rare teachers whose lessons have life-changing impacts on most of his students. Not a few of these, James among them, became his ardent disciples. Reginald forever changed my own approach to Latin and to the Classics, wresting them from the bristling stuffiness and pedantry of Germanic and Anglo-Saxon scholarship and bringing them to life in their Mediterranean home. Once, in his monastery's garden, he challenged us students to sit under the sun, to drink red wine, and to continue speaking Latin using the hard "c" prescribed by commonplace textbooks. An hour into our readings, I, priggish adherent to the hard "c," found myself lapsing into the soft "c." From that day onward I could not help but agree that it was practically impossible that Romans could have spoken with a hard "c" under the steady influence of such sunshine and wine. Since that day I have doggedly used "Church Latin" pronunciation, and in spirit I sneer at those who pronounce "Cicero" as "Kikero."

Those summer afternoons in and after class on the Janiculum, James and I spoke often but never got to know each other well. But we had both been initiated into the group of Reginald's followers, so it gladdened us to recognize each other at Princeton's Graduate School in 2006, where he was to study Classics, I Renaissance history. Over the next two years James and I forged a friendship grounded in our mutual and profound disappointment with Princeton and in our shared despair at the prospect of a future life in the academy. Neither of us wished to continue in this life, and to escape such a fate as well as to pursue many other goals simultaneously I chose to join the Foreign Legion. James was plotting his own escape.

That spring and early summer, James' friendship was a welcome respite from daily toil at the Fourth Foreign Regiment. It was curious to wander with him through the halls of the *École Normale Supérieure*, where I had once longed to study. Not long since I had left behind such dreams, but there I was, and what was James' that semester could have been mine. I had stopped wanting it.

James and I also took these occasions to eat our way through several well-known restaurants in the city, including *Restaurant Hélène Darroze*, where together we enjoyed our first meal made according to the inspirations of a Michelin-starred cook. Of late this restaurant had not received outstanding reviews, but for us *amateurs* it was a meal beyond criticism.

XLI

March 2009

During one of my winter trips to Paris, I was walking with James through the courtyard at the *École Normale Supérieure* when we ran into a young lady wearing a *hijab*. Upon seeing James, she gave him and me a winning smile. James introduced her as an acquaintance from the institution's student group devoted to speaking the Attic variety of Ancient Greek. Her name was Fatima. After this chance encounter the three of us made off for a garden in the Latin Quarter and talked for about an hour. As we parted ways, Fatima and I exchanged mobile telephone numbers and arranged to meet the next day.

We met on the bank of the Seine. From speaking with Fatima that day, quickly I came to admire her audacity. Although it was unlawful at that time in France to wear a *hijab* to schools or universities, she did so brazenly at the nation's foremost cradle of the humanities. When members of its administration confronted her about wearing the *hijab* in public, she simply dared them to discipline her. Given her background and upbringing, her steadfastness in this matter showed remarkable character.

I had grown up with North American prejudices about Muslims that were typical of my time and social origins. In the wake of the destruction of the World Trade Centre in New York City in 2001, Western media quickly assigned the blame for this event to a ragtag group of Saudi Arabian men who mostly planned these attacks in Germany and learned to fly civilian aircraft in Florida. Since the United States invaded Afghanistan in late 2001 in response to this event, our media—especially so-called "conservative" media—consistently portrayed Muslims as terrorists or as their sympathizers. Hollywood films substituted Soviet villains of old with Islamic terrorists. Despite mealymouthed protestations that we should only disapprove of "extreme Muslims," our media deliberately sowed fear, distrust, and contempt for Muslims worldwide. The Anglo-American invasion of Iraq in 2003 amplified these general trends.

In my own religious circles, practicing Catholics in the United States generally revelled in such hostile attitudes toward Muslims. In traditionalist Catholic groups, it was not rarely that I heard favourable comparisons of US military actions in Afghanistan and in Iraq with the Crusades of former centuries. Few notable Catholics in my country questioned these wars. For some time at university, I embraced such war-mongering and anti-Muslim ideas. Even when I later rejected them, I took no pains to combat their general acceptance.

Fatima was the first Muslim woman to captivate me with her charm and wit. She came from a large family of Algerian immigrants and had grown up in wretched circumstances in one of France's industrial cities, Clermont-Ferrand. After trying to take her own life as a teenager and almost succeeding, she devoted herself to studies and to philosophy. In their course she embraced Islam, which she had never before taken seriously as a belief system.

It is an unmistakable testimony to her willpower and intelligence that she rose out of such troubled circumstances to matriculate at *École Normale* studying philosophy. Her research mainly treated mediaeval Christian and Islamic thought, but her knowledge of the Renaissance was remarkable. Her Latin and her Greek were solid, her English elegant and tinged with tasteful British intonations, and her breadth of learning enviable. What is never unimportant in such intercourse, her figure was slender and graceful and her features lovely, if not striking at first glance. Fatima and I enjoyed each other's company, and we ended up seeing each other during all my trips to Paris that spring.

Owing to the tenets of her faith, Fatima did not drink alcohol, so for our second meeting I invited her to take hot chocolate with me at Angelina's. I had not yet developed the loathing for Northern European breakfasts that I did later, but the Legion had already left its mark on me, and I had begun to limit morning consumption in view of afternoon and evening meals. So, Angelina's caloric hot chocolate took the place of our breakfast that day. After an hour or more at Angelina's, we strolled together through the *Tuileries*. During this walk, Fatima remarked that there was one place in Paris with better hot chocolate than Angelina's. I did not refrain from questioning her judgment on this matter, so we agreed to meet at her preferred spot for hot chocolate the next day.

Her favourite place for hot chocolate was a small café near the metro *Odéon*, in the same *passage* as *La Procope*. Its name, *La Jacobine*, was appropriate both to the location and to Fatima's politics. After trying its hot chocolate, I had to admit that Fatima was right. *La Jacobine*'s hot chocolate outdid Angelina's.

From that day we usually met at Paris' most interesting spots for hot chocolate, from *Le Grand Colbert* to new and unknown shops. In this process I discovered exotic varieties that I could not have imagined. My favourite of these was the *chocolat chaud à l'huître* at Jean-Paul Hévin's chocolate bar on *Rue Saint-Honoré.* Over these rich drinks and smoothly switching between French and English, we had what were for me probably the most intellectually pleasing conversations that I had ever had with a woman in my life. Fatima's spirit was indomitable and admirable, her beauty modest but respectable, her other physical features *de mon genre*. Moreover, her interest in and admiration for me did not leave me unmoved.

Every rose has its thorn, however, and Fatima's was radical Islamic politics. Indeed, she had recently been imprisoned for a short spell owing to protests and to other political activities that remained unclear to me.

Whereas today I might approach such matters differently, hers was a thorn that I was unwilling to clasp. James repeatedly encouraged me to begin a romance with Fatima, but I did not do so. After I deployed to Afghanistan in summer 2009, I never saw her again. Years later, I do not remember how we lost touch.

XLII

March 2009

Before joining the Foreign Legion, I had never worried about my weight. Until I quit smoking in 2007 as part of my efforts to prepare for enlistment in the Legion, my steady use of thirty or so cigarettes a day, often unfiltered ones, suppressed my appetite such that I rarely ate. Thus, I kept the wan figure befitting a melancholic young scholar. Once I left off smoking and began a steady regimen of physical activity, my appetite increased as did my weight. I believe that I weighed about eighty-five kilogrammes when I joined the Legion, and this was the strongest and heaviest that I have been in my life.

Save for our stint at the farm, which I left weighing about seventy kilogrammes, I kept to this weight of eighty-five kilogrammes throughout my time in the Legion. No matter the fact that during the week we legionnaires ran every morning anywhere from ten to twenty kilometres, the Legion's hearty fare and my many extracurricular lunches and dinners across the Hexagon kept excess weight on me.

One evening after a long Legion week, I took the train to Paris and met a Princeton acquaintance for coffee near the *Gare de Lyon*. This young man, a French national whose father was an Algerian Freemason, had served for a year as an *aspirant* in the Legion's First Cavalry Regiment in Orange during his studies at the *École Polytechnique*. Therefore, my world was not wholly mysterious to him. Somewhat disappointed that I had not met him outside the station in my full Legion dress uniform, this young man and I set a meeting a few days later at a café near *Place d'Italie*. There our genteel conversation determined that we would only speak again one more time.

After that quick meeting at the *Gare de Lyon*, I sped to the Bastille Opera and met Jean-Paul near the box office. Two of his friends, Mathilde and Geneviève, joined us at our balcony seats with good views of the orchestra. That evening's concert highlighted one of Anton Bruckner's symphonies, either the seventh or the ninth. I was so exhausted from the week that I nodded my way through half of the symphony's performance, which perhaps explains why my memories of it are so few and so blurred.

After this concert the four of us walked to a nearby *bistrot*. This was my first of many encounters with Jean-Paul's friends from his studies and from his subsequent work in the French Republic's bureaucracy, and without fail I enjoyed them all. Whatever the individual foibles of these *énarques*—the common term for graduates of France's *École Normale Supérieure*—and however one might criticize the brutal competition and culture of the French educational system for bureaucrats, it undoubtedly produced brilliant personalities whose professionalism, culture, and competence would outclass all but the most notable exceptions in Anglo-Saxon lands.

Mathilde was a dark-haired and elegant *Marseillaise* who almost embodied that archetype of French beauty that had so recently enthralled me. She lived in a flat that her family owned on the *Île de la Cité*. Although a recent graduate of *École Nationale d'Administration*, she already drove a new black Audi sedan. Over the years we met many times, including during a memorable weekend in Sélestat, when she, Jean-Paul, and I shared a seven-hour meal at *l'Auberge de l'Ill* in Illhaeusern. The day after this meal Mathilde took us in her Audi for a drive through the Munster Valley, where we sought out noteworthy makers of the celebrated local cheese that I especially prized at that point in my life.

The other young lady, Geneviève, was a wholly different specimen. Half-French and half-Brazilian, she was far more outgoing and more beautiful, strictly speaking, than Mathilde. In 2011 I celebrated the coming New Year on the *Isola di San Giorgio* in Venice with her and Jean-Paul. Years later she, Jean-Paul, and several French bureaucrats also came to stay for a week at the *Villa Valmarana ai Nani*, where I lived for four years when stationed in Vicenza. Whenever in Italy, Geneviève took devilish delight in scandalizing Italian waiters by ordering strong red wine for fish dishes and by asking for grated *parmeggiano* to sprinkle in obscene measures on every dish that she ordered.

That evening after the concert at the Bastille Opera, our main topic of discussion was the French language and its peculiar turns of phrase. Of these, the star of the evening was "*coup chrétien*," which, according to my fellow diners, signified a hearty meal. The phrase could be loosely translated as "a Christian blow" or a "Christian punch." I cannot find the term in available books of idiomatic French phrases, but I am all but certain that my memories are correct.

These were some of my first encounters with the levity, irony, passion for culture, and national pride that characterized these young public servants. With time I grew to take for granted such traits in the French, but that night they were new to me. I could not help but to contrast these *énarques*' well-informed and witty conversation with the relatively unpolished chatter that was typical of my peers at Princeton. On this day I began to see that emerging elites in the United States would not stand a chance if they had to compete with their French counterparts on a level playing field. It was a jarring conclusion, but one that has only strengthened with time.

After dinner that evening, Mathilde drove us to Jean-Paul's apartment in the fourteenth *arondissement*, where I spent the weekend. It was only a few blocks from the attic apartment that I had rented a few years earlier, during my aborted attempt to study history at the *Institut d'études politiques de Paris*, or "Sciences-Po." At the time my shaky French and inability to adapt to the strictures of French academic life kept me from seeing this project through to its end. The failure to complete this course remains one of my lasting academic regrets.

XLIII

March 2009

As much as I enjoyed my wonted trips to Paris, some weekends I did not have enough time to travel to and from the *Métropole*. Round-trip travel to and from Paris entailed about ten hours on trains since the nearest TGV station to Castelnaudary was in Toulouse. Therefore, on some weekends I travelled to relatively close locations in France's south. One of these was Lourdes, which I had long wished to visit.

It was still frigid when I arrived in this town of pilgrimage. For some reason my first impression of the place called to mind Karlsbad. By and large it was an uneventful trip in which I was able to confess, to attend Mass, and to absorb the place's unique peace. In late winter Lourde's main square was largely free of pilgrims, and it echoed noises from the adjoining tributary *Ousse*. The evening of my arrival I stopped at an internet cafe—legionnaires were not allowed to own computers on base—and there I took the chance to write an electronic message to my Jesuit former spiritual director who was still at Oxford's Campion Hall, and who had often spoken to me of his devotion to Our Lady of Lourdes. He answered quickly with words of encouragement that did not betray any real surprise at my having forsaken an academic career to join the Foreign Legion.

I found Lourdes drab but serene. Its clean streets were crowded on every side by brightly lit shops selling mass-produced religious items, and its restaurants catering to pilgrims were almost uniformly awful and purveyed the frozen food used by most restaurants in France at that time. The details of this gray but pious weekend have long been overshadowed by memories from later trips to Lourdes, but one memory from it stands out even today.

That Sunday morning, I was one of few who attended Mass at the old Basilica of the Immaculate Conception. There could not have been more than ten churchgoers in the nave throughout the service, although occasional pilgrims and tourists wafted in and out as the Mass progressed. The terse, drowsy liturgy was a typical "low Mass" according to the bland Roman Catholic rubrics of our age, but as I stood up to leave the Basilica after the final blessing, the organ's postlude blared out and seized all my attention. For the next five minutes the organist played with extraordinary expertise a gripping fugue that I had never before heard. As the performance ended, I waited below the organ loft to approach the organist as he left. He was a bespectacled man in his late fifties, thin and dressed casually. I asked him about the fugue and its composer, and he showed me the musical score. This fugue was the work of Johann Ludwig Krebs, one of Johann Sebastian Bach's students.

Had we lived already in the age of mobile telephones and computing devices, by means of which we can easily look up and listen to almost any work of music, I would have immediately identified and recorded this fugue for future listening. As it was, I was not allowed to have any electronic devices aside from a basic mobile telephone for emergencies, and I did not write down the fugue's name or number. So, this piece of Krebs' work will always remain for me "the forgotten fugue." I am not sure that I would recognize it if I heard it today.

Little more than a decade before, French organists helped to set me on the road to conversion to Catholicism, contrary to any expectations at the time. During my first trip to Paris at age sixteen, I stayed for a week at a youth hostel near the *Hôtel de Ville* that, to my knowledge, is still in operation today. Nearby this hostel was *Saint Gervais et Protais*, an unremarkable church by Parisian standards save for one fact—it boasted a spectacular organ on which generations of Couperins had once played. Several days I found myself sitting for almost an hour in the church and listening to the recordings of organ music continuously played on loudspeakers in its nave. The Couperins' music and this church's setting were enough to bedazzle me, as I was fresh from the blandest of suburban regions of the southern United States. They stirred in me for the first time a wish to belong to an institution that fostered things so beautiful and majestic. Two years later I began my conversion to the Roman Catholic faith, leaving behind southeastern Texas' charismatic Evangelical Christianity.

France's national virtues are many, but I would argue that few of them are unmatched or unsurpassed by other nations. In two matters, however, France seems especially fecund—in the rearing of extraordinary organists and mathematicians. It was the former that set me on the road to conversion, and the latter—mathematicians turned philosophers such as Descartes and Pascal—who later kept me within the Catholic Church as my newfound faith began to confront and to clash with the world's dissonant realities, and to butt against the unfathomable limits of rationality and belief.

Ten years after that first trip to Paris I had almost come to take for granted my faith after many episodes of crisis—of faith, of chastity, of reason, of my ability to function as a "sane" member of society. It would be wrong for me to underestimate how much tranquillity and strength my Catholic faith had given me, since it allowed me to function and to survive the Legion, for example, with relatively few psychic troubles and pains. My previous moments of crisis, through which the Church and my faith had accompanied me, were far more troubling to me than any spiritual challenges that I confronted as a legionnaire.

Whenever I go back to Lourdes, I never fail to think of that day when I sat alone and dumbstruck in the Basilica of the Immaculate Conception, wondering who had composed such extraordinary music, and who played it so well.

XLIV

September–December 2008

When Beatrice first summoned Lucia to hasten to Dante's help, she referred to the straying poet as "*il tuo fedele*." I have often wondered about Dante's concrete devotion to Lucia. How much time did he spend in prayer for her intercession and inspiration? At the very least, she played second fiddle to Beatrice.

Throughout my time at Castelnaudary, during and after every Sunday Mass or Foreign Legion ceremony at the *Collégiale*, I made a point of praying at the statue of Saint Theresa of Lisieux that was sequestered in a gloomy side altar on the nave's right side.

This practice that began at Castelnaudary's *Collégiale* persisted throughout my military career, in whose course I have never failed to seek out Theresa's protection and intercession. There is no way for me to know if this saint has indeed helped me or if I have simply been extremely fortunate throughout my time in various national uniforms. Yet I served in the Foreign Legion without injury, without wilfully committing any mortal sin, without suffering significant physical or mental abuse, and without losing my faith. Later, over a decade of training and operations in the US Army, I have never been significantly injured, and I have walked away unscathed from over one hundred jumps from US and foreign aircraft all over the world, under all kinds of parachute canopies.

It would be an illuminating project for well-equipped scholars to examine how three young women took such predominant places in the resurgence of French Catholicism in this nation so thoroughly secularized after its revolutionary upheavals. It would not be an exaggeration to maintain that Catherine Labouré, Bernadette Soubirous, and Thérèse Martin—and to a lesser extent pious women of society such as Sophie Swetchine—comprise the most impactful, far-reaching manifestations of French Catholicism since the seventeenth century. They created distinct and overlapping channels of piety that have shaped and still shape spirituality for millions of believers worldwide. It is impossible to imagine this phenomenon in any other major world religion.

In the case of the illiterate shepherdess Bernadette Soubirous, after reporting her visions at *Massabielle* to appropriate ecclesiastical authorities, she withdrew to a quiet life in a provincial school, where she finally learned to read and write. She died at the age of thirty-five. Yet her visions inspired one of the largest worldwide sites of Catholic pilgrimage, fostering the belief, the faith, and the conversion of thousands, if not millions. Catherine Labouré's life was longer but perhaps even more secluded. After anonymously commissioning a work of jewellery inspired by a vision that she had while at a convent on Paris' *Rue de Bac*, she retired to the Parisian suburbs and worked in obscurity for decades until her death in 1876. Aside from variations on the crucifix, her "miraculous medal" is probably the most widely worn article of religious jewellery for Roman Catholics in the world today. In the case of Theresa of Lisieux, who died aged twenty-four, untold millions of copies of her haphazardly composed and published *History of a Soul* have been printed, such that it is quite possibly the world's most widely sold work of religious literature aside from the Bible itself. Her cult extends to Catholic communities in the world's farthest reaches.

What does it say of Roman Catholicism in the post-Napoleonic Era that its most important saints have been women? Even the spirited devotion to the most widely revered male saint of the past two centuries, the Campanian Padre Pio, does not have the universal reach of the three French women in question here. Henri Lacordaire and Prosper Guéranger made great contributions to Catholicism's resurgence in France in the nineteenth century, but neither is canonized.

Surely part of what we see here is evidence of the Catholic Church's feminine traits and characteristics, far stronger than in any Orthodox or Protestant Christian body, in Islam, or even in strictly observed Judaism, whose matriarchal impulses are especially powerful. Left unchecked, this unique femininity of Roman Catholicism can wreak havoc on orthodoxy. Indeed, I doubt that the Catholic Church will again exert real leadership in the world until it regains and asserts a suitably masculine spirituality that balances the exaggerated feminine impulses of its current dominant subcultures, which have given rise to hysterical "devotional" abominations such as Maria Valtorta's *The Poem of the Man-God*.

Contemporary Western societies' unbalanced femininity was exactly what I was trying to escape by joining the Legion. I refused to continue life without martial experience, and I sought out the most extreme possibilities of military service in the Legion to realize something fundamentally manly and to live out what so many men in our times fantasize and talk about doing, but seldom do.

The effort was not in vain. My time in the Legion stilled a rage at the unsexed creature that I was becoming before I joined its ranks—rage that goads and haunts many civilized men until their last breaths. Yet without the example of Theresa and of other saintly women of the past centuries, it is possible that I would have taken this quest for manly virtue to exaggerated lengths and abandoned Catholicism, embracing instead some modified form of Iago's doctrine outlined in Verdi's *Otello*, in what remains one of my favourite arias: "*Credo in un dio crudele*." My own temptations are to believe in a God of vengeance and of violence, which perhaps explains my keenness on the Hebrew scriptures.

Yet kneeling in so many churches throughout France before Theresa's likeness, usually rendered in extremely bad taste, I often thought back to Guillaume

Apollinaire's bracing commentary:

Seul en Europe tu n'es pas antique ô Christianisme
*L'Européen le plus moderne c'est vous Pape Pie X...**

Although Theresa was frail, short-lived, and the author of letters and autobiographical sketches whose style I now find almost unbearable, for me her image and cult admirably reflect certain divine qualities and realities, in light of which much of the timeworn wisdom of the world appears to be the real *vecchia fola.*

* Guillaume Apollinaire, *Zone*: "Alone in Europe you are not antiquated O Christianity / The most modern European is you, Pope Pius X..."

XLV

April 2009

Until Good Friday in 2007, I considered myself immune to any consequences from drinking too much alcohol. As abstemious as I generally was throughout my years at university, on those rare occasions when I did partake of alcoholic drinks, I had discovered that I could do so with impunity. No matter how much I consumed, by the next day I suffered no lingering symptoms of recent excesses and no loss of memory or other unpleasant side effects.

My penance for Lent in 2007 was to spend its forty evenings at the Princeton Graduate School's *Debasement Bar*, which I then believed to be the most depressing and demoralizing place on earth. So it was not without good intentions that I kept up this habit throughout the *triduum*.

But I did not calculate properly the effects of four large portions of tequila taken simultaneously after observing Good Friday's fast and abstinence. That evening I experienced my first "blackout"—when one loses some or all memory after consuming alcohol. By all reports I was very charming and spoke mostly and quite naturally in Russian while in a state of drunken delirium. That evening I lost my former powers over alcohol, and any overconsumption since then has entailed predictable and painful effects. As I enlisted in the Foreign Legion, I had few doubts about my newfound weakness in this regard, and I made it a point to be careful with drink.

Before joining the Legion, I did not know that alcohol is an essential glue for the Legion's social equilibrium, as well as a leading catalyst for its members' soldierly bonding. I would go so far as to say that many of the Legion's most important decisions are shaped by conversations had under the influence of alcohol, if not actually taken in various states of intoxication. Alongside this pride of place given to alcohol, as I have already remarked, came an expectation for self-control and prudence in its use. Although almost anyone in the organization would have viewed teetotaling legionnaires with the same chariness that one reserves for those suspected of heinous sexual perversions and crimes, or of espionage for unfriendly foreign governments, it was surprisingly rare to see truly intoxicated legionnaires at regimental *foyers* or at any official Legion events. Such excesses were reserved for places far away from the flagpoles.

On Camerone Day in 2009, I experienced my first and only "blackout" in the Legion. Camerone is the second of the Legion's two great holidays. It celebrates the last stand of sixty-five *légionnaires* who, during one of France's ill-fated adventures in Mexico, defended themselves for hours against the onslaught of vastly larger Mexican forces. Some sources claim that over 2,000 Mexican troops loyal to Benito Juárez took part in the fighting that day. There was no happy ending for the Legion, as only three men barely survived the day. This battle, which took place in 1863, was largely forgotten in subsequent years. Only in the 1930s, under the leadership of General Paul Rollet, did the Legion begin to immortalize the military action of Camerone as something uniquely indicative of the Legion's military charism. Since General Rollet's calculated mythologizing of this event, Camerone, celebrated each year on the battle's anniversary, 30 April, has become the Legion's foremost secular holiday.

Unlike Christmas, which focuses on the Legion "family," Camerone is the one time of the year when the normal Legion world is "turned upside down." For Camerone celebrations it has long since become established custom to hold a large festival on each regiment's grounds, and for most regiments these festivities marked the only days in the year when the broader public would be allowed to enter the regiment and to tour its jealously sequestered confines.

To be sure, no Legion holiday would be complete without a *crosse*, a march through the countryside in combat equipment and sporting competitions. That year, our *crosse* took place on the morning of 28 April. The next evening, we conducted an all-night march called the *veillée de Camérone*, which began at various locations throughout the countryside at about 1800 and ended on the morning of 30 April. To finish this event, each platoon had to march in front of the regimental commander in formation singing its own platoon song. This, too, was a competition, as the regimental commander ranked us according to the precision and coordination of our marching as well as to the volume, synchronization, and tonality of our singing. After this march, we began a series of competitive sporting events. Once this long day was complete, we changed into our dress uniforms and the Camerone festivities began.

On that day I was to be promoted to *legionnaire de première classe*. After the brief promotion ceremony, several corporals explained to me that it was a tradition for newly promoted legionnaires to buy a beer and to drink it with each superior in the company. I am not sure if this ritual had any larger validity or whether it simply represented their efforts to intoxicate me. Given the preceding days' events, exhaustion, lack of food, and dehydration, I doubt that I had consumed more than ten beers with various company leaders before I became quite intoxicated. I do not know how many I finally consumed. This was the first and last time in my life that I have been intoxicated by beer. The experience was wretched.

As someone from my company roused me about 0500 the next morning in my bed, I was still wearing my dress uniform, including my shoes. This uniform, which I had ironed and prepared until 0300 in the morning on 29 April, was now so wrinkled that it was useless for any official purpose. Still reeling from intoxication's effects, I do not remember who told me that I needed to report immediately to the regiment's duty officer to serve as the assigned regimental driver throughout the day, and that I also needed to be ready for a meeting with the regimental commander at 1000.

XLVI

April 2009

That blurry morning's first task was to find a passable dress uniform. With the help of a corporal in our company, I cobbled one together, ironed it, and reported as soon as possible to the regimental duty office. There a non-commissioned officer greeted me with some gruffness since I had arrived late for my duty. After noting that I did not have a driver's licence in the French Army, which disqualified me from serving as the regimental driver, he looked me over several times, sniffed at me, and asked if I was drunk. I told him that I did not think so. To investigate further, he gave me a breathalyser test on hand at the office. I do not know what the results were, but after looking at them he laughed and told me that I could not be the regimental driver and that I should go back to my company. He seemed to shrug off this whole episode after I told him that I had just been promoted to *legionnaire de première classe* and that I was still suffering from the effects of a ritual drinking bout from the prior evening.

On any other day, had I shown up to assigned regimental duty late and in a state of questionable sobriety, no mercy would have been shown me. Within twenty-four hours I would have found myself *en taule* for a week or more. Such is the "world-turned-upside-down" nature of Camerone celebrations in the Legion, however, that such grievous missteps were pooh-poohed as inevitable and accepted consequences of the holiday.

That challenge overcome, I had to prepare for the meeting with the regimental commander later that morning—and I had no idea what it would entail. In the remaining hours before this meeting, as sobriety and clarity crept back into my consciousness, I continued ironing my improvised dress uniform as well as practicing my presentation to the colonel. Within a few hours, I found myself with six or seven other enlisted personnel of various ranks waiting to enter the commander's office. Among these enlisted personnel was the Korean corporal who had fractured my sternum during improvised French lessons my first night in Castelnaudary. After some time, one of the commander's secretaries directed us to wait outside the regimental building. The impossibly lanky colonel came out to greet us. We saluted him and prepared to read out our formulaic presentations, but he wished to get to business, dispensed of such formalities with a wave of his right arm, and immediately treated the matter at hand.

All of us assembled before him were going to Afghanistan as temporary attachments to the Second Foreign Infantry Regiment, scheduled to deploy in July. Over the next few days, he expected us to move to Nîmes, the Second Foreign Infantry Regiment´s base, to integrate with our assigned units within the regiment and to prepare to deploy in support of France's Operation Pamir, ongoing in Afghanistan since 2001 but now grown markedly larger in scope and in scale. As a parting jewel of wisdom, he added his observation that at least 95 percent of a soldier's job is to manage boredom and complacency as he awaits those few moments of action, passion, danger, and excitement.

Shocked but elated at this news, the Korean corporal and I walked back almost giddily to the company. For both of us this would be our first operation or mission in a declared "combat zone," so it took time for us to process this forthcoming reality. My company commander and his first sergeant had, of course, nominated us for this assignment, so when we came back to the company, they congratulated us on our new mission and instructed us to report to Nîmes as soon as possible, which meant no later than the next day. As Camerone festivities continued throughout the regimental grounds, the corporal and I stayed at the company packing our bags and organizing our departure.

By early 2009, there were few major worldwide conflicts, and the extent of French colonial or invasionary adventures had been vastly curtailed. It was therefore relatively rare for legionnaires to have so-called "combat experience." What is more, deploying to Afghanistan was still a foreboding, if not terrifying, idea for the Legion's many veterans of armed forces in Russia or elsewhere in the former Soviet Union, organizations still traumatized by the spectre of the Soviet military's experiences in Afghanistan in the 1980s. Yet, it was with excitement and eagerness that I prepared to board a train for Nîmes. Most of my fears were not about Afghanistan, but rather about life over the coming months as an attachment to the Second Foreign Infantry Regiment, where I would be a newcomer with few acquaintances or friends.

The next day I took one of the regional trains from Castelnaudary to Nîmes, with only a duffle bag and a rucksack to my name. Many times I had driven along the highway from Castelnaudary to Marseilles, thereby passing through Nîmes' outskirts, but I had yet to visit the city. By taking these highways I was familiar with the blessed change in climate as one leaves Castelnaudary for the east. This change was familiar and beloved to legionnaires stationed at the Fourth Foreign Regiment, but I have never done enough research to determine why descending only a few hundred metres made for such marked differences in climate. Looking out of the windows on the train to Nîmes, I remarked the rapid changes of the surrounding fauna and landscapes as we approached the department called *Le Gard*. Somewhere between ancient Narbonne and Béziers, the air had already grown arid and warm enough to kindle a large brush fire that filled the countryside with smoke and blocked our train for about an hour.

It was already dark by the time I arrived at Nîmes. I walked out of the station and into the city, making a direct course for the Second Foreign Infantry Regiment's headquarters, a kilometre to the north of the station.

XLVII

May 2009

As I walked out of the train station into a new city, it became apparent that I had stumbled into a civic celebration. Even by the liveliest Mediterranean standards, the streets were far too crowded and festive for a normal Friday evening. To reach the regiment, I followed my memory of a city map displayed on the train station's walls, knowing that veering to the northeast would bring me to *Rue Vincent Faïta*, along which the Second Foreign Infantry Regiment was situated.

I had not gone far before two burly young men in civilian clothes stopped me. Owing to their bearing as well as to their haircuts, their provenance was obvious. They were both corporals from the Second Foreign Infantry Regiment, and they asked me why I was walking through the city in full dress uniform. I answered that to my knowledge I was required to be in full dress uniform in public unless on long-term leave. After gleaning more information from me, they laughed good-naturedly and informed me that unlike in most areas with Foreign Legion bases, in Nîmes it was forbidden for legionnaires to leave the regimental grounds on weekends in military uniform. Later I learned the reasoning behind this exception: after so many fights between legionnaires in uniform and locals, the regiment's commanders had implemented a policy that forbade legionnaires from wearing their dress uniforms on weekends in order to deter brawls.

Before long I arrived at the regiment. The sergeant at the regimental gates instructed me to report to the command and logistics company, whose building overlooked the regiment's *place d'armes*. Unlike Castelnaudary's buildings, whose architecture might justly be called "French military brutalist," the Second Foreign Infantry Regiment's buildings were handsome, if predictable, buildings dating from the late nineteenth or early twentieth century.

I reported to the company. Since it was late on a Friday evening, the only people there were the duty sergeant and his two runners. The sergeant was not expecting me, but soon he figured out why I had come to the company and gave me keys to a room on the building's top floor. He told me to settle in and to take advantage of the weekend before everyone came back for work on Monday.

I climbed up to my new quarters expecting to find a cramped room filled with bunk beds. Instead, as I opened up the door, I was surprised to see a spacious, airy, and largely empty room with many broad windows. It had six beds and lockers spread throughout the room, so I chose one and unpacked my belongings. After settling in and changing into civilian clothes, I took a walk through the unknown city.

Nîmes' streets were filled with revellers during the opening weekend of its largest civic festival, the *Ferias de Nîmes*, which always occurs over several weeks leading up to Pentecost. On this occasion numerous *matadores* arrive from Spain to participate in regular bullfights in Nîmes' Roman arena, one of the best preserved in Europe. For several weeks, crowds from the department, from all parts of France, and from abroad flock into the city for a variety of performances and events. Of all the region's many taurine ceremonies and cultural artefacts, the *Ferias* take first place.

After a winter of living in the Aude, that night the bustle and warmth of Nîmes' streets intoxicated me, and I was thrilled to be far away from

Castelnaudary's damp dreariness. More important than the warmer weather, however, was the markedly different character of the place. Castelnaudary is unmistakably mediaeval. However hard it is to question France's place at the pinnacle of mediaeval culture in Europe, I am far more partial to regions whose terrain, urban structures, and cultures are shaped by tangible Roman legacies.

Therefore, to walk through Nîmes that evening and throughout the weekend was something as pleasing as it was meaningful to me. These were my first days in what I called—imprecisely but in a way that I found convincing enough—"Roman" France. I walked past the *Maison Carrée* and then perched on a bench near the city's arena, admiring its features and its remarkable state of preservation, and thanking my stars for this new mission.

The next day I continued getting acquainted with my new Foreign Legion home. It was hard to believe the luxury of walking out of the regimental gates in civilian clothes. Until then I had always had to wear a dress uniform and then to change into civilian clothes in the toilets of the first train out of Castelnaudary.

Surrounded by stately boulevards, Nîmes' historic centre is relatively small, and much of it limited to pedestrians. Its central market had remarkable offerings, especially on the weekend, and here I discovered many local delicacies and much food for thought as well as for eating.

One stand at the market sold a wide variety of honey made from the region's flowers. I bought several samples and the scales fell from my eyes about something that had always troubled me about the Roman world. As a confirmed *bec sucré*, I had always wondered how Romans got along without cane sugar. I did not think that honey could have properly replaced sugar in pastries and in cakes, and therefore believed that the Romans went without one of nature's sweetest things. Here I finally understood that the Romans had missed out on nothing, but that instead we moderns were missing out on such colourful varieties of sweetness offered by the honey of so many distinct local flowers.

That Sunday, after touring the city, sampling regional fare from the market, and attending Mass at the city's cathedral, I walked through Nîmes' discreet and well-planned gardens. First organized and planted in the eighteenth century, these gardens highlighted a fine Roman building from the early second century after Christ. After this weekend dedicated to getting to know the city, I went to bed early on Sunday to be well-rested when encountering the unknown that awaited me the next morning.

XLVIII

May 2009

About five o'clock that Monday I woke up and presented myself to the duty sergeant. As is customary at every Legion unit, enlisted men began the day with *corvée quartier*. The sergeant assigned me to join a group of legionnaires and corporals engaged in tasks of cleaning and maintenance throughout the company. After cleaning for about half an hour, I was released for breakfast at the regimental ordinary. Until our first formation at 0730, there was little for me to do. Not knowing what to expect, I stayed in my room waiting until about 0700, when I walked down to the duty sergeant's office and asked him where I should go. He told me to report to an office upstairs.

At this office I met a man called "Major" Harold. It bears clearing up here that "Major" in the French Army is not an officer, but rather the highest of all non-commissioned ranks. It is reserved for exceptional or almost incredibly long-serving non-commissioned officers. Major Harold was in his late fifties and probably in the worst physical shape that I had ever seen in a legionnaire. To have reached his rank, however, he must have put in decades of toil. As I learned later, he had spent most of his career in the Second Foreign Parachute

Regiment, the wonted repair of British legionnaires.

By regulation, legionnaires are only allowed to speak French during working hours, even if they share a native tongue. During the first weeks and months at one's regiment this rule can be brutally enforced, depending on circumstances. Afterward there is less active enforcement of this rule, but legionnaires adhere to it out of habit or out of fear of being perceived in the wrong way by superiors. I think that Major Harold simply missed speaking English, as he immediately addressed me in English and made several quick introductions to the personnel in his office. After formation at 0730 on the *place d'armes*, I joined a small group that ran between fifteen and twenty kilometres through the city and the adjoining countryside. We showered and changed before reporting to our respective offices at 1000. Work continued until about 1200, when we had two hours for lunch. Commissioned and non-commissioned officers ate at their respective clubs, the rest of us at the ordinary. As a *legionnaire,* I had to do *corvée quartier* after lunch, but this work was relatively light. This meant that I had time to indulge in a respectable siesta. At 1400 I was back at the office until 1800, when we were released for the day. Soon this schedule had settled into routine.

At the office, I strove to be helpful to my new organization. As I had just learned from Major Harold, my job on the deployment was to serve as a driver of light reconnaissance and armoured vehicles for various staff officers, but primarily for the regimental intelligence cell. I was also to be permanently on hand as a translator of English-language written communications and radio transmissions. During these first days I mainly observed the various paperwork that was underway to prepare the regiment for its deployment.

One worker in the office was a colossal man from Brazil. Bald and with the darkest possible hue of skin, he had the physique of a bodybuilder, and his muscles seemed to burst out of his tightly fitting uniform. To accompany his outlandish physique, he had a girlish, high-pitched, soft voice, and his general disposition was as effeminate and gentle as his presence was intimidating. Such was his obvious strength that he was probably one of few legionnaires who had no need to make pretences about his toughness, for I cannot believe that anyone would have been foolish enough to get into a confrontation with him. While I was waiting for my driver's training to begin, during which I would learn how to operate the French Army's off-road armoured vehicle (the *véhicule blindé légère* or VBL for short), Major Harold told me to sit with this Brazilian corporal and to help him with anything that he wished. The corporal was pleasant and easy-going, but soon enough I was given reason to see something sinister behind his sunny disposition. All the other corporals, and even a few *caporaux-chef*, remarked to me that this Brazilian corporal was an infamous *pédé*—short in French for *pédéraste*—which was the common word in the Legion used to refer to those of homosexual appetites.

I shall leave it to readers to come to their own conclusions about why jokes and innuendo about males raping other males are common in most militaries, as they are in the Legion. During basic training I had become accustomed to threats of forced anal penetration either by corporals' penises or else by some sharp or blunt object inserted by their hands. To my knowledge nothing of the kind ever happened in our platoon, so I had long stopped paying attention to such comments. In this case, however, I must admit that the prospect of being under the supervision of a reputed sodomite of giant-like strength made me take more seriously the arch warnings about the Brazilian corporal.

One day this corporal took me aside and told me that he would explain to me what is truly important to legionnaires—what he called "the three s's." I awaited his theory with some dread, as I assumed that one of these "s's" would represent something sexual—perhaps even sodomy. He proved my fears pointless when he named them: *la soupe, la solde, et la sieste*—food, salary, and siesta. I have remembered these words since they do pithily capture the legionnaire's true priorities in existence—one might even call them the sacraments of our so-called "monastery of the damned." I am not sure if this corporal actually had any sodomitic tendencies or if this was all bad-natured gossip or a joke. He was always kind to me, and to him I owe the foregoing and telling insight into the legionnaire's psychology.

The author and a Venetian friend on Venice's canals in an antique local vessel

The ordinary at Aubagne that we new recruits used during selection and assessment

The "pen" for new recruits at Aubagne and the hills of above Aubagne beyond it

The entrance to the Legion's base at Malmousque in Marseilles

The entrance to the *Direction de Ressources Humaines de la Légion Étrangère*, otherwise known as the 'Gestapo'

The entrance to the Legion's Fourth Foreign Regiment outside of Castelnaudary

The entrance to the *Ferme du Cuin*, which belongs to the second company of the Fourth Foreign Regiment

The author preparing a French ration during the *marche du képi blanc*

During rehearsals for the *remise du Képi Blanc* ceremony, the coldest that I had ever been to date....

Our *remise du képi blanc* ceremony from afar

A typical way for legionnaires to arrange their *képis* during formal ceremonies

The beginning of festivities after the *marche du képi blanc*

Our basic training platoon leader with the author
and a fellow legionnaire from Poland

The outside of the *collégiale* in Castelnaudary

Holiday rooms at the Legion's facility in Malmousque
and sunbathers on the public spaces below

The author with his sister outside the church at *Val-de-Grâce*

The statue of Saint Theresa of Lisieux in a small chapel at the *collégiale* in Castelnaudary

The entrance to the Legion's Second Foreign Infantry Regiment in Nîmes, France

A view of the *Hôtel le Rhul* taken from the *corniche* in Marseilles

View from the *Hôtel le Rhul*

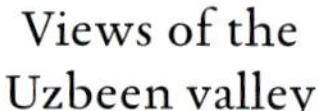

Views of the Uzbeen valley

Views of the 'governor's mansion'

A typical morning hike up *Mont Saint Michel*, near FOB Tora

During a regular trip to the 'governor's mansion' in Surobi

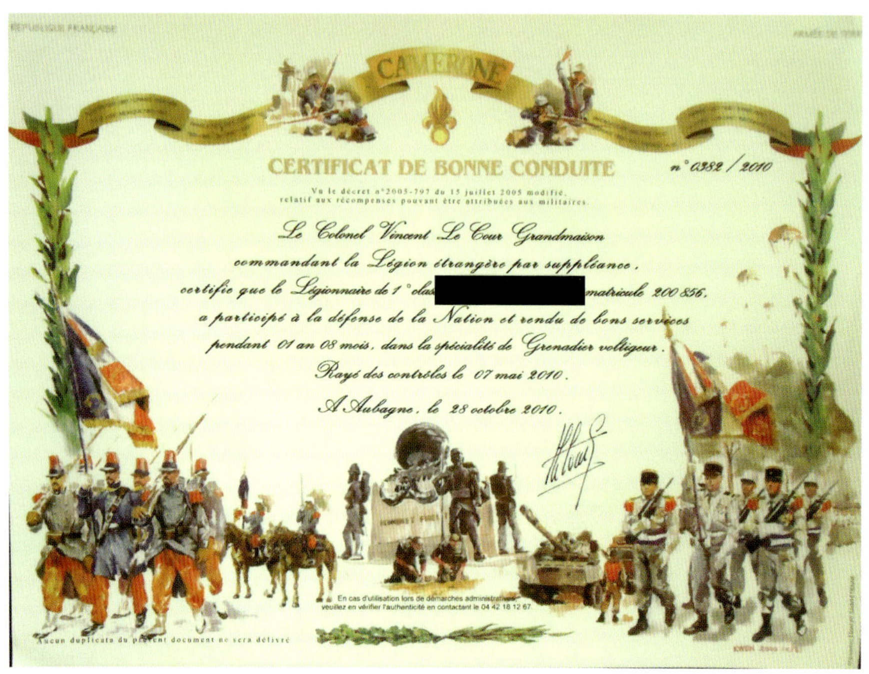

RÉPUBLIQUE FRANÇAISE

CAMERONE

CERTIFICAT DE BONNE CONDUITE

n° 0382 / 2010

Vu le décret n°2005-797 du 15 juillet 2005 modifié,
relatif aux récompenses pouvant être attribuées aux militaires.

Le Colonel Vincent Le Cour Grandmaison
commandant la Légion étrangère par suppléance,
certifie que le Légionnaire de 1° clas[redacted] matricule 200 856,
a participé à la défense de la Nation et rendu de bons services
pendant 01 an 08 mois, dans la spécialité de Grenadier voltigeur.
Rayé des contrôles le 07 mai 2010.
A Aubagne, le 28 octobre 2010.

En cas d'utilisation lors de démarches administratives
veuillez en vérifier l'authenticité en contactant le 04 42 18 12 67.

Aucun duplicata du présent document ne sera délivré

A copy of the author's *certificat de bonne conduit*,
the Legion's equivalent of an honourable discharge

After a few hours at our local shooting range near FOB Tora

XLIX

May 2009

It would take a book unto itself to describe the many characters who made up the company to which I was assigned. Over the ensuing weeks I began to make their acquaintance. On the whole, this company comprised relatively senior commissioned and non-commissioned officers who were disposed to look on a freshly minted legionnaire like me with bemused indulgence. I enjoyed a second weekend in Nîmes before all regimental personnel who were deploying to Afghanistan that summer travelled together to a training location in Burgundy, *Camp de Mailly*. One afternoon we boarded a combination of military and civilian buses and drove for hours to this early twentieth-century encampment.

To my knowledge, by 2009 this training area had become the grounds for preparing French units deploying to Afghanistan in tasks and subjects specific to the environments foreseen in that theatre of operations. Such preparations took especial urgency given the recent and scandalous deaths of ten French soldiers in the hills near Sper Kunday, the same region to which our regiment was heading in July. My new regiment buzzed with excitement as we prepared in earnest for a "combat" deployment where there was a realistic prospect of facing a determined, experienced, and deadly enemy force. At this time, most legionnaires with over five years of service had deployed somewhere abroad, but usually this was in support of ongoing operations in former French colonies in Africa such as Chad, Senegal, the Ivory Coast, and the Central African Republic. Hostilities and combat operations were not unheard of in these areas, but overall, such deployments had become predictable for the Legion, after years of rotating troops to African countries. The prospect of deploying to Afghanistan offered something new and exciting even to our oldest hands.

By the summer of 2009, it had been almost eight years since the United States had begun its operations in 2001 to topple the government of Afghanistan, in large part to respond in some visible and menacing way to the spectacular attacks on New York City's World Trade Centre. These retributive combat operations dislodged Afghanistan's "Taliban" government before the end of 2001, and since then various elements of the United States took a leading role in upholding Afghanistan's government and security. Member states of the North Atlantic Treaty Organization (NATO) also contributed to "stabilization" efforts in Afghanistan—as did other nations, such as France, which had voluntarily provided small and specialized training elements since 2001.

At first, by all reports the situation in Afghanistan was tranquil in the wake of the Taliban government's overthrow. French soldiers who had been to Afghanistan in 2003 reported driving about the countryside as they would have done in West African territories, in open jeeps with no body armour and little supporting firepower. Toward the end of 2006, however, the situation took turns for the worse, and strengthening bands of Afghan "insurgents"—some former Taliban, some regional drug lords or warlords, and some foreign fighters—began to attack Western soldiers, equipment, and installations with increasing regularity and effectiveness. Without any doubt we were deploying to a deteriorating security situation, and at a time when Western governments had pledged to overcome Afghanistan's budding insurgencies by dint of a "surge" of troops and resources.

This period represented what will probably emerge as the high point of the prestige and worldwide reach of the United States' military in the twenty-first century. Having projected power to overthrow the Afghan government in 2001 and the Iraqi government in 2003, tens of thousands of US troops remained in Iraq and Afghanistan. By the end of the 2000s many, if not most, US Army brigades had rotated in nine-month or twelve-month deployments to one of these countries. In this context, French soldiers envied US soldiers in terms of both their combat experiences, and the resources available to them. Soldiers from the US military were widely reputed to be the world's best, and surely the most knowledgeable about how properly to conduct operations in Afghanistan. For this reason, much of our training at *Camp de Mailly* was modelled after US standard operating procedures (or SOPs) forged over the prior eight years of deployments.

No small portion of our training dealt with detecting and counteracting what we called "improvised explosive devices" (IEDs)—which already by 2009 had become Afghan fighters' primary means of attacking Western equipment and personnel. In addition to learning standard US procedures for detecting and responding to IEDs, we trained on communicating with our radio systems and providing basic first aid for the wounded. Our officers focused on planning and executing mock missions. As always in the Legion, the days began with long runs. Afterward we trained for a few hours in the morning and, unless in the field, had two hours for lunch. Since we slept in tents far from garrison, there was no *corvée quartier*. We therefore luxuriated in siestas of sixty minutes.

Major Harold soon discovered that since I did not have a French military licence for driving heavy vehicles, I was ineligible by regulation to undertake the training required to drive the VBL. To his mind this made little difference, but for me this presented the prospect of remaining in an office or in a tent somewhere throughout the upcoming deployment. I telephoned back to my company at Castelnaudary—where the training for heavy vehicle drivers took place—and within a few days we had secured places in the necessary training courses so that I could drive a VBL during the deployment. In order to take part in this training I had to forego the two or three weeks of holiday afforded to deploying legionnaires, but at the time this sacrifice was worth it to me. After completing all the required training at *Camp de Mailly*, I boarded a military van with a few other personnel heading back to Nîmes. We spent the night at the regiment, and by the next afternoon I was back at my old company in Castelnaudary, preparing to learn how to drive military transport vehicles.

L

June 2009

Once I had returned to my old company in Castelnaudary, my mission over the next two weeks was to complete training to get the French Army driver's licence for the Renault troop transport trucks then in use throughout the Foreign Legion. It would take one week to complete the classroom and practical portion of this training, and a second week to drive several hundred kilometres in a troop transport vehicle in order "to validate" my new licence. As it happened, the two weeks for this training coincided with a regimental exercise, so the timing could not have been more opportune for me to get experience driving a truck.

There were only four legionnaires taking the course for this driver's licence. One of them was a new corporal at the second company. His family had immigrated to France from Tunisia when he was a child, and he still spoke French with a strong North African accent. Wiry and dark-skinned, he was an impressive runner and otherwise physically fit, but talkative to a fault. Most everyone at the company disliked him because of his loud voice and owing to a general air of untrustworthiness that radiated from the angry glares that he cast at almost everyone, even his superiors. For some reason, perhaps because I was from the United States, this corporal immediately took a disliking to me and advantage of any opportunity to belittle me.

To train with him over the next week was vexing. Our instructor was a laid-back Romanian corporal who was planning to leave the Foreign Legion soon. That whole week, whenever I made any mistakes as we drove throughout the surrounding countryside, the Arab corporal would scream at me and make me stop the truck, get out, and do push-ups or other physical exercises to his heart's content. It must have been amusing for French motorists to see us with our large, camouflage-coloured Renault military transport truck parked on the side of departmental roads while I did push-ups as two corporals stood over me.

At some point, my Maghrebian nemesis explained to me why he despised me. He told me that I thought that I was better than everyone else in the regiment and that I believed myself to be some type of "superman." Therefore, he was determined to cut me down to size. For that one week he did well in this effort. The passion of this man's hazing was personal rather than professional, which in my experience was rather out of character for the Legion's corporals. It was excessive for the circumstances, because when we finished the training that Friday, the Romanian instructor took the extraordinary step of apologizing to me for the Arab corporal's behaviour.

Was that young corporal correct in his professed reason for despising me? Did I truly believe myself better than my fellow legionnaires, and deem myself some Nietzschean *Übermensch* in comparison with them? As much as I was tempted to dismiss such ideas as the corporal's own delusions, something about his words resonated with me, to the extent that I remember them to this day. All things being equal, he was probably more correct than incorrect. My own arrogance and self-absorption at this time went beyond the individual arrogance that inspires every man's worldview, as described in fragments of the pre-Socratic philosophers: "Although *logos* is common to all, most men live as if they had a wisdom of their own."* Perhaps I did believe that I had an extraordinary destiny before me and that, by joining and serving in the Foreign Legion, I was pursuing and realizing this destiny, whose importance was greater than the fates of my fellow legionnaires, enlisted men and officers alike.

That Friday, as we finished training, the Arab corporal left the regiment to take holiday somewhere for a week. I never saw him again. I had one day off before joining my company and the entire Fourth Foreign Regiment at a training area near Limoges, where its bi-annual regimental exercise was taking place. When I arrived at this training area, I was told to wait in an old, abandoned house for a few days until the exercise finished and my company returned from the field. Afterward I would drive a Renault transport vehicle filled with equipment back to Castelnaudary, thereby logging the approximately four hundred kilometres of driving needed to validate my licence.

For three days I stayed in that house, which I shared with a French *caporal-chef* who had been left behind to watch over the company's property. The weather was flawless and the days long. In the mornings I took peaceful runs throughout the countryside, and then came back and washed myself outside the house with a garden hose and *savon de Marseilles*. I spent the rest of these days reading books and sharing meals of French rations with the *caporal-chef* at regular intervals. When the company came back and prepared its regress to Castelnaudary, to celebrate the regimental exercise's conclusion we held a *pot*—or company party. As always, this event included barbecued meats, snacks, beer, and wine. The *caporal-chef* and I had organized this *pot* as we awaited the company's arrival. Our company's cadres and its tired, hungry, and dirty legionnaires were thankful for our efforts.

The next day we began our drive back down to Castelnaudary, by way of Albi. Since I was a new driver, the company first sergeant sat in the passenger's seat the whole time to ensure that I did not do anything untoward on the road. In between his various, violent exclamations about how bad and how dangerous

* Cited in T.S. Eliot's *Four Quartets*, 77, Fragment II: "τοῦ λόγου δὲ ἐόντος ξυνοῦ ζώουσιν οἱ πολλοί ὡς ἰδίαν ἔχοντες φρόνησιν."

my driving was, we had several interesting conversations about the French countryside, about French culture, and about his experiences over a long and colourful Foreign Legion career, most of it spent at the Second Foreign Parachute Regiment. That evening we were back in Castelnaudary, and I had successfully completed the necessary driver's training and validation of my licence. The next day I was on a train to Nîmes.

LI

June 2009

After arriving at Nîmes over the weekend, I began training on the *véhicule blindé légère* (VBL) the following Monday. For several days a taciturn corporal from Madagascar took me out to drive a VBL through the rocky, craggy terrain at the Garrigues training area, near the Second Foreign Regiment's headquarters. Within a week I was certified to drive the VBL on our upcoming deployment. Thus ended three weeks of training, the result of my dogged politicking and work to become qualified as a driver for operations in Afghanistan. As I would soon discover, it was worth investing this time and energy since this qualification markedly shaped my experience on the deployment. In this process I learned a valuable lesson—that if anyone lets a military organization choose most paths for him and abstains from putting appropriate pressure on that organization in order to pursue individual goals, the military usually takes the path of least resistance and offers relatively fewer interesting opportunities.

We were not due to deploy until late July. Now that I was close to many cities in southern France that I had always wanted to visit, Paris held fewer temptations for me. In late May, my friend James had finished his semester at the *École Normale Supérieure*, and he had decided to spend the summer taking intensive French courses in Aix-en-Provence. Therefore, we were able to see each other many times over the ensuing weeks. Our regiment had already completed most preparations for the deployment, so our daily obligations were few. Leaders encouraged us to travel and to spend as much time as possible with family and friends during the weeks in which we remained in France.

On one of his first Friday evenings in the south, James and I met at *Le Rhul* for dinner. This had already become one of my favourite places in Marseilles, and it was a short walk from our legionnaire holiday lodging at Malmousque. The hotel *Le Rhul* appears modest from the outside, with whitewashed walls and most other architectural elements painted marine blue. The restaurant inside boasted well-chosen maritime decorations. All its broad windows overlooked the Mediterranean, where the early evening's sun, hours before setting, filled the sea with so many glinting reflections of its brilliance that we could not look at it for more than a few seconds without wearing sunglasses.

In theory, *Le Rhul* offers a reasonably extensive seafood menu. Every time I have eaten there, however, I have never seen anyone order anything other than its *bouillabaisse*, which is more a social ritual than a meal. The fisherman's soup comes to each table according to prescribed rites. First the waiter fills patrons' bowls with the soup's steaming, rust-coloured base, or *bouillon*. He then cuts a variety of choice fish before their eyes. The *charte de la bouillabaisse marseillaise*—in part developed and spearheaded by the owners of *Le Rhul*—specifies required and optional fish for any true *bouillabaisse*. Required Mediterranean fish are *rascasse* (red scorpionfish), the *vive araignée* (spotted weaver), *le fielas congre* (conger native to Provence), *le chapon scorpène* (the red lionfish), and the *rascasse blanche* (white scorpionfish). Optional fish are the *Saint Pierre* ("John Dory" or "Saint Peter's fish"), *cigale de mer* (sometimes called "slipper lobster"), *baudroie* or *lotte* (turbot), *langouste* (spiny lobster), and *galinette* (also known in French as the *rouget grondin*, and in English as the red gurnard). The waiter also brings small bowls filled with almost saffron-coloured sauce called *rouille*, which may be consumed directly on small pieces of bread or mixed with the soup's base. Throughout the meal, the waiter attentively watches patrons' tables to ensure that each bowl has enough warm *bouillon*, to bring more *rouille* if needed, and to add additional cuts of fish to bowls if desired.

James and I could not resist comparing this experience with some of our most lavish past dinners. During this artful meal at *Le Rhul*, centred on the once modest local soup *bouillabaisse*, whose imitations have now spread across the world, we admired the restaurant's extraordinary situation, perched on Marseilles' *corniche*. The hotel's stylish, tasteful but modest decoration reflected generations of ownership in one family. The expansive views of the dazzling Mediterranean in this ancient port city filled us two students of the Classics with guarded but deep-running enthusiasms. Both the food and the service embodied the quality and the expertise of family artisans whose secrets are imbibed from childhood and then reproduced and modified for more current tastes, with ambition and sometimes with creativity. Most cultures have some examples of excellence in cuisine and in hospitality, but among such examples there are gradations of objective good and of elegance. To be sure, I have had many more sophisticated and even "better" meals in my life, but I believe nonetheless that the *bouillabaisse* at *Le Rhul* as we enjoyed it that summer evening was one of the purest expressions of culinary culture that I had experienced to that point.

In those days, each portion of *bouillabaisse* cost about forty-five euros. For Princeton doctoral students or for legionnaires without inherited wealth, this amount of money for our *bouillabaisse* meal was easily affordable. In New York or in London, cities of our own native culture which we both knew well, it would have been hard to find similar standards and service at almost any price. A meal of such dependable quality and taste would have been accessible mostly to billionaires who could afford to fly in foreign cooks and ingredients on private aircraft. Yet we meagre students and legionnaires were able to afford this Phocaean luxury in 2009 without thinking about cost.

Whatever the excesses and faults of the European nation-states that have arisen and persisted through numerous, and increasingly disturbing, variations since Napoleon's defeat, it would be churlish not to highlight how general European living conditions have improved since the Second World War, such that common students and workers from "developed" nations can, in theory, afford outings to restaurants such as *Le Rhul*.

LII

June 2009

It bears repeating that it is not so much praiseworthy to know the French language as it is shameful not to know it.

James and I both thought Cicero's well-known quote about Latin no less applicable to French, one of Latin's richest and most culturally significant modern demotics. To learn the language well was one of many reasons that spurred me to join the Foreign Legion. For his part, James chose to spend almost nine months in France to meet the same goal. Given his prowess with languages ancient and modern—at this point James spoke Latin fluently and Ancient Greek well—by his sojourn's end James spoke French better than most non-French scholars at Princeton whose job description implied sound knowledge of the language.

As time passes and as I face greater temptations to believe that I have learnt something of the world, I see even more shame in not knowing French. I remember reading somewhere that Evelyn Waugh, toward his life's end, stated that his "life-long impediment" was that he never gained any real command of French. Once I found this remark fussy and perplexing, but now I believe that

Waugh's regret on this matter was truly heartfelt and appropriate. Not to know French is to be shut off not only from far too many European achievements, but from the formidable culture that enabled them.

It must have been during our dinner at *Le Rhul* that James and I made plans to meet again in Aix-en-Provence. If memory serves, after one night at Malmousque, I took an early local train on Sunday morning from Marseilles to Aix-en-Provence. At half past ten I attended the "Tridentine" Latin Mass at the city's *Chapelle des Pénitents Gris*. This modest structure dates from the seventeenth century, and the much older "Grey Penitents" still call it their home. Their religious association was founded by King Louis VIII, as he performed public penitential acts in Avignon to atone for the sins of Albigensian heretics, whose adherents were once plentiful in this part of France.

The chapel was cosy enough and its pews could not have seated more than two hundred people. The Mass itself was sparsely attended. I do not remember much about it save for a quite beautiful, dark-haired French woman in her thirties. She fit into a familiar archetype of French beauty. Our seating required that I look in her direction during most of the Mass, so I could not help making further observations about her, about her husband, and about their five handsome young children, who scarcely made a peep or budged from their places throughout the hour-long liturgy. The look in this spectacular woman's eyes as they crossed mine briefly both during the Mass and as she left the chapel called to mind one of G.K. Chesterton's better essays, "French and English," where he remarked of the French: "The worried look of their women is connected with the responsibility of their women."

The memory of this woman's tasteful dress of soft red tones with subtle floral patterns brings me to more general observations. However much I admire France and its people, France is not my favourite nation. French women are also not, to my mind, the world's most beautiful and attractive. Greek, Spanish, Italian and Israeli women, and many Levantine Arab specimens, would routinely surpass French women when ranked solely in terms of physical attractiveness. That said, there are some characteristics of French women and of the families that they raise that are especially admirable and worthy of remark.

One remarkable aspect of French women, and especially of French women faithful to Catholic moral teaching in public and within their families, is how they remain attractive well into their child-bearing years, and even after having five or more children. This is in marked contrast to what is customary in Anglo-Saxon or Germanic countries, where women and men alike often see childbirth as an acceptable excuse for subsequent weight-gain and flabbiness. Even in other Latin and Mediterranean countries, women clearly do not show the same discipline as the French after they have children, and there is no other country in the world where mothers of five or more children manage to be as physically attractive and alluring, if not more so, than they were as young brides.

French women also have a way of dressing and of policing their children such that French children are the world's most attractive, polite, and well-behaved. After having attended Catholic liturgies the world over, some common features are infants and toddlers reacting petulantly, even outrageously, to their parents' concerns and doting care, and to strangers' indulgent permissiveness. In any other nation misbehaving children are hallmarks of Catholic religious services, but I cannot remember ever having seen such behaviour among French children. There must be some false memories of mine here, but I stand by my assertion that French children are extremely well-behaved at Mass. This cannot possibly be the result of their virtue and must be due to their mothers.

Never having been associated with a Catholic French woman, I do not know how exactly they manage to do what they so often do, whether it comes to their waistlines, their manner of dress, their children's politeness, and even their uncommon marital faithfulness, writ large—all things envied by us legionnaires who often admired the wives of our officers. I suspect that their personal and family management conforms to an important maxim known to all French women: *Il faut souffrir pour être belle.*

After Mass I saw the celebrating priest outside the chapel smoking a cigarette, so I struck up conversation with him. As it turned out, he was a Dominican, a noted professor, and an accomplished Arabist at the University of

Aix-en-Provence, where he worked whenever he was not at the Dominicans' long-standing establishment in Cairo near Al-Azhar University. In the coming months we shared many electronic messages, as I wished to begin learning Arabic at some point in the future. But to my regret we never met again.

LIII

June 2009

After Mass at the chapel of the Grey Penitents, I met with James for lunch at an unremembered restaurant in the centre of Aix-en-Provence.

That summer James was still struggling with many religious and "existential" questions that we had often discussed at Princeton. After finishing Father Foster's summer Latin course in 2005, in an act of faith Jason left behind a prestigious scholarship and prior studies in Germany to enrol directly in a major Roman university to study Ancient Greek, while also attending Father Foster's regular and raucous lectures at the Pontifical Gregorian University. Although James knew no Italian when he began these studies, he coped with the unavoidable academic challenges and learned to speak Italian as well as Latin and to understand Ancient Greek reasonably well within a year.

During all this time, James' exposure to Catholicism was unremitting, and it would have been reasonable to foresee his eventual conversion. One of our long-standing mutual friends, whose own paths mirrored James', converted to Catholicism shortly after finishing Father Foster's course in 2005. Soon thereafter he embraced a typical outlook for traditionalist Catholics of that time.

Over dinner at *Le Rhul*, Jason told me about one of his obstacles to conversion that summer. As he arrived in Aix-en-Provence after his semester at the *École Normale Supérieure*, he found himself in anguish of mind and of spirit. In a fit of desperation, he sat down in the pew of a local church to pray. There he wound up tarrying at length, hoping to find relief for his philosophical pains.

According to his story, at some point, he looked to his side and saw an attractive girl sitting next to him. The two of them began speaking. That very afternoon James and this girl, so he told, ended up spending hours together in the chambers of his rented apartment in downtown Aix-en-Provence, engaged in most commonplace physical affections aside from coitus.

I found his story improbable and dismissed it as our conversation moved to other matters. Yet, that Sunday, after we had finished lunch and were strolling through Aix-en-Provence, we crossed paths with two young women who knew James. As we stopped to chat with this pair, I understood that one of them was the girl about whom James had spoken at *Le Rhul*. She was in the flower of youth and attractive, but decidedly not *de mon genre*. Something had passed between her and James.

James' carnal temptations in a church pew had seemed to me like something out of Matthew Lewis' novel, *The Monk*, but they did have some basis in fact. It seems that he spent much of that summer in Aix-en-Provence in an association with this young woman or with others. After he and I parted ways that afternoon, we would not see each other again for many years.

On the way back to the train station, I stopped by the house where Blaise Cendrars wrote *La Main Coupée*, a book which I had read the summer before joining the Foreign Legion. The title, "The Severed Hand" in English, refers to the hand of Captain Danjou, who died at the Battle of Camerone in 1863. Having lost his fleshy hand during a military campaign in the 1850s, he had a prosthetic wooden hand made to replace it, with which he continued his military career. Years after Captain Danjou's death, somehow a French soldier in Mexico found his wooden hand and arranged for its transport back to France. Today this talisman is the centrepiece of the Legion's most sacred ceremony at the *maison mère* in Aubagne, where each year on Camerone a prominent legionnaire carries the "severed hand" in procession in front of thousands of assembled legionnaires and admirers at Aubagne's expansive *place d'armes*.

When I joined the Legion, I carried with me a notebook in which I had written one of the best-known passages from *La Main Coupée*. During what we now call "The Great War," Cendrars was badly injured in fighting through the trenches with fellow legionnaires. Years later, as he sat in exile in Aix-en-Provence in the early 1940s, he penned his thanks to the Legion and to what the experience of serving in it had done for him:

> *Être. Être un homme. Et découvrir la solitude. Voilà ce que je dois à la Légion et aux vieux lascars d'Afrique, soldats, sous-offs, officiers, qui vinrent nous encadrer et se mêler à nous en camarades, des desperados, des survivants de Dieu sait quelles épopées coloniales, mais qui étaient des hommes, tous. Et cela valait bien la peine de risquer la mort pour les rencontrer, ces damnés, qui sentaient la chiourme et portaient des tatouages.**

This text shaped many of my own expectations about the Legion and about what it offered. How had Cendrars learned "to be" in the Legion, and "to be a man"? More importantly, what had given him the unusual powers to embrace solitude? In joining the Foreign Legion, I sought answers to these questions.

To pass by Cendrar's house was a literary pilgrimage for me, and it was a fitting way to end that day in Aix-en-Provence as the regiment prepared, over the coming weeks, to ship out to Afghanistan. Soon, I thought, I would come to experience warfare myself, and thereby to share in that experience common

---

* Blaise Cendrars, *La Main Coupée*: "To be. To be a man. And to discover solitude. This is what I owe to the Legion and to those old ruffians from Africa, soldiers, non-commissioned officers, officers, who came to train us and to mix with us as comrades, those *desperados*, survivors of God knows what adventures in the colonies, but who were men, all of them. It was well worth the risk of dying to meet them, these damned men, tattooed and reeking of galley-sweat."

to so many writers and men in history whose works and biographies I prized.

It bears noting that for all the Legion's history and reputation, there are few good books, much less works of literature, stemming from its enlisted men or officers. Aside from *La Main Coupée*, the only other example that readily comes to mind is Alan Seeger's poem, "I Have a Rendezvous with Death." This United States citizen and graduate of Harvard University left behind his posh, rakish life in Parisian literary circles to volunteer to serve with the Legion in the trenches on the Western Front. He died not long after finishing what has since become one of the Great War's best-known poems.

LIV

June–July 2009

The training for which I had volunteered had curtailed my available *permission* before the deployment. Still, I had about ten days available for travel before we were set to deploy in late July. During this time my parents and my younger sister came to visit me in France.

In later years my parents grew accustomed to my deploying to exotic locations featured breathlessly in Western news reports. At this time, however, their son's going to a supposed war zone was something new to them. Only a year before that summer of 2009, they had long known me as a student of the humanities with morose and self-isolating tendencies—who, since leaving university, had been studying intensely but without clear goals and travelling throughout Europe without ever having held steady employment.

Although I announced my intention to join the Foreign Legion to them long before I did so, I am not sure that my parents ever believed that I would follow through with this idea. They probably doubted that I would be successful even at joining the organization, much less at completing its training. Now I was going to Afghanistan, a place fearsome to the North American imagination since the attacks that took place in New York on 11 September 2001. These attacks were blamed on a man named Osama bin Laden, who thereafter was forever joined to Afghanistan in the popular Western imagination. Said to be the early twenty-first century's elusive but most accomplished purveyor of terror, Osama bin Laden descended from a Saudi Arabian family and spent much, if not most, of his time in various Pashtun-dominated reaches of Pakistan. Yet, owing to the nightly televised "news" broadcasts and respectable newspapers of the time, North Americans rarely associated Osama bin Laden with Pakistan or with Saudi Arabia—both allies of the United States. Instead, in the Western imagination as manufactured by its dream-masters, Osama bin Laden was somehow a leading figure in Afghanistan.

To meet my parents, I took the TGV to Paris and joined them at their hotel in the Latin Quarter. The next day we drove a rental car north out of the city. Our first stop as we drove to the northwest was at Giverny, where there is a museum at Claude Monet's former house. For some reason my mother had always claimed Monet as her favourite painter. He was most probably the only European painter that she could name, perhaps because his works were commonly featured on the covers of scores of French impressionist piano music. Later I became more thankful for this visit when it allowed me better to understand Monet's eight great panels at the *Orangerie.*

From there we drove to *Mont Saint Michel*, which we toured before spending the night in Bayeux. The next day we visited several graveyards of my countrymen and US allies who had died storming various beaches in Normandy on 6 June 1944. While I often take the chance to highlight my belief in David Glantz' theory that the Soviet Army would have eventually defeated the German *Wehrmacht* without direct Western intervention in northern France in 1944, this theory in no way lessens my sincere admiration for the heroism and sacrifices of Allied forces as they carried out one of history's few successful invasions over the English Channel.

I took this day in Bayeux to admire an artefact of an older successful invasion over the same waters, the Bayeux Tapestry. While my family continued visiting various historical sites associated with the Second World War, after a visit to the modest but well-kept German cemetery nearby, I spent much of the day in the fine museum devoted to the Bayeux Tapestry.

After this visit, while walking about the nave of the cathedral at Bayeux, I saw a young woman whom I knew from my previous two years at Princeton. Her name was Isabel, and since we shared the same thesis advisor, we had met each other soon after I arrived at Princeton in 2006. A lovely young woman of international background, she was touring Bayeux with a man about her age, to whom she introduced me. Isabel and I spoke earnestly for a few minutes. Given our rather intimate friendship up until that point, we did not even seem surprised to see each other in Normandy. From there we parted ways, but not for long—we ended up meeting in Princeton early the next year.

The rest of the trip was whirlwind and included my only stays in Normandy and in Brittany, where I especially enjoyed sampling Cancale's oysters and visiting the regrettably designed Basilica of Saint Theresa of Lisieux. While heading back to Paris we were able to tour the Cathedral at Chartres, but for some reason I have few memories of this visit to one of medieval Europe's greatest monuments. We then stayed at a religious guesthouse near Versailles with the intention of visiting the park and Paris over the coming days.

That evening, however, I received a phone call in the middle of the night that cut short my leave. It was from a *caporal-chef* in the Legion who told me that I needed to come back to the regiment the next day. He gave no reason for this other than that I needed to load my bags for the deployment.

That morning at half past four my father and I left for Paris. We mostly kept silence as he drove. It had been a fraught trip with my family, since my parents bickered no differently in France than they had done my whole life in the United States. The persistence of unpleasant family habits, developed over decades, troubled me. If something so extreme as my joining the Foreign Legion and deploying to a supposedly dangerous theatre of conflict could not dampen these habits, I understood, then perhaps nothing would ever break them.

Traffic had already reached the full frenetic pace of the morning commute by the time my father left me at the *Gare de Lyon*.

LV

July 2009

Later that morning I arrived at Nîmes and immediately reported to my assigned company to see what was so urgently needed of me. It turned out that the Spanish *caporal-chef* had sounded a false alarm. We still had several days left to load our bags onto shipping containers that would carry most of our equipment for the deployment. My bags were already packed, so I loaded them that afternoon and set about making the most of my remaining days in France.

First of all, I visited Avignon, seat of the Papacy for so many years, but more importantly where Petrarch drew inspiration for much of his *Canzoniere.* Afterward I spent a few days in the Camargue, and especially in the remarkable mediaeval walled city at Aigues-Mortes, whence Saint Louis had embarked for several Crusades. As someone who still entertained ideas of Western cultural and political supremacy and of "clashes of civilization," I found it meaningful to reflect on the Crusades and on how our ongoing engagements in Afghanistan were also historic and important Western engagements against radicalized and aggressive Islamic forces. Soon I would come to hold different ideas about what our engagements in Afghanistan were—ideas that never would have come to me while sitting in comfortable Western libraries.

I have forgotten most details about how exactly we deployed. We must have taken chartered civilian buses to Istres-Le Tubé, a French military airbase near Marseilles from which most French forces deploy worldwide. By 2009, the French Army was still one of Europe's largest and most frequently deployed military forces, and its missions abroad were usually based in former French colonies in Africa. From Istres-Le Tubé we did not travel on military aircraft—I would remember that since the flight would have taken forever and been horribly uncomfortable. So we took chartered civilian aircraft from Istres-Le Tubé to Afghanistan. Along the way we stopped at the recently opened French airbase in Abu Dhabi, *Camp de la Paix*. There we waited for several hours in primitive structures near the base's runways while a sandstorm delayed our progress. As I have always done whenever in Arab-speaking countries, I grew very frustrated with myself that I could not read signs posted in Arabic or speak with the locals.

After this period of waiting, we boarded the same aircraft and departed for the international aeroport at Kaboul. It was early evening by the time we arrived, and darkness was already gathering on the horizon as we disembarked. After collecting our belongings, we boarded French armoured military vehicles called the *véhicule de l'avant blindé*, or VAB for short. Unlike the VABs that I had seen at Nîmes, these were covered in dust, irregularly painted, and included many improvised and non-standard additions specific to this deployment. Eight or so of us legionnaires crowded into the back of one VAB, ushered in by soldiers belonging to France's First Infantry Regiment, one of Europe's oldest continually active military units. Small cloth patches bearing the regiment's insignia were fastened by Velcro to the left shoulders of their dirty uniforms. On one soldier's shoulder I made out the First Infantry Regiment's motto—*On ne relève pas Picardie.**

It gave me a direful feeling when the VAB's metal doors clanked shut behind us and its loud engine cranked and began running. Two First Regiment soldiers

* "No one relieves Picardy."

stood up on platforms in the vehicle's rear and exposed their armoured torsos to the outside world through hatches on the VAB's roof. They had their FAMAS rifles at the ready and scanned their surroundings with the careless confidence that many soldiers show toward the end of their deployments overseas. Through these hatches the remaining daylight flooded into the back of the VAB along with dust and noises from the roadways on which we drove.

As we turned and progressed, I reflected with some foreboding that I was now in a theatre of war, and in this respect, I was sharing an experience known to so many men that I had encountered in studies and readings over decades. It was the most fearful moment for me of the deployment, for I had no idea what to expect when the VAB's doors would open. More seasoned legionnaires took these movements in better stride since deployments were familiar to them, but nonetheless Afghanistan's reputation brought apprehension and thoughtfulness even to their faces as we headed to our first destination.

Before long we emerged from the VABs inside a walled compound in eastern Kaboul, *Camp Warehouse*, where most European armed forces engaged in Afghanistan were then based. It was already dusk when the doors opened, and the air had cooled markedly since the time we had boarded the vehicles. We took out our bags and stored them, and then hurriedly repaired to the base's large ordinary built out of sheet metal, since we had not eaten a regular meal for some time. This was our first introduction to the base's facilities, and I found the ordinary's brightness and cleanliness quite surprising, as I did the food's quality and how much food was available to us. As we walked into the ordinary and sat down to eat, First Regiment and other soldiers ogled us with the thinly disguised disdain that deployed soldiers show for those replacing them. In addition to French forces, numerous foreign soldiers peopled the ordinary, whose individual uniforms we would gradually learn to recognize.

Later that evening we were assigned rooms. Since I was attached to the regimental headquarters for this mission, I shared a room with a *caporal-chef* from Hungary. It was a well-appointed space with two small refrigerators, wardrobes for our clothing, and areas to store our weapons and equipment. After brief tours of the regimental headquarters and of surrounding areas, we were given time to prepare our quarters and to sleep before the next day. As I lay down to sleep, my fearfulness had dissipated and I was filled with excitement, and eager to know what lay beyond the reinforced walls of *Camp Warehouse*.

PART II

Deployment

From wrong to wrong the exasperated spirit
Proceeds, unless restored by that refining fire
Where you must move in measure, like a dancer.

T.S. Eliot, *Little Gidding*

LVI

July 2009

It was only begrudgingly that I came to understand the general logic and good sense of traditional military organization. When I arrived in Afghanistan, I still chafed at military life's many strictures. With the perspective of five months of military experience and four academic degrees in history, I deemed the Legion's strictures and culture outdated and ill-adapted for today's manifold challenges. In my newfound expertise as an enlisted soldier, I scoffed at those more experienced than I who vouched for the wisdom of certain military ways that I found oppressive or ridiculous, such as morning formations.

Experience has since convinced me that, if anything, military efficiency would improve by going back to ruder forms of discipline from ages past, to include flogging. Diverse national armies developed over the past centuries were rarely built up in ideological flights of fancy, but rather they are by and large organic outgrowths, moulded in keeping with constraints in personnel and logistics. It is frustrating to admit that there are indeed sound reasons, if not perfect reasoning, behind much of what we find oppressive in military organizations.

Let us take the example of Leon Trotsky. His very capitalist bankrollers in New York and worldwide notwithstanding, it is hard to question his *bonae fides* as a communist revolutionary or his organizational genius in both the political and military realms. When faced with the realities of warfare, he scrapped revolutionary ideology and embraced traditional military structures and Tsarist officers for the fledgling Red Army. Without this practical response, the Russian Revolution would have taken a far different course.

One sound reason behind the Legion's traditions and regimens became evident in my own response to the new realities of my first military deployment. As unfamiliar as these were to me, within two weeks of arrival in Afghanistan my life had already become ruled by habit. By teaching and instilling routines that we can recreate almost anywhere, militaries teach us how to adapt to almost any circumstances. No matter how bad these become, we can never discount habit's power to sweeten them or at least to make them seem acceptable—as, for soldiers especially, "habit is the gift of heaven."

Every day began with physical training, which, *à la Légion*, entailed running for about eight to twenty kilometres. Since Camp Warehouse itself was only five kilometres in perimeter, we usually ran two to three loops on roads inside the base's walls before moving to one of its many outdoor gymnasiums. To keep us physically fit there were also small indoor gymnasiums with weights and other exercise equipment scattered throughout the base. After sport, we enjoyed an ample breakfast at the ordinary, quite contrary to the Legion's norms in France.

Over these first two weeks our leaders were busy taking notes and tips from our predecessors while preparing for the official change of responsibility for the French task force. At my level, I took part in few of these preparations aside from receiving a light armoured vehicle, or VBL. I took inventory of its equipment and signed papers declaring that I had taken official responsibility for this property, for its upkeep, and for its preparedness. When not building or installing various improvements for this vehicle, I helped several *caporaux-chef* in the regimental headquarters with any number of clerical tasks. When an officer needed something translated into English, he often summoned me to help him, or at least to review his translations.

Here I also got to know the group with which I would be working for the rest of the deployment, the regimental tactical intelligence cell—a name that might sound glamorous and intriguing to civilians with no military experience. The leader of this group was a remarkably short senior captain who had spent most of his career in the Legion. In theory, he should have been a *commandant* by this time, but rumour had it that he was embroiled in some scandal at the Legion's regiment in French Guyana. He was aloof and treated me with mild interest and contempt. His deputy was a tall, jovial, and almost silly-looking Breton whose stomach bulged and whose voice and laughs carried farther than those of most men. The last member of this cell was a French senior non-commissioned officer, a "major," who always seemed edgy and jerked his body in compulsive movements in response to what appeared to be normal daily events. He treated me sternly, held high expectations of me, and demanded that I take good care of our vehicle and weapons and keep them always ready. It would be lying to say that I enjoyed his attentions, but they made me a better and more responsible soldier. Outside of this team, to which I was mainly responsible, any officer of the battalion staff could ask me to do almost anything—which they often did. So I found myself quite busy and the days passed quickly.

On deployment there was usually no *corvée*, so we legionnaires were able to take hour-long siestas after lunch at the ordinary, depending on whether or not we stopped for a beer at the French Army's clubhouse or at the German Army's shop. The days included ample time for physical fitness, a mix of standard and new chores, regular trips to the ordinary, and a customary stop at one of the base's clubs in the evening. On Sundays the regimental chaplain said Mass at eleven o'clock in the morning, where usually I was the only enlisted person present among the few officers in regular attendance. At the ordinary, Sunday "brunches" were extravagant affairs which drew Western soldiers from across Kaboul, since varied and limitless servings of iced cream were available to all.

As of yet, the world outside remained unknown to us, save for the calls of the *muezzin*, the occasional explosion, and the constant, dull din of motors and of automobile traffic. In the measured creation of our new habits, we eagerly and anxiously awaited our first trip beyond the gates of Camp Warehouse.

LVII

July 2009

About two weeks after we had arrived in theatre, we planned and undertook our first journey outside of Camp Warehouse's increasingly familiar walls. It was important to do this before all the First Infantry Regiment's personnel left for France, so that we could ask appropriate questions about their operational experiences in these hostile territories. For this mission we travelled first to what was destined in later months to become our main base of operations in Afghanistan, the Forward Operating Base (FOB) Tora. During this trip we also visited a more isolated Combat Outpost (COP) in the Uzbeen Valley to the north of FOB Tora, from which our task force would be expected to carry out regular operations against local kingpins.

To get ready for this trip I spent days feverishly at work. Having little experience with deploying "to the field" and no experience with operations on deployments, I packed a large rucksack and duffle bag with material fit for any contingency. The deputy commander broke out into open laughter when he saw me lugging this excessive baggage to my vehicle. At the break of dawn on the morning of our movement to FOB Tora, we assembled our vehicles near one of Camp Warehouse's gates and carried out what soon became routine rehearsals of our convoy operations. Commissioned and non-commissioned officers briefed certain aspects of our upcoming movement, such as the probability of attacks by hostile forces, nearby hospitals and evacuation routes, and potential dangers along the way. With these rehearsals finished, we mounted our respective vehicles and ensured that our radios were working and that we all had communications with each other. We loaded our rifles and machine guns for the first time on this deployment as we passed through the camp's gates.

I was driving a VBL with the major and the captain from our intelligence cell. The former sat quietly in the back while the captain stood up through an opened hatch in the vehicle's roof, casually manning an austere-looking, steely French AA-52 7.62 calibre machine gun. We left the base and turned eastward.

For me it was thrilling to be out of the camp and to see the world beyond our walls that I had been trying to envisage for weeks. In our base's immediate surroundings, shops and kiosks abounded and lined every space along the two-lane highway, selling all kinds of wares. Children on foot, motorcycles, wizened men in robes, and cars darted in front of and between our motorized columns. Already I could see a range of brownish mountains to the east. As we drew nearer to them, most evidence of urban life stopped abruptly.

Either no one had mentioned the Mahipar Pass in sufficient detail, or else I simply was not paying attention when someone did warn us about its hazards. It was a winding two-lane highway of surprisingly good quality that includes countless dangerous twists and turns through cut-outs in the mountains, where it skirts parts of the Kaboul River until it ends in an extremely steep, almost spiralling descent. This descent transports travellers down most of the thousand metres of elevation that separate Kaboul and the largest city in Afghanistan's east, Jalalabad. The driving conditions were challenging and the traffic more so, but to my surprise the Legion's training had prepared me well for these difficult moments in the "real world."

Within a few hours our convoy turned right off the highway between Kaboul and Jalalabad onto a dusty trail, veering southward. A few minutes later we had already reached the gates of FOB Tora. Legionnaires from the Second Foreign Infantry Regiment's third company were manning the encampment's gates and waved us through to enter without stopping. In these chaotic first moments of our arrival at FOB Tora, we parked our convoy in as organized a fashion as possible. As the dust stirred by our vehicles settled, my superiors told me to take a nap somewhere or else to stay otherwise occupied until lunch.

Curious about my new surroundings in these relatively austere grounds and conditions, I wandered into a tent where the regimental reconnaissance group had already established itself. I admired and envied this tent's "orientalist" decorations, replete with local rugs and teapots, not to mention various souvenirs gathered from the surrounding countryside. At the time I had too little experience to understand that these reconnaissance troops had scant authentic intelligence about the surrounding areas and that their expertise was probably limited to rudimentary knowledge of local geographic features and various local personalities busy with the manipulation of our presence. In my innocence I stood in awe of these men who put on airs of "going native" after a few weeks in that area, and with no knowledge of its languages and customs.

In their tent a television blared out bizarre European music videos, including the Italian rapper Fabri Fibra's hit song at that time, "Do You Speak English?" I had barely finished watching the video, which I found quite amusing, when a sergeant asked me what I was doing in the tent. He quickly surmised that I had no business there and told me in no uncertain terms to leave.

Later that morning I walked FOB Tora's perimeter. It had been built on the ruins of a former Soviet Army base that, so the story goes, was overrun by Afghan forces during the Soviet-Afghan War. From the Soviets we inherited about five hard structures occupied by our headquarters. The rest of the base comprised a few dozen shipping containers converted into living quarters, a small ordinary made of sheet metal, several other similarly constructed buildings and two trailers that included showers and toilets. Until recently, Italian NATO forces had intermittently manned this base, and their neglect showed. With nothing to do, I walked over to a nearby guard post with no occupants, stretched out on the bare earth, and fell asleep. About an hour later the French major found me, woke me up, and brought me to lunch at the ordinary.

LVIII

July 2009

In the United States, popular culture broadcast prejudices against the French that I absorbed throughout my youth. Many of these concerned French hygienic practices, as seen in common claims that French women did not depilate themselves like their North American counterparts, or that Paris was "dirty." In my university years, when the French President Jacques Chirac exercised his nation's last burst of independence by gingerly opposing the impending Anglo-American invasion of Iraq, US bombast took new heights.

In response to this unaccustomed resistance to North American imperatives, an overweight journalist from an agonistic US publication popularized the phrase "cheese-eating surrender monkeys" to describe the French nation. Such pathetic blather overlooked our own relatively short and questionable military history, while omitting facts that this journalist either never knew or ignored—for example, that for one thousand years the French were probably Europe's most accomplished martial people, or that "The Great War" alone brought more deaths to France's male population than the combined number of all US combat deaths throughout our adolescent nation's relatively brief existence.

During a few sojourns in Paris before I joined the Legion, I grew suspicious of such provincial prejudices about the French. Any city in the United States even approaching the size of modern Paris is ridden with crime and with filth, whereas most parts of central Paris remained pleasant, safe, and clean. This is to say nothing of the general quality of life. By French standards, Paris was a frenetic, stressful city, yet it seemed composed and calm to me when compared with the cities I knew best—Baltimore, New York, and Washington, DC.

In the Legion, I came to take for granted standards of cleanliness that I had not often known in the United States. Indeed, I do not think that there is any other military in the world that requires its soldiers to clean their rooms, their lavatories, and all their company's offices and common areas three times daily. After six months in the Legion, I had become used to such cleanliness, however much I found the acts of cleaning burdensome and vexing. It was therefore a shock to me to see the relative slovenliness of my countrymen in Afghanistan when compared with the French, something which I experienced in a memorable way during our first regimental reconnaissance in the Uzbeen Valley.

We spent the first night of our mission at FOB Tora, sleeping under the open skies in French Army cots enclosed with mosquito nets. About six o'clock the next morning, the regimental headquarters and robust security elements set out to our new combat outpost, or COP, approximately twenty kilometres to the north. We left FOB Tora in a convoy, crossed the bridge over Lake Surobi, and drove along dirt trails toward the COP. Along the way we passed Sper Kunday, where ten French soldiers, including two legionnaires, had been killed in an ambush the day that I was travelling to join the Legion. Given such recent history, all were watchful. We younger soldiers saw danger and combat lurking everywhere.

We arrived at the COP before noon. It was still high summer in Afghanistan, and the COP was situated in a treeless valley and surrounded by foothills that led into mountains to the north and the west. As the colonel and his staff took their bearings and got to know the lay of the land, I walked about the COP and spoke with some of my own countrymen stationed at this outpost.

The first fellow citizen with whom I remember speaking was a lieutenant from the United States Marine Corps. Graced with an enormous torso and biceps bursting out of his uniform's rolled-up sleeves, he was curious to speak with a fellow citizen serving in the fabled French Foreign Legion. He showed me about his tent, equipped with rows of laptop computers and all kinds of electronic gadgets. No US tent was complete without an enormous air-conditioner. Perhaps revealing my own budding sense of propriety as a legionnaire, I asked him how he and his platoon kept themselves clean at this remote location. He stunned me by answering that there were no showers on the base, and that every week or so he would sprinkle water over his body to wash himself. His platoon had been there for almost six months.

A second interaction with my countrymen betrayed similar attitudes. Also on the COP was a small US Army Special Forces detachment. While talking with one of its non-commissioned officers, he regaled me with a story about the COP's only latrine, a lonesome plastic chemical toilet coated with thick dust. Its container for human waste was not working, so this detachment's members had fastened a plastic trash bag about the rim of the toilet to collect droppings. They paid a local man whom they called "Shitter 6," to haul away their solid waste once a week.

Amused by this tale, it was with some concern that I walked up to this chemical toilet and opened its door. What I found inside was worse than anything that I could have imagined. The plastic bag fastened to the toilet bowl's rim was brimming, its overflowing contents attended by swarms of flies. In the chemical toilet's urinal, enterprising soldiers had stashed away several pornographic magazines. A small vat of Vaseline, a petroleum-based lubricant, and liquid alcohol hand sanitizer dispensers completed this chemical toilet's mournful offerings.

Men sometimes tell of events seared into their memory. Although I would usually avoid using the verb "to sear" to describe the forging of my memories as an unduly dramatic choice, my few moments of exposure to that chemical toilet's humid and fetid air make one such "seared" memory for me.

It was not unheard of for tribesmen in the surrounding hills to direct random small-arms shots at the COP, and we were all jittery in this new setting. Yet the prospect of inaccurate direct fire from afar was far preferable to the idea of having recourse to that plastic "thunderbox."

LIX

July 2009

To stand guard became one of my regular duties whenever we moved beyond Camp Warehouse. This task is one of the most boring and unwanted but also one of the most meaningful responsibilities of soldiering, and for its guard shifts the Legion set high standards. Indeed, one of the first things that we learned to do at Castelnaudary was to maintain uninterrupted nightly watches in all circumstances. Quickly we grew adept at organizing and executing these adequately and with only the occasional supervision of our cadre.

Today, when one thinks of a Roman legionary, his thoughts would most probably conjure up film-inspired images. In motion pictures about ancient Rome, legionaries are usually presented as anonymous but admirable and muscular figures that hew down hordes of barbarians owing to their superior organization and *esprit de corps*. To be sure, legionaries of yesterday had more than their share of fighting, but for many generations the common legionary's fate was probably to spend most of his twenty or so years of service standing guard in largely peaceful times—or enforcing rules on those standing guard. Some fifteen centuries since the last plausibly Roman legions policed European territories, to stand guard is still the soldier's most important task. The Foreign Legion unfailingly understood and reinforced this.

Our first evening in the Uzbeen Valley, I witnessed a ritual wholly new to me. In this remote location our regimental commander hosted a dinner with a select group of his officers in a tent. I was privy to all this since I had become acquainted with the commander's two servants—one a kindly and pudgy Romanian who was his official driver and uniform keeper, the second a short and perpetually exasperated Frenchman who was his assigned cook. That evening the cook and the driver gathered a variety of French Army rations (which have consistently ranked among the world's best military rations for decades) and "augmented" these rations with products somehow procured from local merchants. To accompany such dinners came bottles of wine from the Foreign Legion's vineyards at Puyloubier, or else a specific maker of *Côtes-du-Rhone* who may have had an exclusive contract with the Legion. That night at the COP, the regimental commander and eight of his officers dined formally in a rustic tent, while the colonel's two servants managed a handful of legionnaires who served as the officers' waiters throughout the meal. Later I would serve as a waiter several times during the colonel's nightly dinners with fellow officers.

The French major from our intelligence cell told me to take part in a guard shift that night. Therefore, about midnight, after a few hours of sound sleep on a cot in one of the COP's warm, dusty, and sparsely inhabited tents, I woke up for my assigned shift and reported to a tower on the outpost's southwestern corner.

There I was surprised to find an almost elderly non-commissioned officer from the Tennessee National Guard awaiting me. He must have been well into his fifties and his teeth were in a state of distress. The accent and twang of his speech betrayed Appalachian origins. That night he shared a two-hour shift at the guard post with me. For the better part of these hours, he told me all about the various and dangerous combats that had taken place at this outpost over the past six months. When I expressed to him my concerns about the COP's lack of showers and sanitary facilities, he confirmed that he had not properly bathed or cleaned himself for almost half a year. He seemed to reckon it somehow beneath his station and contemptible to think about doing so.

In this valley outpost, the stars' brightness dazzled me throughout the night's shift, much of which we spent looking through night-vision goggles that worked by magnifying the intensity of natural nocturnal lights. Ever since I took a course on Goethe's *Faust* as an undergraduate—in which our stereotypical German professor once explained that we, surrounded by electric lights at all hours of the night, could never imagine how bright the moon and the stars were in Goethe's time—I had longed to see stars undimmed by interference from the earth's electric lighting. Standing alert in our guard tower, I called to mind lines from *Faust* that I had long since committed to memory, and which I was wont to repeat to myself in times of especial melancholy or self-pity:

> *O sähst du, voller Mondenschein, Zum letzten Mal auf meine Pein,*
> *Den ich so manche Mitternacht, An diesem Pult herangewacht....*
> *Dann über Büchern und Papier, Trübseliger Freund, erschienst du mir!*[*]

In this outcast place the moon's radiance was overwhelming and washed the entire landscape in colour that was indeed milky. Stars that I never could have imagined littered the skies, and those known to me shone with unfamiliar intensity. When I looked up to the skies with our night-vision devices, stars were brighter and more numerous still. Next to the earnest and bumpkin-like Tennessean, I marvelled at the skies above us, believing that I had, for the first time in my life, caught glimpses of heavenly lights more closely resembling those known to Goethe, and indeed to all men before our electrified ages.

As I looked out toward the moonlight-soaked mountains that surrounded us, the only manmade lights visible were gas-powered lanterns that shone out of the windows of occasional mud buildings. Here I perceived something of

---

* "O full moonshine, if for the last time, you would look upon my torments / You that I have so often watched, at midnight, while awake at my desk / Then you might appear to me, my melancholy friend, shining over my books and papers."

ancient worlds about which I had studied in books and classrooms, but which had heretofore seemed unfathomable realms of myth.

That night Afghanistan gripped me with a fascination that endures today.

After our first night in the Uzbeen valley in simple tents, we moved directly back to Camp Warehouse the next morning. During this visit several of our senior non-commissioned officers had seen enough of North American squalor, and they had already planned to build two amenities that no self-respecting Legion base could be without: facilities for showering and a well-stocked bar.

LX

September 2009

Once back at Camp Warehouse, before long we had set up a routine that lasted for the next three months. About once every two weeks we deployed to FOB Tora and, from there, to its northern satellite COP for three or four days. During these trips we carried out missions throughout the Uzbeen Valley. Such missions usually comprised movements in formations of ten to twenty vehicles. Our moving about the valley in this manner kept locals from taking random shots at us from the surrounding hills with their AK-47s. Few of them were suicidal enough to attack us, even though shadowy elements based in Pakistan offered handsome sums of money to locals for even the smallest attacks on NATO forces and their local supporters.

To my knowledge, during our deployment we did not conduct any foot patrols in the Uzbeen Valley, probably owing to the recent and deadly embarrassment at Sper Kunday. Our usual missions entailed driving to one of the valley's settlements, surrounding it, and then summoning local strongmen to sit and to have tea with our commanders—what we euphemistically called *shura* (in this context meant to indicate a gathering of relevant authorities). Although of little effect, these engagements allowed us to train many military procedures, and the dangers were sometimes real, if small by twentieth-century standards.

At Camp Warehouse I was usually responsible for a variety of menial tasks associated with the headquarters' equipment and radios, and in the evening I shared turns with a senior corporal in the headquarters buildings to serve as a runner for the duty officer, or *officier du quart*. This task usually lasted until about 2200, after which time we runners were allowed to go to sleep while remaining on call. Owing to this regular employment, I was exempt from standing watch in Camp Warehouse's guard towers, which was a duty common for most legionnaires throughout these three months in Kaboul.

Wild and probably exaggerated stories from happenings at the guard posts were often shared in the evening at the French Army club, where most of us headed to enjoy a few beers after dinner at the ordinary. One widely spread rumour was about a bug-eyed Bulgarian legionnaire whom I remembered from in-processing at Aubagne. It was told that his platoon leader, a lieutenant fresh out of the French military academy at Saint-Cyr, had caught him in onanism's throes—*in flagrante delicto*—during a routine inspection of his soldiers' guard posts. Whether true or not, everyone believed the story. Beyond any question was legionnaires' use of local *hashish*. It seems that some well-meaning regulation was in place whereby NATO soldiers were required to man their guard posts with Afghan military counterparts. The latter would regularly bring powerful *hashish* to their guard duty. Not every legionnaire resisted the temptation to partake of these provisions, which enjoyed a brisk trade throughout Camp Warehouse.

Was buggery a common practice at this base? For my part, I saw no evidence of it throughout my three months there. That said, toward the end of our time in Kaboul our company first sergeant, a disappointed and irritable Pole, assembled the whole company and stated that there was a serious and growing problem with sexually transmitted diseases in our ranks. For that reason, he said, he would be leaving boxes of condoms outside of his office from which we were all free to take as many as needed, with no questions asked. At that time, there were no more than twenty or so women at Camp Warehouse. Given various limiting factors, I cannot believe that there would have been even a remote possibility for legionnaires to have had sexual relations with more than five of these women.

It is possible that legionnaires were servicing their fleshier needs at Kaboul's infamous "Chicken Street," where a variety of brothels, most of which were said to be run by Chinese entrepreneurs, catered to the capital's teeming population of Western bureaucrats, diplomats, and soldiers. One legionnaire whom I knew from our selection process at Aubagne, a young and muscular black man from Houston, once invited me to sneak out of base with him and several peers to go to a Kaboul brothel. Curious as I was to learn more about exactly how legionnaires did such things, I turned down this invitation for many reasons. Such an invitation leads me to think, however, that the practice was not uncommon. It would have been easy to walk out of the base with cooperative colleagues at the guard post, to take one of the numerous taxis near the base's entrance, and to paint Kaboul red. For commissioned and senior non-commissioned officers, it would have been even easier to do this since no one would have asked questions about their taking official vehicles off base.

How much did any of this happen? I do not know, but furtive, lusty jaunts were probably not uncommon. The French Army has long taken a pragmatic approach to soldiers' fornicating with local populations, since until recently it maintained officially sponsored and regulated military brothels. Although the practice was long-standing, by the 1920s the French government had codified the provision of prostitutes to soldiers in what were labelled *bordels militaires de campagnes* (BMC). These survived in the Foreign Legion long after they had disappeared from the rest of the French military, and some older Legion officers even had some experience of them—whether as clients or else in supervisory roles. In French Guyana the "BMC" lasted well into the 1990s. If we had been deployed to Africa, I would have witnessed many more traditional legionary recreational activities at established *maisons de tolérance*. In Afghanistan, however, such activities were kept hushed-up and underground.

I would not be surprised if the German Army's discotheque at Camp Warehouse, the *Wolf's Lair*, played some important role in upholding the ancient trade of female bodies that for men in desperation become…

> *…des Christ d'une autre forme et d'une autre croyance*
> *Ce sont les Christ inférieurs des obscures espérances.**

* Guillaume Apollinaire, *Zone*: "Christs of a different kind and of a different religion / The inferior Christs of obscure hopes."

LXI

September 2009

Every other evening at Camp Warehouse, I manned the desk of our regimental headquarters after normal working hours, from about 1800 until 2200. Here my charge was to help the regiment's duty officer who stayed in the headquarters throughout the evening, where he monitored radios and electronic messages in case any emergency should arise.

During these shifts I enjoyed much uninterrupted time for reading. Happily, I had managed to bring my Lewis and Short Latin-English Dictionary (which I fancied, probably incorrectly, to be the only copy in Afghanistan) and a few trusted editions of Latin Classics. So these evenings I occupied myself with re-reading Caesar's *Commentaries on the Gallic Wars* for the umpteenth time. I also used our headquarters' resources to print articles about Erasmus of Rotterdam, whose patristic scholarship later became the subject of my doctoral thesis.

As somewhat of an expert on Caesar's *Commentaries*, I could not avoid drawing parallels between our engagements in Afghanistan and Caesar's "pacifying" ventures in Gaul. On one of those evenings at the duty desk, as I read about Caesar's bloody and thoroughgoing suppression of the Veneti revolt, it occurred to me that until we could terrorize our would-be "terrorists," and so long as we tried to conduct warfare according to seemingly random selections from post-Christian bourgeois morality, any efforts in this country, where we strove against generations of hardened fighters, were doomed to failure.

While serving as the duty officer's runner, gradually I got to know most of the regiment's staff officers. As they entered the headquarters after hours and saw me with books or scholarly articles, invariably they asked me what I was reading, often with true curiosity. What surprised me about these French officers is that every one of them knew who Erasmus of Rotterdam was. What is more, many of them were able to ask me informed questions about him. Even the most unintellectual of the regiment's officers, the Fourth Company's pimply and short executive officer, knew who Erasmus was and made lewd remarks about the European Union's eponymous foreign exchange programme, implying that he had good reason to refer to this praiseworthy effort as "orgasmus."

By far the most amusing officer was Captain Michel. He was a Corsican who had served in the Legion's Second Foreign Parachute Regiment and later risen through the ranks to become an officer *à titre étranger*.* At this point he had served in the Foreign Legion for over thirty years. A short and portly chain-smoker, he hardly cut the figure of a dashing officer. His decades of service, however—which included his participation as a young legionnaire in the Foreign Legion's legendary airborne operation in Kolwezei in 1978—had made him almost impregnable to criticism. He served as the chief of staff to the regimental commander, and in this capacity lorded over all the other officers at our headquarters with benign neglect. Rumour had it that his career had been significantly undermined by an episode in Calvi, where he had seriously injured someone by breaking a chair over his head in a drunken brawl. He affected outrageously reactionary political views redolent of *Radio Courtoisie*'s broadcasts with *commandant Pierre Guillaume*. He refused to attend Mass unless it were offered in the so-called "Tridentine Rite."

---

* This is a particular class of officers authorized by French law who, nowadays, usually serve in the Foreign Legion.

My favourite officer was Captain Xavier. Rare among officers in the Legion, he had not graduated from Saint-Cyr, the French military's main source of officers, but instead from the *École Polytechnique*, after which he chose to pursue the career of a professional officer. His conversation suggested a sound Jesuit education. One evening he entered the regimental headquarters and saw me reading an article about Erasmus. He stopped me and, with excitement almost unbecoming an officer, explained to me that he had just finished reading Stefan Zweig's biography, *Erasmus of Rotterdam*. I had read the book but did not remember much about it, and this seemed to disappoint Captain Xavier.

This episode is illustrative of the marked difference between officer cultures in the United States and in France in my days of service, a difference that I first began to appreciate during this deployment. In general, I found that French officers from Saint-Cyr or other commissioning sources had more basic knowledge about Erasmus and about his accomplishments than my graduate student colleagues at Princeton University's history faculty. After nine years of serving as an officer in the US Army, it is hard for me to imagine a fellow officer who could pose intelligent questions about Erasmus or, even more bizarrely, had just finished reading a well-known biography of Erasmus. Yet, most officers in our French task force in Afghanistan could do so. In the French Army I consistently found officers of respectable intellectual depth and culture. Our regimental commander himself had a doctorate from a prestigious Parisian university and had published a large book and numerous articles about Clausewitz' legacy in the French military tradition.

It was during these shifts with various duty officers that I began to understand more about French officer culture, where many men who probably had little allegiance to the Fifth Republic nonetheless undertook to serve their ancient nation, perhaps carrying on family traditions. Far be it from me to extol French officers writ large, but I would estimate that in the early twenty-first century, their intellectual and cultural formation stood remarkably above those of officers from any other Western nation. What is more, they appeared to relish belonging to the specific caste of officers, something markedly different from the United States military, where enlisted men and non-commissioned *sous-offs* are lionized for their extraordinary virtues and heroism, whereas officers are customarily viewed with suspicion and thinly disguised disdain.

I think it fair to state that we legionnaires respected our officers when we could believe that they were learned, intelligent, and well-bred men as well as tactically proficient. To take an example of this, the rude and experienced soldiers under Captain Xavier's command generally held him in high esteem despite his intellectual bearing and effeminate, often stuttering voice.

LXII

September 2009

By 2009, distrust, even hatred, of the United States was growing in many circles in Afghanistan. For this reason, NATO military authorities in Afghanistan sometimes sent French officers to parlay with powerful Afghans who refused to speak directly with agents of the US government. One morning at Camp Warehouse, I was assigned as a driver for a mission of this kind to a compound on Kaboul's outskirts.

Ever since our arrival in Kaboul, in addition to driving our VBL, I also maintained and drove an armoured Toyota Land Cruiser designated for driving officers in our battalion staff to meetings elsewhere in the city. These unwieldy vehicles, whose engines strained almost pathetically under the weight of armour added to their frames, were most probably inherited from the US embassy or from some other US agency. It is hard to imagine any European government, whatever its faults, acting so wastefully with its limited funds as to buy dozens of such armoured vehicles that guzzled outrageous amounts of petrol.

Before this mission I had already grown familiar with driving in Kaboul, so it was somewhat routinely that four of us left the camp's gates that morning. Our party comprised Captain Michel, the lieutenant from our intelligence cell, and a local translator whose name I do not remember, but with whom I had become familiar over the prior weeks during our trips in Kaboul and the Surobi area. In his youth he had attended Kaboul's prestigious *lycée français* before the nation's Communist revolution, back when Afghanistan's elite was largely francophone.

This translator's sense of humour was delightful. He also matter-of-factly explained to me how he approached his work as a translator. To him, to represent speech and conversations faithfully was a fool's errand. In his translations between French and the local dialects of Persian, he took care to twist meaning such as to keep his paymasters happy and to ensure as few untoward reactions as possible from Afghans. He doted on his wife and proudly repeated a phrase in English that I had never heard to explain his philosophy on this matter: "Life without wife is fifty without five!"

We left that morning for an unknown location. The French lieutenant gave us directions while peering at a map unfolded on his lap. I remember passing several rows of gaudy new buildings and "wedding halls" before reaching an isolated location along a dirt road. I believe that this compound was somewhere along the way to Gardez, but I cannot be sure.

Guards armed with AK-47s, many with bandoliers of ammunition draped decoratively about their shoulders, surrounded the compound. Captain Michel and the lieutenant went inside to speak with whoever was calling those AK-47s' shots—they never told me who this person was or why he was important. Most improbably, I was the security detail for our engagement—one soldier with a FAMAS surrounded by at least twenty armed men in sight, with countless others within the compound or within earshot. At the time I was too unaware of our overall situation and too foolhardy to be frightened. I stood by our vehicle for most of this wait, save for when some of the guards invited me to take tea in one of the house's outer rooms. It seemed unwise to spurn their hospitality.

Our officers' conversation dragged on for some time, during which I took stock of our surroundings from my limited vantage point. This compound appeared to be the centre of economic and social activity in an otherwise isolated settlement on Kaboul's outskirts. Several roads of packed dirt separated houses and compounds built from the region's distinctive mud-based *pahkta* bricks. There was one above-ground electricity line that led into the compound where we had parked our vehicle. Barefoot children ran through the streets and armed guards stood at every corner. Not a woman was in sight. The guards did not seem overly pleased at our presence, but their behaviour toward me was genteel, if curt.

About an hour later Captain Michel, the lieutenant, and our translator came back to the vehicle. Quickly we hied our way back to Kaboul's relatively comfortable familiarity. Everyone seemed jittery and conversation was limited. At a busy roundabout somewhere in the city centre, our translator asked if we could drop him off close to his apartment instead of making him ride all the way to Camp Warehouse. Our officers obliged him, and the translator assured us that the way back to Camp Warehouse was simply a matter of taking few left turns.

Contrary to commonplace military prejudice, I am wont to defend lieutenants and their orienteering skills since they often have the most up-to-date and recently reinforced training in these matters. Yet, in this case, following the lieutenant's directions, the three of us promptly got lost somewhere in downtown Kaboul. The lieutenant protested that he knew where we were until we drove right into a crowded market impossible to navigate with a vehicle. Passers-by ogled us and both officers almost broke sweats in their anxiety that bordered on panic. A similar armoured vehicle drove slowly by us, and through its tinted windows I could make out what seemed to be four North Americans, one of whom wore a cowboy hat. Both vehicles' occupants seemed to question each other with their gazes: "What are *you* doing here?" The frazzled lieutenant made a few telephone calls and eventually we left the market and found our way back to Camp Warehouse.

For my part, I found the market itself fascinating. Objects for sale included antiques that would fetch small fortunes west of Suez, and I very much wanted to come back to this bazar on a shopping expedition. It surprised me to see how helpless our officers looked without our translator. Had our phones failed us I do not know how we would have managed to return to Camp Warehouse.

If we could not do something as simple as drive in a capital city without translators, how could we run military operations?

LXIII

September 2009

It was over caviar that I spoke at length for the first time with Father Gaël, our regimental chaplain. A member of our regimental staff had secured several tins of Persian caviar and offered it to all the staff at headquarters late one afternoon. On rickety wooden tables squeezed between dusty Hesco bastions, we washed down this excellent caviar with beers.

As the lowest ranking person in this group, I was careful about appearing too chummy with anyone. Noting my reticence, the chaplain struck up conversation with me. Hitherto I had spoken with him only briefly after Sunday Mass, since I was the only enlisted legionnaire in regular attendance. From this day forward I confided in him more often. Little did I know it, but this chaplain was well-known in the French military chaplain corps for various reasons.

Firstly, he had countless deployments to missions and combat operations throughout the world. Decorative medals are relatively hard to come by in the French military, but Father Gaël had more campaign and service medals than any other officer, save for the regimental commander. He could not reasonably fit all his authorized decorations on his uniform, so he only wore his favourites.

Second, by all reports he was an excessive drinker. Perhaps too naïve at the time to remark this, I am now more inclined to believe this rumour because I have since heard many stories relating colourful incidents involving this priest and alcohol, including one episode in Guyana when he was supposedly too tipsy to say Midnight Mass. That said, I myself saw no reason to believe such rumours during our regular interactions, and military gossip is not known for its accuracy.

Third, he was a charming personality with a profound understanding of the military condition. His father, a minor noble of old lineage, had served as a career officer and retired as a colonel, so Father Gaël had a knack for perceiving the subtleties of military politicking.

Last but not least, Father Gaël was a fabulous storyteller, such that even if one suspected him of embellishing or fibbing, one paid no heed, simply out of desire that his story be true. He embodied two of the three types of "greatness" identified by Baudelaire: *Il n'y a de grand parmi les hommes que le poète, le prêtre et le soldat. L'homme qui chante, l'homme qui bénit, l'homme qui sacrifie et se sacrifie.** Perhaps in his storytelling Father Gaël also figured as something of a poet as well! I cannot remember a dull moment with him, and I learned much from this kind, generous, and astute man.

Father Gaël was a "high church" type. He owned a three-storied house in a mediaeval village in the Aude whose *collégiale* had inherited a chasuble made from the fabric of a dress belonging to Catherine de' Medici or Marie-Antoinette—it escapes me which queen. Father Gaël wore this magnificent vestment as often as possible when celebrating Mass in this village. Later, when I was travelling to Florence and to Rome, he asked me to seek out lacey surplices from specific makers in both cities. All the same, Father Gaël was also stridently critical of France's many "traditionalist" priestly orders. His venom against the *Institute of Christ the King Sovereign Priest* knew few bounds, as he had met its founder at some point in Gabon. They did not part on friendly terms. I do not

* "The only great men among us are the poet, the priest, and the solider—he who sings, he who blesses, and he who kills and sacrifices himself."

know if Father Gaël's piquant story about why the order wears its distinctive light blue colours was true or not, but it was most entertaining.

For months Captain Michel had refused to attend Sunday Mass at Camp Warehouse because it was not the Latin "Tridentine Mass." Father Gaël was dyslexic and found it hard to read the appropriate liturgical rubrics in Latin, but nonetheless he agreed to humour Captain Michel and to say this older Mass one Sunday at Camp Warehouse. It was a sparsely populated celebration, as most were, but Captain Michel was present, along with the regimental commander. Father Gaël continued to say the Tridentine Mass on Sundays until Captain Michel stopped attending them a few weeks later, at which point he became convinced that Captain Michel mainly talked about the Tridentine Mass to appear to others as appropriately reactionary. Father Gaël was probably correct. Captain Michel seemed to have little interest in Christianity but much zeal for the philosophies of organizations such as *Action Française.*

In English it is often said that "there are no atheists in a foxhole," which is meant to convey the idea that military realities and coinciding fears of death make men more likely to contemplate the afterlife and to turn to God for strength or forgiveness. I saw little evidence of this in Afghanistan, although it must be admitted that the dangers which we experienced were few when compared with those of the previous century's great wars. Aside from Christmas Masses that were more or less obligatory for officers and senior NCOs, I cannot remember seeing more than a handful of enlisted men at Mass throughout the deployment. None of them attended regularly.

As for the officers, it bears noting that whereas most officers attended Mass weekly in France, on this deployment they did not, even though to attend Mass was much simpler at Camp Warehouse—where it was held at convenient hours and a stone's throw from our headquarters—than it could have been anywhere in France. Aside from our regimental commander and a handful of others, few officers came to Father Gaël's Masses. This did make me wonder whether our officers' regular Mass attendance in France, then, was perhaps expected of them by their peers or their womenfolk, and not something they believed necessary to guide their progress through this world and into the next. A weekly thirty-minute liturgy is a small threshold for faithful practice, and although we can never know one's interior disposition, it is hard for me to take anyone's faith seriously who cannot make such a paltry effort.

LXIV

September 2009

During one of our stays at FOB Tora, we diverged from our usual activities in the Uzbeen Valley to carry out operations in the south. We knew little about this area aside from rumours about its Jegdalek ruby mines. Locals managing these mines were said to be men of fabulous riches, and I imagine that some of them did have impressive bank accounts in the United Arab Emirates.

It was in this valley that I saw for the first time the poverty and want that affected so many Afghans, something largely incomprehensible to me before encountering it. We began the operation by moving to the south some ten kilometres, mostly along dirt roads but sometimes on trails that we improvised ourselves. At one point along the route our lead unit, led by a competent cavalry captain, became lost. It was something easily done, for to navigate we were using a combination of unreliable old maps and modern geolocation technology whose effectiveness in those areas was often limited. Toward noon we ended our journey in an open plain, where our regimental headquarters set up a mobile command post while other combat units accompanying us provided security. As often was the case, after driving to this place I had little to do. Once

I had parked my vehicle alongside those of a few staff officers, I sat inside and switched between reading Caesar and napping.

Locals had long noted our presence, and soon children came and started begging beside our vehicles. They were dark-skinned, short, and dirty, wearing gowns that had probably not been changed for weeks or months. This area was Pashtun, but the children begged in Persian, time and again asking me for a pen using the Persian word for it. At first, I could not understand why they would ask for a simple ball-point pen made of plastic, something whose cost in Western countries at this time would have been negligible even for society's poorest elements. It took a more experienced *caporal-chef*'s explanation to make me understand that these children had probably never owned a pen, and that for them the opportunity to draw pictures with one was a rare treat.

After several hours in this location, an impromptu marketplace began to form about us. Someone brought bread and other foodstuffs and sought to exchange them for French Army rations. Others brought canned and bottled drinks for sale. It surprised me to see that the Coca-Cola Company's products featured more prominently among these drinks than anything of local manufacture.

In the late morning's heat, we all drank water and other fluids in abundance, and soon enough I had the urge to urinate. For this purpose, I walked over to a lonely tree to shield my genitals from potential onlookers. After I had urinated, a different *caporal-chef* walked over to me and remarked that I had behaved badly, since trees represented a limited source of shade in this unforgiving climate, and that locals might find my urinating on it offensive. Again, it made me think of how much I had taken for granted in life, including something so simple as a tree's shade.

Whatever the officers were doing in that location, it soon came to an end. Thereafter we headed toward a different settlement to the north, nearer to FOB Tora. It was already approaching evening when we parked near an inhabited area. While our officers met with the village elders, we tried to set up a secure area as men and children gaggled between our vehicles, angling to communicate with soldiers by hand gestures and unmistakably begging for military rations.

A company from the US Georgia National Guard, which intermittently came to stay at FOB Tora, accompanied us for this mission. Already I had spoken with its commander several times since I was curious to learn more about the US soldiers in the area, and he keen to hear more about the Foreign Legion. In the US National Guard, soldiers were frequently mobilized and taken from their civilian jobs to take part in nine-month deployments to Afghanistan or to Iraq. This company commander was a kindly, stout banker from a town near Atlanta, who spoke with a thick southern accent. His company had parked its vehicles next to ours. Even in this isolated area the children could distinguish between French and US soldiers. This became obvious when a gang of children came to us and, pointing at the US soldiers, suggested that we shoot at them.

As our commander spoke with whomever we believed to be the foremost local authorities, our Civil-Military Cooperation (or CIMIC) team did its customary work. This largely comprised throwing bags of flour, rice, and other foodstuffs from the back of its vehicles to locals' outstretched hands. Crowds formed about their vehicles, and shouting and chaos grew. Watching from about ten metres away, I could not help but to marvel at such actions and to wonder what we hoped to accomplish with such crude "charitable" performances. I have few doubts that the locals ate the food given to them, but I have even fewer that they did not do it with any senses of gratitude whatsoever.

Until this time, I had been largely isolated from local populations, and this was my first chance to walk among Afghans. It was jarring to witness the meeting of two worlds—one that had probably not changed very substantially since Alexander the Great's invasion of these same territories; and the other a decaying offshoot of the past two centuries' industrial economies.

Many of the Afghans in this village must have found us bewildering, but in the end, I think that they were less naïve and less deceived in this episode than we were. For too many of us participating in this bizarre ritual of almsgiving believed that we were doing something good for these people, that they would bear better will toward us for our action, and that we were somehow pursuing France's skilfully crafted military and political goals.

LXV

October 2009

Internet-based "social media" were in their infancy in those days, but already they had noteworthy effects on our task force's operational planning. This became apparent one day as we were preparing a four-day operation in the Uzbeen Valley. Our company commander summoned us all to a formation where he told us that owing to indiscreet online messages, our coming operations were better known among women in France than they were at Camp Warehouse itself. It could therefore be assumed that our adversaries had even more intimate knowledge of such plans.

It remains unclear to me how this could have happened. Even for privileged officers at Camp Warehouse, in 2009 it was hard to come by internet connectivity. In general, it was only possible to send emails from a few designated "internet cafes" scattered throughout the base. Yet, somehow, in Kaboul, the tentacles of social media were already latching onto collaborative prey. That they did so is a testimony to the rapidly growing power of electronic devices and internet-based mediums of communication at that time.

Since I served as a legionnaire from 2008 until 2010, I was rather isolated from the revolution in human interactions that was occurring in those very years, when for the first time a majority of people in Western or "developed" countries began carrying "smart phones." As legionnaires we were not allowed to have any mobile telephones without special permission. At Castelnaudary, I was told to buy a small, simple Nokia portable telephone so that my cadre could get in touch with me when I was travelling, but I know that legionnaires in other regiments were often not allowed to possess any personal electronic devices at all. Of course, many legionnaires kept telephones, computers, and electronic gaming devices hidden away in their quarters, but to be caught with such items by strict-minded superiors was a sure ticket to a week or more *en taule*. Although it was possible for some aspects of the revolution ushered in by smart phones and social media to creep into the Legion's sequestered culture, it was nonetheless out of the question for us as legionnaires to experience this revolution as fully as those outside our unique environment.

Until that company formation at Camp Warehouse, I had never taken seriously the phenomenon of social media, deeming it a fad that was destined to fade away into the electronic voids. From the beginning I found such media distasteful, but never could I have believed that their proliferation could somehow affect military operations in Afghanistan. When I matriculated at Princeton in 2006, the most used "social media" was a now-defunct platform called Myspace, which no serious university student would have considered an important medium for social interaction, and much less for pursuing the free-wheeling sexual gratification promised in consumerist societies. In 2006 even "internet dating" was still considered somewhat "kinky." Facebook had just started, and it was only available to university students in the United States.

At first I found the meteoric rise and widespread popularity of this Facebook platform bizarre. It surprised me that nubile women would take so keenly to disseminating photographs of themselves—often revealing or compromising photographs—such that thousands of young men could study them much too frequently, and often in the most inappropriate ways. Were such Facebook photographs an online "fifteen minutes of fame" for these would-be starlets?

I now understand that I vastly underestimated the power of this and of similar online platforms. In hindsight, the logic of Facebook's viral spread is, after all, easy enough to understand. Women are predisposed to prize and to share photographs of themselves and of their loved ones, and men to studying photographs of women. Facebook served as a devilish medium to capture, to distort, and to amplify these unwholesome natural tendencies. For my part, to succumb to any instinctive elation at a Facebook "like" always made me feel utterly abject and pathetic, and I found the idea of studying the Facebook profiles of others, and especially of women, invasive and perverse.

That said, I can understand the siren's call of this platform for lonely legionnaires in Afghanistan, who, through this medium, were able to do things that soldiers of the past could only dream about doing while on distant deployments, such as sending quick messages to loved ones, sharing photographs of children and relatives, and hearing the latest news from home.

In addition to such sentimental exchanges, in Afghanistan our soldiers had already found ways to use Facebook to share with their loved ones and lady friends details about our ongoing operations. Indeed, among the translators through whom we conducted most local coordination and in whom we placed childlike faith, were many who were selling information to spies in Kaboul. Now they only had to look at Facebook to learn about our latest movements.

By the time I left the US Army in early 2022, social media platforms had come a long way from the relatively minor, if shocking, nuisance that our task force experienced in Kaboul in 2009. They had instead become full-fledged weapons of high-stakes information warfare, and one that no senior military leader could afford to ignore. In this context some general officers in the US Army assigned entire teams of officers to manage their official social media accounts. As absurd as this might sound, it was absolutely necessary given the abundance of fake accounts created weekly, if not daily, in these senior leaders' likenesses, and these accounts' outsized potential for harm.

Although it is of course historically impossible that such social media technology might somehow already have been available by 1914, I try to imagine soldiers in the great wars of the twentieth century indulging in such ruinous vanity as posting details of their upcoming operations online for the world to see. I must admit that it is entirely possible that many legendary men of this era would have quickly succumbed to such unmanly impulses had only technology made it possible for them to do so.

LXVI

October 2009

For the past five centuries at least, the invasions and machinations of imperial powers have dominated local economic activity in Afghanistan. Our presence at FOB Tora brought large sums of money to regional authorities, and I would wager that many locals met violent ends in power struggles that determined who would service our contracts and provide manpower and oversight for our construction projects.

As a lowly legionnaire, I believed that our many contacts with and widespread employment of locals were things thoroughly vetted and understood by competent military authorities somewhere, somehow. I have since learnt that this was in no way possible. We were probably employing the cousins or even the brothers of those whom we were supposedly fighting in the Uzbeen Valley—something that I already suspected from reading the daily intelligence briefs and summaries that I translated from French to English for our NATO headquarters.

The much-vaunted prowess of British colonial administrators of yesteryear is overblown. That said, the East India Company, and later authorities of the

British Crown, sometimes gave meaningful support to men who were adventurous or tasteful enough to wish to leave the sceptered isles behind them. Some of them installed themselves in regions of Afghanistan for years or even for decades, giving priceless context and services to the British administrators who watched over and pacified this tumultuous territory with relative success.

Among the NATO forces in 2009, including its British contingents, I saw no such support for or interest in understanding our situation. The consequences of our deliberate ignorance and two decades of stumbling in our self-made darkness were broadcast the world over as NATO operations abruptly ended in August 2021, with one of the most humiliating defeats and retreats in modern history.

To staff our ordinary, to clean our public facilities, and to do our laundry at FOB Tora, we relied on contracts with a mysterious local chieftain. He supplied us with a motley band of young Turkmens who spoke basic Persian after years of working in Afghanistan. We saw little of these young men outside of the ordinary's kitchen or the laundry facilities, housed inside a rusting shipping container. Every now and again we saw them in the mornings walking in groups to and from where they lived outside our walls. At the time, I had some command of basic Persian words, and thus I took to greeting these boys whenever they passed by or whenever I saw them working on base. One of them, who could not have been more than ten years old, asked me for my running shoes whenever he saw me wearing them. He did not have any shoes and walked barefoot every day, so his petitions did stir pity in me—but not sufficiently so that I would part with good running shoes.

For weeks the boy asked me for my shoes, and always I laughed and told him no, since I needed the shoes to run. This repeated dialogue in basic Persian became a joke between us. As weeks became months, I had already run enough kilometres to wear off much of the shoes' soles, and the boy's regular entreaties had an effect. After I had bought a new pair of running shoes from one of the shops at Camp Warehouse, I gave the boy my shoes during our next trip to FOB Tora. Doing so gave me the comforting sensations that charity often gives to those inexperienced with its true rewards.

A few days later I saw this boy, and he was barefoot again. I asked him what had happened to the shoes. Although I could not develop the conversation owing to my limited Persian, he communicated to me that either he did not like the shoes or that they did not fit. This angered me, as I could not imagine why this Turkmen pauper was not still beside himself with joy at my gift. Only with time—and after expressing a wish to do more for these destitute young men to Father Gaël—did I begin to understand how little, in fact, I could imagine about their situation. Wearing my shoes may have subjected this boy to beatings or to worse. Someone may have stolen them from him forcibly, or perhaps he sold them as soon as possible to have money for something else.

Here I began to understand that seeming acts of charity or goodwill often do more harm than good. Their help to intended beneficiaries is usually limited at best, and charitable gifts can easily upset established local norms, which brings the ire of the powerful upon the weakest. This new understanding shaped my judgments about many of our official acts during this deployment, since at least half of these were "charitable" in nature, as we attempted to buy locals' goodwill by distribution of food and bestowing other gifts such as water wells, school supplies, and books. Thus, we collectively repeated on larger and vastly more costly scales my individual foolishness in giving shoes to a young Turkmen. After reading Madame de Staël's *Delphine* in my early twenties, I believed that generous impulses not restrained by reason and by religion are some of the world's most dangerous things. Yet it took years of seeing misguided government generosity before I could resist the siren's call of pity and altruism, and discern when charity would probably hurt more than help others.

One day I spoke briefly with a different Turkmen who usually did my laundry. He asked me if I was Muslim. I answered in limited Persian that I was a Christian. "Why are you not a Muslim?" he asked. To answer this question, I told him that I believed that the Catholic faith was the truth. He stuffed my dirty laundry inside a worn cloth laundry bag and tossed it into a metal cage. After ridding his hands of my clothes soiled by dirt and by sweat, he replied by unwittingly echoing one of our age's most fateful judgments:

"What is truth?"

LXVII

October 2022

To my mind, Caesar's *Commentaries on the Gallic Wars* embody the heights of Latin prose style. Throughout our deployment, I rarely went on operations without my worn hardcover edition of the work made by the French publisher *Les Belles Lettres*.

From my studies of the dictator's life and writings, I do not believe that Caesar was prone to order wanton ruthlessness and savagery for their own sake, especially given the relatively violent standards of his age. Of all the "cruel" actions recorded in the *Commentaries*, his repression of the Veneti, in modern day Brittany, stands out for its brutality. Here Caesar terrorized and wasted the region's peoples, thereby setting a terrifying example for all Gaul. After his desolation of the Veneti, other Gallic tribes generally refrained from rebellion. It is entirely possible that Caesar's calculated cruelty therefore set conditions for France's relatively quick absorption into the Roman Empire thereafter, which perhaps saved it from additional centuries of tribalism.

In the twentieth century's latter half, a foremost question of warfare as waged by Western powers has remained how to win the "hearts and minds" of civilian populations whose territories they invade. Local elements of resistance have routinely resorted to tactics of "terror" to maintain their control and to undermine the forces of Western occupiers, whereas Western forces have usually chosen to pretend to take moral high ground by showing sometimes fastidious concerns for civilian casualties. In the so-called "War on Terror," the United States had a reputation for caring less about collateral damage and for being more trigger-happy when it came to engaging local populations. In my experience, however, I saw little difference between North American and European approaches.

A few years before I had ever set foot in Afghanistan, the US Army had published its newest "doctrine" on counter-insurgency operations, supposedly drafted by its greatest minds of that day. By the time I was in Afghanistan, local commanders, including French ones, were eagerly trying to implement the clever suggestions made in this doctrinal publication. In doing so we all overlooked a salient twentieth-century fact, and one whose underlying causes remain valid in other historical periods: to wit, that the Germans of the 1940s conducted that century's only truly effective counter-insurgency because only they were ruthless enough to terrorize local populations far beyond the capacity of any resistance fighters to terrorize them. Therefore, throughout four years of warfare beyond the scale and scope of any war in recorded human history, the Germans enjoyed largely tranquil conditions throughout the vast territories of non-Germanic peoples that they occupied.

Reflecting on Caesar's treatment of the Veneti made it clear to me that our NATO engagements in Afghanistan were doomed. The moral codes of contemporary Western societies, not to mention their powerful bureaucracies, would not allow their own military forces to use those "cruel" and "immoral" means of prosecuting warfare in ways needed to achieve an acceptable, sustainable peace. It took twelve more years until the whole world understood this in summer 2021.

Quaint projects to win the "hearts and minds" of the local populations took their own French twists in our regiment. Halfway through our engagement, the regimental commander introduced a new captain to his staff. His name was René. Alsatian of origin, he looked the part with his large, tall frame, blond hair, and blue eyes that seemed deferentially to seek acceptance from us legionnaires. In civilian life he was a freelance journalist, and he had been brought into the French Army's reserves, and attached to the Foreign Legion, owing to an official requisition for someone with his professional skills.

René and I became friends since, owing to his reserve status, our relationship was not constrained in the Legion's customary ways. I enjoyed having someone of considerable intellectual depth and human experience with whom to speak, and he enjoyed speaking in English with me. His English was excellent owing to a lengthy stay in the United States, where he worked for National Public Radio. He left it in disgust, but kept his deep admiration for the United States, for its peoples, and for cultural icons such as Johnny Cash, whose lyrics he often asked me to explain to him. René was one of the few real journalists whom I have ever known.

Our regimental commander asked him to create a radio station based at FOB Tora, one that would serve as a local version of *France Culture* for the surrounding valleys' inhabitants, without broadcasting any implicit or explicit content in support of NATO. For this purpose, René occupied an old mud brick building on FOB Toba, said to be the location where, during a daring Afghan raid in the late 1980s, the last surviving Soviet soldiers holed up before the Afghans overran and killed them all. Cyrillic graffiti on the building's inner walls bore witness to that Soviet presence, if not to any dire situation.

René's efforts were at first successful. The radio station became popular in the surrounding valleys. Its foremost weekly event was a radio-based poetry competition where Pashtun bards from across those rugged hills spun lyrics of almost shocking sentimentality about first loves and other similar topics. Its presenters and producers risked life and limb to come to our base to work for the radio, but they did so with obvious commitment. The radio was René's pride and joy for years, and once I heard our regimental commander suggesting that creating *Radio Surobi* was the one good thing that he managed to achieve during the six-month deployment. René refused all pressure from higher commands to introduce materials supporting NATO into the radio's broadcasts.

Two years later the radio was no longer itself. Once the Foreign Legion left Afghanistan, gradually the radio became a mouthpiece of NATO talking points, and I have no idea what became of it after 2013. I also do not know if any of those Afghans who worked for the radio have survived, but I doubt it. Local powers that outlived our short presence cared little for "hearts and minds."

LXVIII

October 2009

After about three months at Camp Warehouse, our task force relocated to FOB Tora for the duration of the deployment. Since our arrival in July, the Legion had steadily done what it probably does best—build. While our headquarters remained at Camp Warehouse, the number of legionnaires posted to FOB Tora as well as to our COP in the Uzbeen Valley steadily grew. At both locations large building projects had begun almost immediately after our arrival. Three months later, legionnaires' hard work had all but transformed the FOB and the COP beyond recognition.

The first building to go up at FOB Tora was a spacious open-air tavern, named *La Hacienda* in memory of the Legion's expeditions to Mexico in the 1860s. It never lacked beer and snacks for sale, and it boasted large televisions and sound systems. We also started building numerous hard-structure barracks, a large ordinary, and a new wing of the base for vehicle maintenance. At the COP, legionnaires likewise cobbled together a fine bar, and within two months of our arrival the COP also had respectable field-showers and plentiful, clean chemical toilets.

Although I had grown accustomed to life's rhythms at Camp Warehouse, I was excited to move to FOB Tora. It beckoned with more frequent missions throughout the Uzbeen Valley and surrounding areas, and therefore increased potential for the light, not-too-dangerous combat for which most of us longed. In part, my expectations proved correct. Drivers were always needed, so various task-force officers, units, and cells frequently drafted me for their missions. Not long after our move, I became an intermittent part of the regimental commander's personal protection team, led by a French *sergent-chef*, who let me shoot his team's machine guns to my heart's content. I also tried to leverage my native English to secure a place with our regimental reconnaissance unit. Since its leader was a Briton from Newcastle, this was to no avail.

Charlatanism must be as ancient as the military profession itself. To its great credit, the Legion's leadership created a climate of professional humility among legionnaires—an ethos quite contrary to what we often find in the US military, where every unit commander is expected to proclaim that his company or battalion is the world's best. I never witnessed such boasts in the Legion. Indeed, I remember reading an impressive essay from the Legion's commanding general in which he stressed that while legionnaires should strive for excellence, they should never boast about themselves. Instead, their goal should be to make their excellence so obvious that others remark it and praise them for it, while modestly refraining from useless and dangerous self-praise.

The British *adjudant-chef* in charge of the regimental reconnaissance unit did not share such an ethos. Braggart and barrel-chested, he is one of the few men that I have known who swaggered in real life. He often treated his commander, and indeed all officers, with barely disguised contempt. It was not beyond him to call our regimental commander a "coward" in drunken conversations at *La Hacienda*. For most of us, he was the object of envy since his small team regularly went on missions with the US Special Forces unit that holed up within an isolated compound adjacent to our FOB. I was never there to witness these occasional armed scuffles with local warlords (the military jargon of the time labelled these "kinetic engagements"), but since no legionnaire on the *adjudant-chef*'s team was ever injured, we can assume that they were not epic battles. How could they have been when our forces, supported by attack helicopters and even fighter jets, used the latest technologies to attack farmers armed with AK-47s at night, when the latter could scarcely see anything?

This *adjudant-chef* had once been a bartender in an industrial slum in northern England. His brother had joined the British Paratroopers, but he was disqualified from doing so owing to a problem with his eyes. Therefore, he joined the Legion, where he had served for almost fifteen years in a variety of sought-after roles. His French, which he still spoke with a plebeian northern English accent, was excellent. All legionnaires bought much of their own military equipment, but he stood out for his extravagance in this regard, as he had paid to have his FAMAS rifle rebuilt to accommodate the latest military gadgets.

After my own share of active military service, I believe that this *adjudant-chef* was typical of characters whom I have often met in military formations and whom I would immediately distrust today. Yet back then he held me and many other legionnaires under his spell, and we wished to be in his place and to emulate him. We admired his apparent confidence and derring-do, and we envied his team its "firefights" in the coveted company of US Special Forces.

Had we been in the trenches in the First World War, this man's peacock-like bravado probably would have earned him scorn. To my mind it was only in our relatively safe warfare that his reputation was possible—a world of "good guys" and "bad guys" where many soldiers seemed more intent on living out Hollywood scripts than on embracing as reality their own experiences as legionnaires.

To be shot at by one's foes would have been nothing remarkable in most major twentieth-century conflicts, but in our comparatively cosy conflict in Afghanistan in late 2009, to be shot at and to shoot back was a privilege sought out and thirsted after by many of us. It was usually afforded only to those few who could escape our authorities' safety nets, such as this *adjudant-chef*.

All told, I cannot fault myself or my fellow legionnaires for our desires. Many of us had joined the Legion to forge and to steel our manhood in what we perceived to be an overly feminized world. We had taken extreme steps to escape its safety. But even in war, in Afghanistan's harsher reaches, that world conspired to keep us safe. In this conspiracy, it largely succeeded.

LXIX

October 2009

Immediately to the northeast of FOB Tora, a large hill, or small mountain, towered above the surrounding countryside. According to what was probably recently invented lore—routinely repeated, embellished, and exaggerated by legionnaires throughout our deployment—control of this mountain allowed Afghans to raid the Soviet base at this location and to slaughter all those in it. Legend had it that one evening Afghans managed to sneak a *DShK* (or "doushka") to this mountain's top, which the Soviets had somehow failed to secure. From this advantageous terrain, so the story went, the Afghans used the legendary and fearful Russian heavy machine gun to keep suppressing fire on critical locations throughout the base. Meanwhile, Afghan soldiers crept up from valleys to the base's south and west, overran the base, and killed every Soviet soldier in it.

Without undertaking detailed research and interviewing dozens of Soviet veterans of this war, I have no way of knowing if any aspect of this story was true. Although possible, it seems nevertheless unlikely that Soviet officers would have left this mountaintop unsecured. In any event, after our arrival we immediately secured this location. A sentimental legionnaire dubbed our new mountain outpost *Mont Saint Michel.* At its modest summit legionnaires built a small wooden structure to protect our guards on duty during harsh weather. There we also placed a large antenna that helped our task force to relay radio communications throughout the Uzbeen Valley. Although the sky was seldom clear enough to see far into the distance, on the clearest days with a naked eye we could make out our COP to the north in the Uzbeen Valley.

To climb *Mont Saint Michel* soon became one of our preferred morning physical training events. On mornings when we climbed *Mont Saint Michel* we would walk up and down its forgiving slopes several times, always in full body armour and with combat equipment, and sometimes with rucksacks. This was valuable training for me as I learned to walk up and down mountainous terrain under heavy loads with considerable confidence and ease, something that would have intimidated me before this deployment.

It was quite a steep walk to the summit, and I must credit the Legion for ensuring that even its less physically capable and seasoned soldiers like me had considerable cardiovascular strength. Whenever US soldiers climbed the mountain, they reckoned it an extreme physical challenge. Even the local US Special Forces team hated climbing this mountain, complaining about it on the rare occasions when the team's impressively athletic commander forced them to do it. By contrast, even the most lacklustre legionnaires were accustomed to climbing the mountain twice or three times during each morning session.

We also climbed *Mont Saint Michel* for its views. From its summit we could see not only the whole Uzbeen Valley, but also far to the south, to the east toward Jalabad, and to the west, where a ridge of mountains announced the steep ascent toward Kaboul some fifteen or so kilometres in the distance. Whenever French forces used either the 155mm CAESAR howitzers or the new Tiger attack helicopters, from this vantage point we could clearly observe their manoeuvres and fires.

It is important to note that climbing *Mont Saint Michel* became a favourite legionnaire pastime during this deployment not only because of its physical challenges, but also because of our sensibility to its beauty. During this deployment I climbed *Mont Saint Michel* countless times with many ranks and nationalities of legionnaires, and not once did we reach the summit without taking time to sit down and to enjoy its panoramic views, often when dawn's lights were still stretching across the horizon. Usually someone in any group of climbers would make remarks about the beautiful and spectacular views from the summit, and no one ever contradicted or disrespected such statements.

For all their supposed gruffness and hardihood, I believe that most infantry soldiers—and perhaps most foot-soldiers in general—share sentimental and almost romantic ideas about the deserted and isolated places to which we deploy. We always wake up before dawn, and the treat to observe the dawn skies is something that we usually experience with our morning exercise regimens, a rare privilege for most Western mortals nowadays. We are often deployed to countries that are supposedly "under-developed" as compared to Western nations, and therefore we experience natural beauties and marvels beyond the reach of most civilians. We also have the unique privilege of regularly seeing the spectacular allure of military exercises and operations.

Having had more exposure to beauty and its sundry manifestations than most legionnaires, officer or enlisted, I have found that few of the world's artistic achievements or natural creations rival or outdo modern warfare's aesthetic glories—the fading of tracer bullets' fiery glare into the night to machine guns' steady echoes and under the magnifying influence of our night vision's green, grainy, unreliable displays; the launches of rounds from mortars and from howitzers, and their magnificent impacts thousands of metres away, seen in bright explosive flashes and in coloured columns of smoke; the graceful, gallant swoops and turns of attack helicopters as they roared through valleys toward their next objectives; the sight of long columns of vehicles as they kicked up clouds of dust from the dirt roads that led them through hostile territory toward their mission or back to their base.

As much as greenhorns thirst for their *baptêmes de feu*, they would not last long in the military profession if fighting were all that they could truly appreciate. Moments of fighting are rare, and even in our past century's most harrowing wars, there were periods of quiet where many soldiers might have missed out entirely on combat actions. Infantrymen may be loath to admit it, or even be unable to explain it to themselves, but they yearn for and cherish the natural beauty that we alone enjoy in our historic walk of life, beauties simultaneously dampened and enhanced by our customary physical and mental anguishes.

LXX

October 2009

Before long we had established a new rhythm of life at FOB Tora. Since there was no *corvée* there, we legionnaires began our days later than usual. Physical training usually took place from about 0630 until 0830. In order to take more time for sport, I often forewent our Turkmen-prepared breakfast at the ordinary, for doing so gave me time to exercise alone, a rare treat for any legionnaire. After working at our task force's intelligence cell all morning, I made for lunch as early as possible and then took a long siesta before the afternoon.

For sleeping quarters, at FOB Tora I shared a converted shipping container equipped with air-conditioning with a senior Hungarian *caporal-chef* and a junior French sergeant from our headquarters. Cramped as we were for space, these seasoned legionnaires were expert at creating acceptable living conditions out of lousy circumstances. Somehow the *caporal-chef* had even found us a small refrigerator, which we kept well stocked with beer.

After working in the afternoon—for me this entailed various duties, including guard details, weapons and equipment maintenance, and translating French documents into English—we usually had time for more physical training before taking dinner at the ordinary. Each night about eight select officers joined the regimental commander for dinner in his tent, diligently prepared by his cook. Legionnaires from the task force were chosen to serve as waiters for these dinners, something which I did several times. Over bottles of *Côtes-du-Rhone* or the Foreign Legion's *rosé*, the commander learned from and taught his company-level officers and his staff. Legionnaires mocked this practice and dreaded the duty of serving as waiters, but I believe that this aversion was mostly owing to envy rather than to any authentic proletarian ideology.

By this time *La Hacienda* had become an all but obligatory stop after the working day. An additional stimulant to our usual beer and wine was a foul-tasting brew called *Desperados*, a light beer with Tequila-like flavours. Throughout the bar several large screens played music videos from France or from Eastern Europe. The French starlet Alizée's videos were especially popular, as were the crudely suggestive videos from the Ukrainian girl-band "Viagra." *La Hacienda* was soon a well-trod watering hole where carousing often continued into the next morning. I chalk up my gaining four kilogrammes during this deployment to *La Hacienda*'s malty beverages.

Early that autumn, a French journalist came to visit FOB Tora. I knew nothing of his arrival until one of my officers asked me if I would be willing to sit down with him for an interview. To my lasting disappointment, I was the only legionnaire on this deployment with prior studies at some of our era's celebrated universities, so this fact alone made me a curiosity to the journalist. I knew nothing about him and declined the interview, but later I asked Father Gaël who this journalist was and what had brought him to FOB Tora.

In France, this journalist was an accomplished "war correspondent." He boasted a well-known surname graced with a particle that commanded instant attention among our officers. I did not really follow his comings and goings at FOB Tora, but later that November, by way of the Associated Press, I did see his final article that came out in numerous publications throughout the world. This article was interesting and well-written for a general audience, but there were a few inaccuracies. For example, it claimed that *La Hacienda* displayed "hard-core porn videos" on its screens throughout the bar, and this was untrue. Given how regular a customer I was at *La Hacienda*, I would have witnessed such a thing had it ever occurred. He also reported that one legionnaire who refused to be interviewed—me—had been to Harvard and to Princeton. But I had studied at Oxford University, not at Harvard. Such almost inevitable inaccuracies notwithstanding, his article was clever and compelling, and accurately captured the widespread sentiment among us legionnaires at FOB Tora that our deployment was "dull."

As would be expected, the first legionnaire whom the journalist cited in his article was our swaggering British *adjudant-chef*, who echoed many legionnaires' thoughts when he declared over beers at *La Hacienda*: "We're meant for fighting. There's too much chatting around here." Over the prior months we had conducted countless missions throughout the surrounding valleys. But our tactics of moving in formations with numerous combat vehicles, whose firepower would quickly overwhelm any local attackers, ensured that our firefights with locals came few and far between long stretches of quiet and eventless engagements. We contrasted these practices with what seemed to be the swashbuckling approach of the local US Special Forces team, which would drive through the surrounding countryside in unarmoured pick-up trucks, thereby inviting the locals to shoot at them—which they usually did. Almost all of us wished to satisfy our urges to participate in such relatively safe episodes of low intensity conflict. Unable to do so, legionnaires often expressed their disappointment by criticizing our officers and our regimental commander, some even accusing them of "cowardice."

Only later did I come to pay no heed to such bluster and to see the truth in Father Gaël's assessment that our regimental commander was remarkably brave and wise. I have no doubts that he, too, would have enjoyed the bracing effects of small-arms engagements and, more enticing still to him, the rare treat of manoeuvring companies in combat. Yet he correctly understood that France's engagement in this theatre was largely for political purposes and that, in the end, we could have little impact on this war's course or outcome. In this context he refused to risk his soldiers' lives to tickle his own fancies or to bolster his subordinates' fickle opinion of him. He knew that any legionnaire's death under his command would be especially pointless. Looking back on it, I admire him greatly for the integrity of his leadership and for his courage, which we legionnaires were mostly unable to appreciate and to recognize.

LXXI

October 2009

To encounter my countrymen at various places and moments throughout this deployment usually came as a welcome experience. Soon after our arrival at Camp Warehouse, US officers often stopped by to visit our headquarters. Since US citizens in the Foreign Legion were a novelty, many of these officers wished to speak with me. In one amusing incident, a group of officers from the United States promised our staff officers not to ask about our regiment's supposedly numerous "black operations," clandestine and known only to the highest authorities. Repeated assurances that no such operations were taking place only seemed to reinforce their suspicions about dark happenings behind the seemingly quiet front of our daily rhythms.

Sometimes we visited US military posts throughout Kaboul. French officers greatly enjoyed these trips, especially when they allowed for meals at US ordinaries or extended shopping tours at well-stocked "Post Exchanges." In my many conversations with them, US soldiers found my engagement in the Foreign Legion somewhat surprising, but admirable and exciting. To my memory, none of them ever questioned my patriotism or my motives, and many US soldiers told me that they had once thought about joining the Foreign Legion, but for various reasons never did so.

Once we moved to FOB Tora our engagements with US soldiers became more frequent. In addition to the Special Operations Team, or "Operational Detachment Alpha" (ODA), located on FOB Tora, for several months a company from the Georgia National Guard stayed in the base's makeshift barracks and took part in most of our missions. US Marines also frequently travelled through our base and spent the night there if necessary. Of all these interactions, those with the local Special Forces' ODA were the most memorable and would have significant consequences for my military career's subsequent course.

This detachment's commander, Theo, was a strapping man who lived up to most stereotypes that we could imagine about West Point officers in the Special Forces. Barrel-chested and with flowing black locks, he rarely wore standard Army uniforms and instead walked about in civilian clothes or else in a combination of such clothes with his own personal tactical gear. Most of us envied him for his ability to wear civilian clothes on duty, thereby conforming to an almost universal and paradoxical dream among twenty-first-century soldiers: to wit, to be able to do our military work dressed as civilians.

Over the months I grew to admire Theo's team as well as to develop lasting perceptions about it. Given the Special Forces' reputation and vast funding, it was easy to believe that Special Forces soldiers had enviable linguistic abilities and could speak in Dari or even Pashto with their Afghan "partners." That said, I had my doubts since Theo had finished the Special Forces' six-month specialized training in Russian but could barely string together a sentence in the language. Such misgivings notwithstanding, over the course of this deployment I decided to leave behind the Legion—where a medical restriction would forever limit my advancement—and to pursue a career in the US Army, with the goal of becoming a Special Forces officer like Theo.

Of all the US citizens on FOB Tora, I became closest with an older US Army sergeant first-class named Patrick, who was assigned to our regimental staff as a liaison officer. Having spent most of his career as a helicopter mechanic, this was

Patrick's last mission overseas before retirement. His kindness to me outlasted this deployment, and years later he hosted me during several weekends at his suburban house near Williamsburg, Virginia.

Since Patrick had already deployed to West Asia four times over the past decade, such engagements had long since lost any enchantment for him. His own opinion, which he expressed to me on numerous occasions, was that the US would be better off launching a few nuclear missiles to destroy Afghanistan's large cities, and then leaving the place for good. I have no doubts that Patrick believed himself to be a good Christian of evangelical persuasions, but I also have few doubts that he would have thought little wrong with his suggestion to use atomic weapons on Afghan civilians and population centres. I found Patrick's ideas at the time more than troubling, but they were hardly foreign or surprising to me, since I had heard members of my extended family and many acquaintances make similar statements. Indeed, "make the place a glass parking lot" was a well-known phrase in US slang at the time, referring to the supposed effects of nuclear explosions on the dry expanses where Afghans, Arabs, and other dangerous and terroristic peoples were known to live.

For me, this deployment was the first time that I had met Muslims in their own countries, and it was the beginning of a long process whereby I learned to consider Afghans and other West Asian populations as humans like me, and not lesser beings who were expendable objects in our era's evolving "great games." Throughout that deployment I still actually viewed Afghans as lesser beings, even if I showed uncommon desires to understand them and their perspectives. To view others in this degrading way was probably the natural consequence of years of socialization and propaganda in Western countries, where carefully scripted mass media films and "news" had warped my ability to think about Afghans and about their civilization.

For many US soldiers like Patrick, for many US citizens, and for many legionnaires at FOB Tora, our inability to achieve any lasting results in Afghanistan owed little to our own ignorance, to unclear political aims, and to poorly directed operations throughout the country, but rather to unfair limitations on our violence, imposed by our own military and political leadership. To some extent I shared these views, but I still found it unacceptable and deeply troubling when I heard fellow soldiers echoing what "Mistah Kurtz" had scribbled at the end of seventeen pages of "close writing" for the International Society for the Suppression of Savage Customs: "Exterminate all the brutes."

LXXII

November 2009

To win "hearts and minds" has become a phrase used to point out bad policy and self-deception ever since US military campaigns failed in the Vietnam War, but this does not mean that winning hearts and minds is impossible. Hollywood films are one example of how the United States has reliably created and distributed cultural artefacts that, in hardly believable ways, transcend national and linguistic barriers and win "consumers" throughout the world. On one of our missions to the Jegdalek Valley, remote even by Afghan standards, I remember seeing aged "eight-track" videos of *Star Wars* and Coca-Cola products for sale in a shop built of mud and sticks.

Our translators' favourite US products included Jack Daniels and pornography. They concealed their indulgence in alcohol, but they took no pains to hide their smut. Indeed, when seeking out translators for various missions, often I found them stretched out on their beds and matter-of-factly paging through pornographic magazines. On one memorable occasion, a cheeky translator, having draped the open pages of a pornographic magazine across his chest, berated me about Western decadence and asserted that he had no respect for "Western culture." As I walked out of his room after relaying the message intended for him, he turned back to his Western pornography.

What does it say about a nation when its most conspicuous worldwide exports are fantastical and predictable films, chemically modified food and drinks, financialization, pornography, costly weapons of war, and psychotropic medications? From the worldwide success of such exportations, I have drawn one unshakable conclusion: decadence and consumerism rarely have trouble winning over hearts and minds of the most stubborn and nationalistic tribes.

For the most part our translators preferred to stay out of the limelight and to carry out their services discretely. They rarely interacted with French officers beyond giving their inventive "translations," and they confined themselves to their relatively comfortable living quarters near the regimental headquarters at FOB Tora. One evening, however, they caused quite a stir and created bad blood between us legionnaires and themselves that lasted until our departure.

It all started when a wild-eyed Hungarian *caporal-chef*, the deputy commander's driver, obtained a pig in Afghanistan—perhaps the least *halal* thing imaginable. That he did so surprised no one since he had often shown himself to be as enterprising as he was resourceful. This *caporal-chef* was one of my favourites among our headquarters' fascinating enlisted personnel. A former regimental sniper, he had honed his legionary skills in French Guyana. For almost a decade he had made a practice, before every weekend when he was able to travel, of throwing a dart at a map of France with his eyes closed. Wherever the dart landed, thither he travelled that weekend. From this practice he had amassed formidable knowledge about the French countryside. He was also infamous for an earlier feat of having used his FAMAS rifle to kill a wild boar to enrich a company barbecue while on a training exercise in southern France, to his company commander's horror, since it was quite illegal at the time.

This Hungarian procured and prepared his pig for a planned Saturday evening barbecue, and the whole headquarters was looking forward to this rare treat. In an open area next to our living quarters, we set up a roaring fire and a spit, and we gathered an impressive quantity of cases of beer and boxes of wine. As the night approached and the pig was brought to the spit, our translators, housed in the same area, began to protest. They claimed that our festivities were defiling holy ground, since a mosque had once stood in the area where we were setting up our pig-roast. They took their complaint to the deputy commander, threatening to broadcast our sacrilege throughout the surrounding valleys should we go ahead with our barbecue as planned.

Their logic was specious, and to this day I cannot understand what led them to craft such a bogus protest. In the end, sincere stupidity seems the most likely explanation. There was no evidence that there had ever been a mosque on this former Soviet base and in our living area. It is highly unlikely that these strangers to the region had access to accurate historical or archaeological information. What is more, soldiers had been living in this same area for over five years. Countless episodes of drunkenness and masturbation—to say nothing of the large portable toilets nearby, or of the translators' own questionable sexual practices within their shipping container—had hitherto raised no concerns from anyone about our defiling these sacred precincts. Yet, the pig's presence spurred them to action and inspired them not only to invent a tale about a long-lost mosque, but also to threaten the people who were employing them, at substantial salaries.

Their complaints to the deputy commander did not fall on deaf ears. He came to our barbecue site and directed us to move it to a different place on the camp, near *La Hacienda*. The translators seemed pleased at their victory, whereas all the legionnaires in our headquarters were enraged at them for their sanctimonious meddling with our elaborately prepared feast.

That evening almost all the enlisted men at our headquarters grew decidedly drunk as we ate the pig. At some point during our feast we walked with a purpose to the location where we had first planned the barbecue, supposedly the holy site where a mosque had once stood, and took turns urinating luxuriously throughout the area, ensuring that our long-lasting and heavy streams of urine covered as much of the ground as possible. We continued to drink alcohol and to urinate in these areas well into the morning.

The next day the grounds of our living quarters reeked. In our drunken spite, we had overlooked the fact that most of us lived quite near to the spot now bathed in gallons of our own urine. To address this smell, we shovelled out the sullied soil and replaced it with fresh dirt.

LXXIII

November 2009

Our regimental task force in Afghanistan comprised one troop from the Legion's First Cavalry Regiment, based in Orange. The Foreign Legion's only cavalry regiment had a reputation for being its most pampered unit. For all this prejudice, the regiment's unique capabilities—it was the Legion's only unit capable of fielding the French AMX-10 light tanks—meant that it had deployed to more operations abroad than any other regiment over the past decades. The regiment was formed in the 1920s as the Legion was incorporating numerous Russian soldiers from the White Russian General Piotr Wrangel's dissolved forces into a new unit that served with distinction throughout the Maghreb. No small recommendation accrued from the regiment's situation in the middle of vineyards that made *Châteauneuf-du-Pape*. While the rest of the Legion depended on Puyloubier for its *Côtes de Provence* plonk, the cavalry regiment's neighbours ensured that its fabled *pots* served more rarefied vintages.

The troop that deployed with our task force was the First Cavalry Regiment's most distinguished and decorated. Its commander was a tall, lanky, handsome Frenchman of unmistakably aristocratic origins. He was one of my favourite officers since he was of good cheer, intelligent, and very physically fit. He talked kindly to legionnaires without pretending to be one of them, and he was one of few who regularly attended Mass whenever possible, whether at Camp Warehouse or at FOB Tora. He relished operations, but not with the desperation for action that many other junior officers and enlisted showed. In this respect, he seemed to understand better than most that Fortune is a woman, and that no matter how deft your dissembling, she can always understand when you truly need her attention and her embraces. For desperate military men, Fortune's affection can be more destructive and painful than her rejection. For most junior officers and soldiers of my generation who needed "combat experience" to make peace with their manhood, Fortune would prove disdainful and aloof, as she did to most of us during this deployment.

One day, this captain, scion of the *ancien régime,* was assigned to escort an embodiment of our new regimes, Dr. Bernard Kouchner, to a small village to our south. The honourable Dr. Kouchner was then serving as France's Minister of Foreign Affairs. This celebrity of ministerial rank came to visit us one evening at FOB Tora with little notice. Before his arrival I, like several other legionnaires, spent the whole day and much of the prior evening preparing for the *piquet d'honneur* that would greet him as he walked from the FOB's helicopter landing pad to our headquarters. The afternoon of his arrival, we stood for two hours awaiting his helicopter. Good form on his part would have been at least to acknowledge our existence as he passed us. Politicians of populist inclinations might have even seen fit to stop to greet us and to ask questions about our origins and about our service to the Fifth Republic. Dr. Kouchner, however, did not so much as look in our direction as he walked by us to the headquarters.

The next day, Dr. Kouchner toured some villages in the Jegdalek Valley, escorted by the young troop commander from the First Cavalry Regiment and accompanied by our regimental commander and much of his staff. Although I was not there to witness the event, several sources, including our chaplain always ready for gossip, told me that Dr. Kouchner had scandalized his aristocratic escort. While processing in a military vehicle through a thronging Afghan

village, so goes the story, Dr. Kouchner grabbed candy and other food products from a bag and threw them out to the assembled Afghans, as though they were spectators in a parade. This spectacle of ministerial largesse shocked many legionnaires and especially the young cavalry captain. Whereas this son of the *ancien régime* could see perfectly well how insulting and demeaning it was for this socialist politician to throw candy and foodstuffs to the peasantry from his mechanical steed, I doubt that it ever occurred to Dr. Kouchner that he was doing anything untoward. He had, after all, graced both us and the Afghans with his magnificent presence, which none of us deserved.

Whatever the faults of the old and dead European aristocracy, at one time it did at least have to pretend to military virtue and prowess, and in this respect meaningful contact with people and worlds outside of aristocrats' own was necessary, even desired. Dr. Kouchner's own past was not without its share of adventures, so it shocked me to note that of all French ministers who visited us, he was by far the most aloof and deaf to criticisms circulating in his presence.

Our progression into the cycles of generational decline and decadence is most evident to me in our elites' general refusal of military service, and in the parallel fact that military service has little positive impact on the career progressions and political possibilities of the rich and powerful. In France and in some other European countries, a sense of *noblesse oblige* still attracts many old aristocratic families into military service, but in general these are the aristocrats whose social and economic means and clout are increasingly marginal. In the United States, our powerful families have almost wholly recused themselves from military service ever since the Vietnam War, leaving such dirty work to a small caste of families that go to West Point, to lower middling classes that largely fill the ranks of US officers, and to minority groups and Southern whites that overwhelmingly make up the US military's enlisted ranks.

Over a decade later, whenever I think of old and new aristocracies, I think of the surprising contrast between Dr. Kouchner and the young captain from the First Cavalry Regiment. The latter, almost surely a monarchist who frequented "Tridentine Rite" Masses back in France, showed far more understanding of

Afghan peoples than a supposedly socialist humanitarian and activist who had long since made his peace with the powers of high finance.

LXXIV

November 2009

One of my favourite duties at FOB Tora was to work with the regimental commander's personal protection team. Such duties gave me the chance to travel wherever and whenever the commander engaged with powerful men in that remote part of Kaboul Province. In addition to many unforeseen and unusual journeys, we had regular meetings at the local administrator's palace. We called him a "governor," but I do not know what his true title was. His residence was a ramshackle concrete building perched on the edge of Surobi's marketplace, overlooking the town's adjoining lake.

Nearby, the last Afghan king, Mohammed Zahir Shah, had built a respectable palace. It is easy to understand why the king had chosen this area for its construction. Waters from the Kaboul River collected into a charming lake framed by the surrounding mountains, and this region's lower elevations ensured warmer temperatures. So many were this area's natural advantages that had we been in Italy, it would have been filled with pricey resorts.

I enjoyed trips to Surobi since we were able to walk into the local market to buy fresh bread and to shop for other items. It would not surprise me if the *caporal-chef* who found a pig had negotiated its purchase with some enterprising merchant in this very marketplace. We grew used to driving through the city and even to walking as pedestrian shoppers through its main street, actions that became unthinkable a few years later as the security situation worsened.

Sometimes we visited the local police headquarters, with whose leaders we were supposedly cooperating to secure the area. Our regimental commander viewed most of the violence in the region as matters for the police, not for the Afghan military—and surely not for us. So, as a matter of course, we provided some information to and held discussions with local policemen.

To imagine this Afghan police station in Surobi, one would do well to envisage the opposite of Max Liebermann's *The Courtyard of an Orphanage in Amsterdam*. Instead of clean and fair-skinned young women, the station's inhabitants were swarthy and dirty young men who looked as though they had not changed clothes in weeks. Sunbeams framed no green leaves or plants, but instead highlighted dirt, sand, mud, and flies. Rooms reeked of urine, and the station's underlying odours derived from the stenches of solid human waste as they wafted either from malfunctioning toilets or else from open areas designated for such use immediately outside the station's buildings. The building itself was made of degraded concrete. The glass panes of its barred windows were either broken or missing. Instead of bristling activity and conversation, sullen silence reigned. It is not my wish to overlook positive aspects of this police station, but I remember none.

The "governor's palace" was more colourful. Here we usually parked our two armoured vehicles. The regimental commander, his translator, and one bodyguard entered while the rest of us stayed outside and watched the vehicles. Our potential as guards was doubtful as men with AK-47s and dozens of locals swarmed about us, most often taking little notice of our presence. Men of all ages defecated in the open, right next to the governor's palace, squatting and raising their robes in distinctive poses to do so. Wild dogs bounced and barked throughout the courtyard. Once I witnessed a group of boys savagely beating one of these dogs. To see this was shocking to my North American sensibilities, such that I was tempted to take my FAMAS and to shoot in these boys' direction. It would have been an apt time for a mental fit like Nietzsche's episode over a whipped horse in Turin, but I kept my wits.

The regimental commander usually remained in the building with the governor for about an hour. Sometimes we saw them walking together with a translator along the governor's private gardens that bordered the lake. To judge from our commander's remarks, it seemed that the governor was mainly worried about money. Local US teams reportedly canvassed the area giving away suitcases full of cash to Afghan dignitaries with few strings attached. If this was true—and I have reason to believe that it was—this governor must have found French thriftiness vexing. Once our commander exclaimed that this governor was trying to garner resources to build a spa resort on the lake, a venture whose potential for sustainable patronage and profits did not convince him.

From all these welcome excursions, one of the most surprising observations came from the protection team's leader, a well-built French sergeant. This man had little wit or eloquence, and in general he only talked about his children and his family's creative holidays throughout Europe in his camper van. After one of these visits, however, he brought to my attention something that I had not yet noticed—namely, that these villagers lacked anything feminine in their civic life. The sergeant was quick to protest that he may not always like the role of the feminine in French society (in his words: "*ça nous fait chier*"), but he admitted that it was necessary and that it distinguished us from the Afghans.

The more I pondered his observations about the lack of feminine influences during subsequent visits, the more I came to see their basic accuracy. Over several months of driving through Surobi and standing for hours at the local governor's residence, I never once saw a woman's face. Only occasionally did I see female figures from afar, walking about the town's mud shacks.

By 2009, for almost eight years NATO leaders had been engaging this and similar Afghan populations in contexts about which they had absolutely no understanding save for analysis provided by military and civilian intelligence agencies—in which, incidentally, almost no one spoke appropriate local languages. If I learned anything from months of engagements at the governor's residence, it was that the nature of our presence kept us shielded from the means necessary for right thought and action in these foreign places.

LXXV

November 2009

To work in "military intelligence" is a stated goal of many young men with yearnings for military life. The enterprise of "military intelligence" implies cloak-and-dagger fantasies. It beckons with prospects of intriguing mixtures of action for the body, challenges for the mind, and mystique for the romantic, not to mention car chases to dramatic music and far-fetched sexual exploits.

It is worth investigating the rise of commonplace ideas about "military intelligence" and their association with motion pictures. Spying is said to be one of our older professions, but I doubt that it was the stuff of worldwide popular fantasy until the rise of films. Rudyard Kipling's *Kim*, acclaimed as one of the best "spy" novels of all time, is as phoney as his *Barrack-Room Ballads*. Yet Kim's eponymous character was a possibility in the British Raj, however remote. The notion of action-packed military intelligence officers blazing new trails, fearless and often far away from headquarters, seems to have reached its maturity with the Hollywood epic, *Lawrence of Arabia*, which, in my opinion, has influenced subsequent military officers in Western countries far more than T.E. Lawrence's *Seven Pillars of Wisdom* ever did. The world has now been flooded with enough motion-picture fantasies that flattering and fearful images of US and British intelligence agents and military officers have all but universal reach.

Such images and "on the ground" realities could not be more distinct. To cultivate officers capable of learning foreign languages and communicating with and understanding different peoples—men like T.E. Lawrence—it took a gentlemanly officer culture where sound education in the Classics was a given. Lawrence, for example, had written his doctoral thesis at Oxford on Crusader castles in the Levant, long before he reported to the British military in Cairo. To raise crops of officers capable of developing real human intelligence, it also took lack of management by and interference from "human resource" clerks. Militaries had to be inefficient enough to leave officers marooned in far-off posts, free to live for years in isolated luxury and to take up local concubines.

Such conditions are impossible today for many reasons, and thus to cultivate effective intelligence officers in any major bureaucratic Western military is a rare feat. I have met many military intelligence officers of great sensitivity and finesse when it comes to working within their respective organizations. None of these would have been capable of collecting basic first-hand human intelligence in Afghanistan without the help of compromised local translators.

The organization of modern militaries will continue to prevent the development of capable intelligence officers. During my last deployment to Afghanistan with the US Army, the commanding general of all our military operations in the theatre—a man with over fifteen deployments to Afghanistan under his belt—explicitly recommended that all his officers read Charles Allen's *Soldier Sahibs*. I did. This recent work of history aimed to show how British military and colonial administrations in Afghanistan produced a few, but enough, officers competent in local languages and expert in regional politics, whose efforts were of great importance to British successes. No matter the general's recommendation, the US military's impersonal bureaucracies, whose power far outdid his, precluded the making of any *Soldier Sahibs*.

At some point in the Afghan conflict's first decade, owing to the initiative of several concerned and sensible US general officers with imagination, the Army created a programme meant to mould officers into *Soldier Sahibs,* who could foster the success of long-term national missions in Afghanistan. This innovative and promising initiative proved stillborn from its start, wrecked by the incompetence of US military language instructors, the strictures of US Army Human Resources Command's career timelines, the provincial instincts of US officers themselves, and superior officers' embedded beliefs and prejudices about how to manage and to promote their juniors.

In the French Army, back in 2009, I had not even been in the Legion for a year when I found myself working directly in the military intelligence cell of a tactical regimental headquarters. At the time, I did not understand how fortunate I was to have this revelatory experience. In this capacity, my main role was to translate appropriate bits of information gathered from our task force from French into English. For the most part, the senior captain in charge of the intelligence cell sent off these translations with few edits or comments to NATO headquarters. There was a limit to how much I understood about what our captain and his underlings did every day, partly because they kept much of it from me and partly because of my inexperience. It seems that our intelligence came mostly from our soldiers spread throughout the surrounding valleys, or else from a small "human intelligence" team that was based in Kaboul.

I imagine that all this intelligence served a purpose. If nothing else, our intelligence cell gave our regimental staff information—even it was partly or mostly wrong—needed for the staff to begin its planning process for missions and operations. Some information that we were getting through our translators' indirect speech could have approached accuracy, and maybe select pieces of intelligence were, as the saying goes, "good enough for government work."

Still, after months of working in this environment, I became sceptical about the concept of military intelligence, or at least about how it is envisaged and developed within military staffs organized on the pervasive Prussian model. For me, an honest assessment of the situation would have been that we had no real knowledge of the cultural and political realities outside of our base aside from what our translators—all local nationals and therefore cautious and compromised in their work—chose to tell us. Likewise, I would have said that our abject reliance on these local nationals compromised our position and all but ensured wrong action. For officials in both the French and the US Armies, whenever I tried to mention the above problem, there was never any real interest in admitting it, and much less in addressing it.

LXXVI

December 2009

Never underestimate what a junior officer will do to slake his thirst for glory. As our deployment drew on, and as mission after mission dashed the hopes of young officers and of legionnaires alike who yearned for the thrills of light combat, we began to undertake operations with a dangerous sense of routine.

One legionnaire died in a motoring accident while driving through the Uzbeen Valley, and it is surprising to me that we did not have more such incidents. As a driver, I had several close brushes with disaster on the roads. Also, prior to the deployment I had not conducted any training under night-vision goggles, but in Afghanistan I was expected to drive treacherous roads with no lights and under night-vision. Surely I was not the only legionnaire facing these and similar challenges as we drove on local highways and the Uzbeen Valley's trails.

There were occasional moments of alarmed hubbub. Legionnaires cannot forego running daily, so at our COP members of our regiment had established a running route outside of its Hesco barrier walls. Sometimes the sight of men running in shorts outside the base was too tempting for hostile-minded peasants in the surrounding hills, and they would take pot shots or launch a few homespun mortar rounds toward the COP. Improvised mortar rounds were also quite common whenever we explored the Tagab Valley to our west. Some of our units had small arms engagements, but for the most part Afghan fighters avoided our large columns of armoured vehicles, graced with fifty-millimetre machine guns and sometimes even with the M621 twenty-millimetre automatic cannon. It was a hostile area filled with rough men, but its seasoned warriors were not suicidal, and so long as we deployed with overwhelming force, they let us be. Only those few legionnaires who went out with the US Special Forces in small Toyota pick-up trucks and other unassuming vehicles drew fire.

Of all company commanders in our task force, the commander of one infantry company was the most high-strung. He also appeared to seek to be like "one of the men," a ridiculous trope that seems to have infected Western militaries at some point in the twentieth century. All of us wished to get a *croix de valeur militaire*, especially career-minded officers, but this commander showed an exceptional desire for action. His best chances for it came in the months of November and December, when his company was assigned to occupy our COP in the Uzbeen Valley. Soon he made its presence felt throughout the valley.

It was under mysterious circumstances that his company began what turned out to be our regiment's longest engagement throughout our six months in Afghanistan. This incident began one afternoon when his company was on mounted patrol in the Uzbeen Valley. No one knows how the fighting began. Some soldiers claimed that Chechen snipers active in the valley had been identified and had shot at them, while others said that they had received small arms fire from a compound of mud huts. In any event, this commander's trigger-happy legionnaires did not waste any time in responding to all possible threats. They immediately engaged suspected enemy positions with astonishing rates of fire, such that by this incident's end our regimental ammunition stores had been all but consumed.

At several points our regimental commander tried to get involved in this situation from his position at our headquarters on FOB Tora, but for unknown reasons the company commander's radio had stopped working soon after firing began. Later Father Gaël related to me damaging rumours that the commander had disconnected or turned off his radio so as not to suffer any interference from higher echelons. Given that our leaders knew little about the developing situation, French attack helicopters were mobilized, and our mortars and artillery pieces—including the 155mm CAESAR howitzer that had recently arrived at FOB Tora—were on high alert for fire missions. Several platoons from our quick reaction force deployed and all units scrambled to get ready for battle. From FOB Tora we could hear gunfire and explosions from the valley.

In this engagement's aftermath, it did not take long for videos of it to surface on the internet, as enterprising legionnaires had taken footage of its progress with their mobile telephones. These videos showed excitement, confusion, fear, and panicked movements—all components of the fabled "fog of war." Nowhere in these videos was there any evidence of hostile forces firing upon the legionnaires, nor any unquestionable sight of enemy fighters or positions.

When it was all over, the casualties of this battle were several local asses. This alone was scandalous, given that the company's "fighting" had lasted over an hour and had used up critical supplies of ammunition. More scandalous still was that at least one of these asses had been obviously and deliberately slain by French sniper fire. Legionnaires claimed that in accordance with NATO regulations, the French government had to pay local farmers handsomely for their killed beasts of burden. After numerous inquiries, it was never established that any enemy was in the area at the time of this battle.

Such events did not reflect well on the commander, and his company became the butt of many jokes after this escapade. Yet he did get the *croix de valeur militaire* during a later engagement in the Uzbeen Valley. However inappropriate his legionnaires' actions may have seemed during this "battle," they were logical given the mentality of many officers and enlisted men. I have no doubt that this commander believed that enemy fighters had engaged his men, and his legionnaires that they were under fire. After all, most of the men at FOB Tora agreed that there was "too much talk, not enough fighting."

This company commander demonstrated at a small level and in this laughable example what too many senior military leaders do matter-of-factly without suitable leashes for their *ids*. If they cannot fight real enemies in real wars, they will invent *bona fide* windmills to slay.

LXXVII

December 2009

During this deployment, soldiers of our regiment recorded over thirty engagements in which they and hostile forces exchanged small arms fire. There were also serious injuries to supporting US personnel. During one of our larger operations in the autumn of 2009, Soviet-made mortars from hostile forces landed near a group of US Special Forces National Guard soldiers who were watching over a valley to our east. Four of these men were badly hurt. Later our regimental commander decorated them with the *croix de valeur militaire*.

Whatever the faults and follies of our engagement in Afghanistan, men's wounds were as real as those received in any war. Thousands of US and allied soldiers lost their lives fighting in Afghanistan before the scrambled US retreat in summer 2021, and many more thousands went home with lifelong and sometimes debilitating injuries.

When I was a new company commander at the 82nd Airborne Division, I spent one evening in Raleigh, North Carolina, with the families of veterans wounded in Afghanistan. The authoritative leader of this group of families was a young woman whose husband had already undergone dozens of surgeries to enable him to function in a minimal way. When I met him, it was clear that his face had been reconstructed by plastic surgery, and he could not spend much time out of a wheelchair. Someone that evening asked his wife if she thought that Afghanistan was worth her family's sacrifices. She said that she made herself believe that the war was worth it to keep her wits together in the face of her family's many financial and logistical challenges.

Another young man with whom I had attended specialized training in Nevada in 2018 had most of his body below his waist blown off by a booby-trap set in the door of a building when he was on operations with US Army Rangers in Afghanistan. He was a thoughtful, hilarious, and intelligent sergeant with a beautiful wife and his best years ahead of him. Owing to his injuries he would never again lie properly with his wife or become a father. Throughout the United States and nations that joined US efforts to prosecute the war in Afghanistan, there are thousands of men who live with similar injuries from these wars, and thousands more who killed themselves after coming back from these wars.

All of this tells nothing of the hundreds of thousands of Afghan soldiers and civilians who died in our favourite "savage war of peace" from 2001 until 2021. Whereas the sacrifice of Western soldiers is often overlooked or forgotten by civilian populations, the sacrifice of Afghan soldiers is never even considered. Our war in Afghanistan was relatively safe by historical standards, and by the 2010s Western soldiers often lived in conditions that were outright cozy. Yet thousands of them gave their only lives in this war. They did not die for nothing. They gave their lives to support unclear and amorphous strategic objectives and to bolster the profits of Western defence contractors.

Given the region's hostile population, our regiment was lucky that its only combat injury took place in late December, shortly before we were due to head back to France. At this time a young British legionnaire was injured in one of the largest operations of the deployment, which pushed far up into hostile lands that we could see from our guard towers at the COP.

The operation's concept was simple. We would advance into the largest settlement in the valley to our north and plant an Afghan national flag near its only public building. This flag represented the pretence that the few Afghans who deployed alongside us in painted Toyota trucks—our "partners" with whom we rarely spoke—were conducting these operations and responsible for their outcomes. This was a "plant-the-flag" mission, and in theory the concept could have made sense within what our regimental commander had labelled his "oil-drop strategy"; that is, creating small blots of security that would ooze out and at length overcome the whole valley.

The weather was cold when this overnight operation began. I was meant to serve as a driver for one of the captains on this mission, but at the last moment my participation was no longer needed. By this time, I did not believe that I would see any significant direct-fire engagements on this deployment, so I was not upset by my unexpected removal from the vehicle and from the mission.

As it turned out, there was some limited small arms fire on our formations as they entered the valley's northernmost areas the next morning. We could see muzzles flashing and ordinance exploding from the COP's walls. Before fleeing into their mountains, assailants launched a rocket-propelled grenade, or RPG, at one of our vehicles. It landed near the vehicle, exploded, and sent shrapnel flying through the air. A shard lodged itself in the buttocks of a Briton whom I had got to know in our English-speaking group in Aubagne the prior August.

This young man was the stereotypical English "Tommy." Short, wiry, blond, freckled, and with unsightly teeth, his drunkenness was dangerous, his hygiene wanting, and his resort to prostitutes religious. He spoke loudly and excitedly with an accent of the English lower classes. His French was still all but non-existent after almost eighteen months of service. I saw him coming back to our COP in the medical evacuation vehicle and spoke with him soon afterward. Owing to his injury, he was one happy "bloke."

That shrapnel wound entitled him to immediate French citizenship owing to a French law that established a principle for legionnaires wounded in battle; that they become *Français per le sang versé.* Also, this young man would be entitled to wear several medals that showed that he had been wounded in battle, rare for any legionnaire at that time. His injuries healed quickly. When I saw him back at Nîmes after our deployment, he sported, as a legionnaire first-class, more decorations than most enlisted men in the regiment.

LXXVIII

December 2009

By the end of November our regiment and its supporting units had overhauled FOB Tora. Brand new brick-and-mortar barracks covered formerly open areas where we had once camped out in tents alongside our vehicles. We had built new and expansive areas for maintenance, and we had our own well-stocked shopping and laundry facilities. Our Turkmen cleaners and cooks had long since disappeared. Now we ate at a brand new ordinary where the French food services giant, Sodexo, furnished and prepared everything. There was even a fast-food pizza franchise under construction. If we could be proud of nothing else, we had done a remarkable job of building up FOB Tora and our COP in the Uzbeen Valley. A few local Afghans had made millions of dollars in these construction projects. Reports had it that some of them were sympathetic to the Taliban and hostile to our presence.

As Christmas drew near, the pace of missions slowed down markedly. No matter where and no matter the circumstances, legionnaires always celebrate their major holidays—Christmas and Camerone. Our replacements were scheduled to arrive during the first weeks of January, and already we were planning for our departure and for life after this deployment. As the likelihood of further missions lessened, and as our boredom grew, nights at *La Hacienda* became longer and more intoxicating. The club's music grew so boisterous that it pulsated throughout our living quarters until well after midnight. It took the regimental commander's complaints to tame the volume.

Over the prior months I had gathered a clearer picture of my situation in the Legion, in large part thanks to Father Gaël, who told me what others would not. In the course of completing several translation projects for our regimental commander, I had the chance to speak with him privately many times before he granted my request to speak with him in my company leadership's presence. During my formal meeting with him, I restated my desire to continue serving in the Legion, to overcome the limitations imposed by my medical record, and to become an officer in the Foreign Legion *à titre étrangère*. I had even combed through French laws and found one that might facilitate my goals.

It became clear to me from this meeting, and at long last, that there was no realistic way to overcome the ruling of one prickly audiologist in Marseilles. I would not become a Foreign Legion officer and my service in the Legion would remain significantly constrained by my permanent medical profile. The regimental commander's most alluring proposition was that I finish my five-year contract and then go to work for the French civil bureaucracy. During this meeting, the regimental commander also approved my going on leave in the United States after this mission and before reporting back to my unit in Castelnaudary—an exceptional privilege for a legionnaire of my rank.

This meeting determined my next actions. Having talked for hours with US Special Forces members and two different ODA team leaders over the past months, I had decided to ask to leave the Foreign Legion in order to pursue a commission as an officer in the US Army. I knew that this path would be a trying one, and it frustrated me to have to begin from scratch in a new military organization after I had just proved my worth and earned some respect in the Foreign Legion. Yet I became increasingly convinced that I should cast this die. Whatever my continued qualms about US foreign policy and military actions, the fact is that I, as a legionnaire, was working for US interests and directly subordinate to US commands. This experience in Afghanistan helped to dampen many concerns that I once had about service in the US military.

That winter I had already begun negotiations with Princeton to return to its doctoral programme in the coming summer of 2010. My plan was to finish my general examinations at Princeton's history faculty and then to complete the US Army's Officer Candidate School. The secretary at Princeton's history faculty was as cheerful as ever when I phoned her from FOB Tora. I had taken a two-year leave of absence from Princeton in June 2008. If all worked out, I would be back in Princeton at the two-year mark—in June 2010.

As I was busy hatching such plots and stratagems, we approached the Christmas holiday. Shortly before the holiday, the French Army's chief of staff came to visit us, and we welcomed him with numerous ceremonies and a raucous evening at *La Hacienda*, where we sang Foreign Legion songs for hours and finished all the bar's available *Desperados*. For Christmas itself we held an elaborate ceremony—catered by Sodexo—in one of our large maintenance tents of US manufacture, made for servicing heavy vehicles and helicopters. After a well-attended Christmas Eve Mass in our makeshift chapel near the regimental headquarters, we dined, shared gifts, and sang all night. Holiday festivities continued until New Year's Day, when at last we began focusing on transferring our responsibilities to the Foreign Legion's newly arrived Second Foreign Parachute Regiment.

Legionnaires buzzed with excitement. Married officers and enlisted men could hardly stop talking about their wives and their families. Six months ago, we were all excited to deploy, to leave our homes, and to fly off to Afghanistan. Now it seemed that most of us had already grown tired or bored with what was so important and exciting to us not long ago. In this way we, too, exhibited and felt weighing on us the soldier's sempiternal contradictions—the desire to fight and the desire for peace; the wish to make war in faraway lands and the yearning for home; the powerful ties of military comradery, as ranged against the consolations, routines, and obligations of family life. Back then it seemed to me that seasoned and mature legionnaires had learned to balance these contradictions in ways that were still beyond my powers.

Now I doubt that they ever did.

LXXIX

January 2010

Legionnaires from the Second Foreign Parachute Regiment had begun arriving at the FOB. The parachute regiment's commander was a Breton of aristocratic origins whose nickname among senior enlisted men was *Le Roi Soleil.* Years later I had many interactions with him when I was serving as an officer at the US 173rd Airborne Brigade in Vicenza. In 2017, I organized *Le Roi Soleil*'s formal visit to our US Army unit. In part owing to his splendid reception (which included lodging at the *Villa Valmarana ai Nani*, in whose *Foresteria* I lived, and an excellent dinner at my favourite restaurant for *baccalà vicentino*, the *Trattoria di Palmerino* near Sandrigo), he invited me to spend two days as a guest at the *Palais Niel*, the French Eleventh Parachute Brigade headquarters in Toulouse. I took him up on the offer and stayed two nights at this Second Empire creation, a few blocks away from the apartment of my North American friends whom I used to visit as a legionnaire. All these things I could have scarcely imagined as *Le Roi Soleil* walked by me in all his glory when I was a legionnaire first-class at FOB Tora.

One morning, as we were putting our packed bags into a shipping container that would be leaving FOB Tora the next day, I came across the familiar face of a young legionnaire from Texas. He had been a great troublemaker in my company's basic training platoon in Castelnaudary when I served as an *aide-moniteur*. For the past four months he had been living out the dream that had inspired me to join the Legion—to serve in its celebrated parachute regiment in Corsica. He told me that he was thrilled to be in Afghanistan, since his daily life in Afghanistan was vastly more comfortable than his conditions as a junior legionnaire in Calvi, his regiment's home base. Just before the deployment, he had taken his first two weeks of leave. He took the ferry from Calvi to Marseilles and, after checking into his hotel, went to a night-club with over a thousand euros of cash in his pocket. He began to enjoy alcoholic drinks. Late the next morning he woke up dazed, alone, and naked, and it was only by telephoning his mother in the United States that he was able to get enough money to catch the last ferry back to Calvi before the deployment. As we parted ways, he told me that he would probably desert after this deployment.

When I was packing my bags into the container, I took the chance to step onto a scale. To my horror I saw that I weighed some ninety-one kilogrammes. Granted, I was wearing my combat uniform and heavy winter boots, which probably added about four kilogrammes to my bodyweight. Nonetheless, this figure unsettled me. I had been exercising regularly throughout the deployment and I had gained considerable upper-body strength, but my increased weight had become noticeable to others. Heavy portions at Sodexo's new ordinary as well as lunch and dinner drinks at *La Hacienda* had taken their toll. It was the shock of that moment that led me to change radically my dietary habits and to weigh myself daily until I consistently weighed fewer than eighty kilogrammes. To this day I weigh myself every morning and every evening, keeping in mind always the horror of seeing ninety-one kilogrammes on the scale under me.

The day of our departure approached. At first, the plan was for us to take US Army "Chinook" helicopters from FOB Tora straight to Bagram Air Base, whence we would catch our commercial flight back to France. This plan was soon scuttled, however, and one day in early January we lined up and got ready to take French Army VABs on the long ride from Surobi to Bagram Airfield.

Tedious and bumpy as it must have been, I do not remember anything of this journey. We dismounted from the VABs next to a hangar at Bagram Airfield, where we shared a large tent with US Army soldiers who were getting ready to go back to the United States after a twelve-month mission near Kandahar.

At Bagram we spent two days and two nights on open bunk beds in well-lit tents, with little to do but to wait. Aside from chatter with US soldiers, the only conversation that I remember from this time is the chance that I had to compare English and French lifestyles with an engineering officer, who agreed with my assessment that the English had entirely lost their *savoire-vivre*, and that the French would face great struggles to preserve their own over the coming years.

Since our stay in Bagram included a Sunday, I had the chance to attend Mass at Bagram Airfield's main chapel. After sixteen months in the Foreign Legion, I had grown accustomed to its conservative Catholic liturgies. Although the French military did, in theory, have Muslim and Jewish chaplains, I had never met one, and they must have been few. In the Legion we celebrated every major regimental and corporate event with a Catholic Mass, and even if legionnaires rarely attended such liturgies voluntarily, by necessity they took part in many religious ceremonies as guards, as members of the choir, or in *piquets d'honneur*. When I walked to the Bagram Chapel it shocked me to see advertisements for religious services with such descriptions as Baptist, Gospel, Mormon, and "contemporary worship," not to mention weekly "Wiccan" ceremonies to boot. Such expression of religious diversity came as a jarring reminder of the United States' radical pluralism. That Sunday afternoon I went to Mass said by a kind chaplain from Texas. Although thousands of Catholics were serving at Bagram, there were only a half-dozen soldiers in attendance.

At the appointed time we boarded a civilian aircraft out of Bagram, and once again we stopped for fuel in Abu Dhabi on the way back to Europe. It unsettled me to learn that our flight from Bagram was not back to France.

LXXX

January 2010

To our surprise, our commercial aircraft landed in Cyprus. Dimly aware of this island's ancient and recent histories, the first thing that came to my mind when learning of our destination were lines from one of my favorite poems of Paul Verlaine, which I had long since committed to memory:

> *Ce vieux vin de Chypre est exquis / Moins, Camargo, que votre nuque.*[*]

None of us legionnaires knew what to expect. All reports were that we had come to Cyprus for *décompression*. Legionnaires could be forgiven for viewing anything unforeseen with edgy suspicion. For us *décompression* could have meant something harrowing indeed.

From Limassol's aeroport, chartered buses took us to a hotel located on the beaches near Paphos. It was January, so this hotel was deserted, and we

---

* Paul Verlaine, *Fêtes Galantes*, "Pantomime", Stanza V: "This old wine from Cyprus is less exquisite, Camargo, than the nape of your neck."

legionnaires its only customers. Our task force's personnel were re-deploying to France in three or four different movements, so at one time this four-star hotel hosted about a third of our regiment. Its enterprising managers greeted us hundreds of legionnaires in the hotel's spacious entrance hall with remarkable aplomb before introducing us to the French military psychologist who would oversee our *décompression*. This psychologist explained that we would stay in Cyprus for three days and two nights in order to help us to manage the abrupt transition from our deployment's realities back to the tamer ways of living in mainland France.

All told, this was not a bad idea. To my knowledge, the French Army had implemented its own *décompression* sessions following similar efforts by the US and British militaries. As frightening as we must have been to the hotel's management, I am sure that legionnaires were less dangerous to its interests than US or British troops. Whatever legionnaires' faults, thanks to the Legion's purposeful and forceful training they are a relatively civilized bunch among soldiers, with higher standards of decorum. As a retired Foreign Legion colonel explained to me years later at his office in Bethlehem, many of the Legion's officers take pride in their charge to form legionnaires as much as possible in the ways of French civilization. In this effort they have some success. This is not to say that our stay did not become riotous in Cyprus. It is simply that legionnaires tend not to destroy property, and that they are tidier and clean after themselves within the Legion's properties and especially in public settings. Failure to do so results in punishments including days or weeks *en taule*.

I was fortunate in that I was assigned to share a room at this hotel with a quiet corporal from Madagascar who worked in our headquarters' communications section. Taciturn but good-natured, this man in his mid-thirties wanted quiet on the beach, massages, and time alone to speak with his wife over the telephone. Thus I was spared the ordeal of sharing a room with younger legionnaires of my rank, who together probably managed to employ scores of the island's prostitutes of Eastern European vintage available in this off-season for Mediterranean tourism. In the Legion of that time, Romanian prostitutes and cocaine were widely accepted forms of "rest and recreation," and both were in plentiful supply over the coming two nights. Of these the young Briton with shrapnel recently removed from his backside was an especially avid consumer.

French military psychologists had arranged several events for us, including group "therapy" sessions and massages for every legionnaire, entry to the hotel's spa, and trips to sites of cultural importance at Paphos and throughout the island. Since the enlisted men were mostly engaged in different cultural pleasures, usually I found myself in tour buses filled with our task force's officers. For the first time, I was able to have lengthy conversations with Captain Xavier. One night, as we went to a bowling alley on the island, the two of us talked the whole evening about European history. He seemed disappointed that I had not taken time to study the development of canon law, which he saw as fundamental to all subsequent European civilization. I do not think that his knowledge on this matter was expansive, but it outdid mine, even though my professor at Princeton had long urged me to study in earnest Gratian's *Decretum*. It is a skewed and flattering point of view, but to this day Captain Xavier is my idealized image of a graduate of the *École Polytechnique*.

However interesting our hours of conversation were that evening in Cyprus, in buses, and at the bowling alley, between this young captain and me there was a void, our many similarities in age and educational experiences notwithstanding. It was the void of military rank, which was new to me at the time. Perhaps not as definitive as that abyss between Lazarus and the rich man, this void must be real for militaries to function, and true friendship between ranks cannot be. In the Legion these divisions were almost excessively respected, as officers and enlisted soldiers would often have familiarity only with those of their own rank. But even in the much less formal and hierarchical US Army, I have found that successful soldiers understand how dangerous and destructive it is to make friends outside of one's rank.

In our Western societies today, which like to keep their rigid hierarchies hidden under burkas of egalitarian pretences and of joshing familiarity, hierarchies' visible limitations on human interactions frustrate us. But whereas our egalitarian prejudices are fantastical, hierarchies are real and permanent, and I owe it to the Legion that I learned to appreciate the importance of hierarchy, to respect its limits, and to understand its necessity for the best possible shaping and regulation of human mores and conduct.

In the end, I enjoyed our time in Cyprus, which did "decompress" me. Throughout our *décompression* I drank little, forewent Eastern European embraces, and prayed where Saint Paul may have been whipped with forty lashes less one. Three days of soft Mediterranean sunshine in wintertime, enjoyed at empty beaches, bleached much of Afghanistan from my mind.

PART III

Demission

*Furchtbar ist das Allensein mit dem Richter und Rächer des eignen Gesetzes. Also wird ein Stern hisausgeworfen in den öden Raum und in den eisigen Athem des Alleinseins.**

Friedrich Wilhelm Nietzsche
Also Sprach Zarathustra I

Никакая свобода не может устроить человека раз и навсегда без той духовной работы, которой она оплачена....а внутренняя свобода дана изначально каждому, только надо иметь мужество и решимость ею воспользоваться, осознав общественную значимость своего внутреннего опыта.†

Андрей Тарковский
Запечатлённое Время

* "It is terrifying to stand alone as the judge and the avenger of one's own law—it is like a star cast out into the barren emptiness of space and hurled into pure solitude's icy breath."

† Andrei Tarkovsky, *Sculpting in Time*: "There is no freedom that we can possess once and for all without the spiritual work that pays for it....Inner freedom is initially given to everyone, but one must have the courage and the determination to use it, keeping in mind the social significance of his inner experience."

LXXXI

January 2010

Once back on French soil, all legionnaires were subject to searches for contraband. At Camp Warehouse I had bought a small computer, allowed to us legionnaires in Afghanistan but forbidden in France. This was the only item in my possession that worried me, as its discovery could have landed me a week *en taule* immediately after our deployment. As we legionnaires lined up to have our belongings searched, with no other recourse I shoved the computer into the back of my trousers and covered it with my uniform. As it turned out, the search was decidedly *pro forma*, and no one bothered to check the back of my trousers or my pockets for any forbidden items.

Taking chartered buses from the Istres aeroport, we arrived at our regiment late in the night. Alone I trudged up the stairs of my company building with two duffle bags in tow. As I opened the door to my barracks room, I remarked that little had changed since my departure. A few more of the room's lockers were occupied, but it did not look as though anyone had begun to live there. Our last instructions were to report to our regimental motor pool the next day in normal duty uniforms, wearing our *képis blancs*.

The next morning all those who had just returned to France—some one-third of our regiment—assembled in the motor pool. After the usual jumble and chatter of morning formations, we marched together in orderly ranks and sang the Legion's well-known song, *"La Petite Piste,"* as we crossed over *Rue Vincent Faïta* and onto our regimental *place d'armes*. There a small ceremony marked our arrival. Once we had fallen into regular formations looking toward the centremost point of the *place d'armes*, loudspeakers blared out *"La Marseillaise"* as the French tricolour climbed the mast while keeping time with the national anthem. At no other time in my short Foreign Legion career do I remember having such a powerful response to *"La Marseillaise"* as I did that morning. At its familiar strains my heart welled up with pride at my service to the Fifth Republic and at the privilege I had to be in its Foreign Legion. With the full force of my once respectable baritone, I sang as loudly as I could my favourite line from this anthem: *Qu'un sang impur abreuve nos sillons!*

Over the coming days we prepared for a few weeks of leave after our deployment. At the regiment we ran across many legionnaires who had stayed behind in Nîmes during our operations abroad. In their eyes I was no longer a greenhorn, and I even merited some respect and consideration. My six months in Afghanistan had changed how others in our organization would henceforth look at me. Already, at a junior level, I had taken part in our unit's most desirable deployment, and owing to this I was entitled to wear four medals—something that looked impressive in those days on a young legionnaire's uniform. I think that it was during these days that I first understood how much military decorations determine how others in our formations look at us. This seemed "superficial" to me at the time, and I chaffed at the increased respect that corporals and sergeants showed me, when I believed myself to be the same man whom they had treated some six months before with indifference or scorn. I did not yet understand that I was no longer the same man.

In Afghanistan's winter my hands had chapped badly, such that they were covered in almost permanent sores. No matter how much lotion I put on them or how I took care of them, their skin remained painful and broken. Yet within a few days of our arrival at Nîmes, my hands became whole again, and the sores that had plagued me for months turned from reality to memory. No less quickly did I forget our deployment, its rhythms, its concerns, its personalities, its privileges, and its limits. As I walked through the streets of Nîmes, quiet under the fickle winter skies, I rejoiced at being back in Europe, even as I plotted to leave the Foreign Legion to join the US Army.

Whereas our regiment strictly governed legionnaires' movements outside the base in normal times, there was a welcome chaos in the days following our return from Afghanistan. This permissive environment gave me the chance to spend days and evenings walking through the city, reacquainting myself with its Roman monuments, eating *brandade de morue* and other local delicacies at its markets, and partaking of pastis and good wines. It took me several days to get used to encountering women in the streets, as for almost half a year I had barely seen one. After these few days, I was on my way to Paris. I spent the weekend with my friend Jean-Paul at his flat in the fourteenth *arondissement*. Early the next week I flew back to the United States.

It had been almost a year and a half since I had taken a Lufthansa flight from Houston to Marseilles. Much sooner than I had foreseen, I was already heading back to New Jersey to organize my return to Princeton University.

When I left Princeton for the last time in May 2008 before joining the Legion, I bid farewell to my professor in his office. I had no intention of ever setting foot again in Princeton, whose environment I found depressing and whose intellectual life seemed tiresome and limited. My plan was to continue any future studies either at the *École des Hautes Études en Sciences Sociales* in Paris or at the University of Oxford. Yet during that meeting with my professor, I had the foresight to understand the fragility of our plans and the mockery that Fortune makes of them. I said to him something to the effect of: "Who knows, maybe I'll be back here one day." He shrugged in agreement and with a measured smile that acknowledged Fortune's whims.

LXXXII

January 2010

Life-changing experiences seldom live up to our expectations. However much they change us, they usually do so in slippery ways that we do not understand or even remember.

As I flew back to the United States, I left France quite disappointed with my Legion experience and with our deployment to Afghanistan. I had just undertaken an adventure scarcely imaginable to me two years before, when I was a fretful young man with no military experience, to whom the very word Afghanistan would have stirred up frightful and far-fetched images. Now I was frustrated that I had not seen what I believed to be "real" combat, that I had not had the chance to dodge bullets or to feel them whizzing and cracking past my ears, that I had not faced the challenge of pointing a rifle or machine gun at my fellow man with the intention to kill him—that I had not done so, and then shown the resolve to pull the trigger and to accept the burden of murder.

At Princeton on leave, my task was simple. I had arranged to spend about a week at one of the Graduate School's apartments on University Place, and as soon as I arrived, I met with my professor, with our faculty's secretaries, and with the dean of Princeton's Graduate School to iron out my return. A few weeks before, I had been running laps about FOB Tora each morning and climbing *Mont Saint Michel*. Now I took morning runs on trails along the Delaware Canal.

When it came to my fellow students at the history faculty, not much had changed. Its new students were as little interested in me as I in them. The students with whom I had begun my journey at Princeton welcomed me back kindly and with curiosity. I spent several evenings with them at parties in familiar haunts. Two years before, I was shy about speaking in French, but now some French graduate students even mistook me for one of their countrymen, so fluent and off-the-cuff had my French become. Little had changed in Princeton's small Catholic community. My same confessor from years past was there and welcomed me as though I had just come back from summer holiday. The chapel of the Blessed Sacrament at Princeton's university chapel was as quiet as ever in the early afternoons. Whereas I had formerly thought little of this university chapel and its quaint surrounding courtyards, I now appreciated their clean, faux-gothic charms.

During this trip I finalized all arrangements to re-matriculate to Princeton's Graduate School in June 2010. I secured an apartment on University Place for the summer, and I arranged to take my "general examinations" in European history before September. My renewed scholarships and stipends would already be in effect that June. The possibility of spending the next few months and years studying European history, which filled me with dread as recently as the spring of 2008, now excited and inspired me.

Princeton had not really changed, but, in foreseeable and unexpected ways, I had. One evening I went to eat dinner at one of Princeton's undergraduate dining halls named after the Rockefeller family, whose members had donated lavishly to the university and therefore had undergraduate living quarters named for them. I sat down at a table dedicated for an informal club in which everyone had declared a commitment to speak in Latin over dinner. Across from me a young man sat eating barbecued beef and drinking a tall glass of milk. Horrified at the sight, I asked him what on earth he was doing drinking milk at dinner, and to accompany sauce-soaked beef at that. He answered that this combination was "healthy." Before my time in the Foreign Legion, I would not have been able to notice, and much less to understand, this situation's absurdity—a young man of means at one of the United States' most prestigious universities washing down beef with milk while believing that he was making "healthy" choices to do so. After not even two years in France, immersed in the Foreign Legion's military culture, what before would have escaped my notice now unnerved me.

My former peers' reactions to my return were interesting to me. Some sheltered young women went so far as to suggest that I had joined the Foreign Legion mostly to build social *éclat* in academic circles. Many students had barely made any progress in their studies since I had left in early 2008. In the main, those who had moved ahead in their academic lives were still possessed by the same "spleen" that I had left behind me. Before joining the Legion, I believed that there was something wrong with me that made me miserable at Princeton. In this I was correct—I simply did not have the context to appreciate Princeton's luxuries. During those two weeks in Princeton on leave from the Foreign Legion, I could already recognize opportunities and appreciate simpler pleasures that hitherto had not interested me. I looked forward to continuing my progress at Princeton as much as I had used to loathe living and studying there, a loathing that many of my peers still shared.

For a few days I travelled to Texas to visit my parents, whose isolated lives had barely changed since my departure in 2008. As I prepared to go back to France after this period of leave, I had resolved to quit the Foreign Legion and to take my next steps at Princeton. Never would I have done this, I think, had my initial hearing tests gone better, and had I been allowed to serve in the Second Foreign Parachute Regiment in Corsica.

At any event, in late February 2010, I returned to France to fulfil my contractual obligations and to make my official request to leave the Foreign Legion. When I returned to my assigned company at Nîmes in spring 2010, many officers were surprised that I had not deserted while on leave in the United States.

LXXXIII

February 2010

Once back from leave in the United States, I had to travel back to Castelnaudary's Fourth Foreign Regiment. According to the Legion I was only attached, or "on loan," to the Second Foreign Infantry Regiment for the deployment to Afghanistan. Now that this engagement was over, my old company at Castelnaudary awaited me. Before taking this journey, I spent one weekend in Nîmes.

At Nîmes, one of the more typical legionnaire activities for weekends was to take a train across the Spanish border to a brothel in Catalonia. This brothel's name was "dallas" or "adallas"—I never saw its name in writing. Although I have long believed that honest recourse to prostitution is preferable to the sterilized and consumerist sexual relations now prevalent in Westernized lands, owing to my natural prudishness and Catholic morality I was never tempted to visit this brothel so beloved of Nîmes' legionnaire population. Instead, during this weekend in Nîmes, perhaps my last, I was determined to try out one of the city's two restaurants graced with Michelin-starred chefs. One of these, *Alexandre*, was in Nîmes' peripheral zones, but the other, *Le Lisita*, sat right across from the city's Roman arena. Owing to its enviable setting, I chose the latter.

That Saturday afternoon, by chance, I ran across two soldiers from the United States who were also in Nîmes that weekend. One of them had plans to spend his time and pay at our regiment's favourite Catalonian brothel, but last-minute duties at the regiment had kept him from leaving Nîmes. The second was simply lazy and, I think, planning to spend most of the weekend playing video games. I invited them both to have dinner with me at *Le Lisita*.

Were I to have this same dinner today, I would probably find myself criticizing the food and the environment. At the time, however, I had dined at relatively few such restaurants, so the creations of any Michelin-starred chef impressed me. Six months of meals catered by Turkmen and by Sodexo had also heightened my appreciation for the handiwork of well-appointed French kitchens.

For my two North American colleagues, this was their first dinner at a restaurant of this quality. It left them flabbergasted. Such food, service, wines, ingredients, and presentation were unthinkable in most provincial parts of the United States, much less in their wonted lower-class environments in Utah and in rural Virginia. After the dinner they both left outrageous tips that together amounted to almost half of our bill's total charge. The young man from Virginia remarked to me that he was glad that he had been kept from going to Catalonia, and that this meal was, in the end, far more enjoyable than "lines of coke snorted off a Romanian hooker's butt"—or words to that effect.

That week I left for Castelnaudary and went back to my old company. Familiar sergeants had left for various operational regiments, and my old platoon leader had secured a coveted position at the Legion's small detachment in Mayotte. Of our former leadership, only the blustering first sergeant remained. Most at the company welcomed me warmly and seemed both envious and proud of me for my deployment. I had brought back a pennant from Princeton for my new company commander, which he displayed prominently in the company club. As always in the Legion at any moment of change or transition, he received me for a formal interview. Unlike most officers in the Legion, who usually come from Saint-Cyr, our new commander was a former enlisted soldier with almost thirty years of military service. I answered this seasoned veteran's questions about my recent mission in ways that I thought to the point and honest, but which probably came across to him as petulant and childish. I did not take pains to hide my disappointment with the deployment—an experience that he and almost anyone else in our company coveted. No matter how inappropriate my answers, he received me kindly and informed me that I would soon be transferring back to the Second Foreign Infantry Regiment owing to its commander's specific request.

I spent only a week or two at Castelnaudary before going back to Nîmes for good. It was a sombre time for me since I had accepted that my Legion career was finished. One Russian sergeant new to our company, whose relatives had fought in the Soviet Union's war in Afghanistan, took me aside and asked me many questions about our deployment. He concluded from hearing my observations that the war of NATO forces in Afghanistan was not as brutal and as violent as that fought by his Soviet forebearers. This thought consoled him.

One evening I spoke with the first sergeant for hours. He understood my disappointment with the deployment, but also made me understand how impertinent it was for me to show any disappointment to others. Here I inferred that this man, whose presence I had formerly avoided and whom I had intensely disliked, was probably the non-commissioned officer in the company who took the most interest in me and who gave me the best counsel. I also saw that my former platoon leader was, in fact, somewhat of a charlatan, and at least deceptive and manipulative. So much that was once mysterious to me was now clearer; so much of what I believed true was false. Six months of operational experience had changed my understanding of this company.

Once back in Nîmes, I met up again with my North American colleagues and we began eating at more fine restaurants in Nîmes and in surrounding areas whenever our weekend schedules allowed us to do so. Our informal club of dining enthusiasts had even gained renown among certain legionnaires. Had I stayed longer in Nîmes, I believe that we would have developed our budding arrangements and started a regular and popular group of legionnaires interested in fashionable local restaurants and chefs with Michelin stars.

As it was, I only had a few months left in the Legion.

LXXXIV

February 2010

Soon after arriving at Nîmes, I had to report formally to our regimental commander. Before this meeting, the regimental commander's officer in charge of manging personnel greeted me and offered suggestions as to where I might best serve the regiment. To the unsuspecting legionnaire like me, this thin, balding, and frail-looking officer, rather aged for his rank of *commandant*, appeared the embodiment of a mere military pencil-pusher, one whom young soldiers could hold in justified contempt. Since this officer had not taken part in the deployment to Afghanistan, I even wondered if he had somehow contrived to avoid the mission, or if he had volunteered to stay behind in France to forego the deployment's hardships and to enjoy the leisurely life of an officer on rear-detachment while his unit was fighting beyond the hills.

A few weeks after meeting this man, I learned from Father Gaël, always the overflowing fount of gossip and often a source of good information, that this "human resources" officer had spent at least three tours at the Legion's Third Foreign Infantry Regiment in French Guyana, whose prestige and renown rivalled that of Calvi's Second Foreign Parachute Regiment. What is more,

Father Gaël told me that this officer had graduated from the Colombian Army's "Lancero School," which at the time was one of few training events outside of the Legion that filled any legionnaire with awe. To me, mention of the "Lancero School" seemed as fantastical and as mysterious as Macondo's muddy streets, Aureliano Buendia's fourteen firing squads, and his family's venturesome and often incestuous sexual unions. Never could I have believed that fewer than ten years later I would find myself serving in Colombia as a student, and later as an instructor, at the same Lancero School.

Prior to my meeting with the regimental commander, through backdoor channels Father Gaël had already set the stage for our formal conversation. Therefore, when I answered the commander's question about what I wished to do in his regiment, it came as no surprise to him when I requested demission from the Foreign Legion owing to the medical constraints imposed on me. At these words, all in the room save for the colonel almost jumped in their seats at my audacity. The colonel's calm and thoughtful reaction to this outlandish request only redoubled their shock.

The colonel proposed a few options to me whereby I might stay in the Foreign Legion. Of all these, the most tempting was the idea of completing my five-year contract in relative ease and then competing for a place at the *École Nationale d'Administration*. Fanciful visions of life as a provincial bureaucrat in southern France sorely tempted me, but my time in the Legion had too much whetted my appetite for things military. Therefore, I remained steadfast in my resolve to leave the Legion and to seek out a career as an officer in the United States Army and to become a leader in its Special Forces. The colonel understood my request and forwarded it with his endorsements to the Legion's headquarters in Aubagne. In the meantime, he directed me to stay in the regiment's headquarters and to work for the Hungarian *caporal-chef* who had guided me throughout the deployment.

Life at the Second Foreign Infantry Regiment resumed its predictable rhythms. Since we had just come back from a deployment, most of us longed for an easier pace of life. The weather warmed up and summer beckoned as the days grew longer. My request to leave the Legion had already been submitted to the deciding authority in Aubagne, the Legion's commanding general, and there was little for me to do but to complete my assigned tasks, to wait for a decision, and to get ready for an uncertain future outside of the Legion. Days were remarkably alike in garrison. After morning *corvée* and formation, we had about three hours for physical training. Months of running predictable routes in Afghanistan made our diverse daily routes in Nîmes and its surrounding countryside enlivening. Soon I devised a way to forego lunch at the regimental ordinary in order to eat in my barracks room more refined foods that I bought every weekend at local markets. As a veteran of the deployment to Afghanistan, I had the implied right to a reasonable daily siesta, so most afternoons I indulged in Sancho Panza's "universal currency" in my barracks room.

I spent most weekends shopping at the city's central market after attending Mass at the Romanesque Cathedral of Our Lady and of Saint Castor. Given my growing penchant for fish, at the lively Sunday market I usually bought several portions of *brandade de morue* (a speciality of the area made of salted cod and potatoes), local wines to accompany it, and bread from *Maison Villaret*. On Sundays it was usually about 1330 when I came back to my barracks room with produce sufficient for lunch and for the week to come. At my table looking out westward, I ate the *brandade de morue* and perhaps later hearty sausage with pieces of a baguette, washing them down with local vintages. Only two things remained to conclude this Sunday ritual. The first step was to walk outside and to smoke a weekly Gauloise cigarette—for after a relapse into occasional daily smoking in Afghanistan, I was trying to limit myself to one cigarette every Sunday. I drew its plumes of smoke into my lungs with purposeful sensuality. The second was to take a siesta in my barracks, one bathed in the rays of the afternoon sun as they flooded through the ample windows.

Weeks flew by me. Aside from outings to Nîmes' finer restaurants, I avoided most company and I turned down Father Gaël's repeated invitations to attend cocktails and other events hosted by high-ranking military officers in the area. Father Gaël believed that I was being petulant, but I knew that he had ulterior motives. Moreover, I thought it unseemly to be in situations where I would necessarily be a spectacle.

LXXXV

March 2010

In our daily process of gathering up fragments of memory to piece together our life's story—that ever-changing narrative through which we understand present sensations as they flit imperceptibly from future to past—many of us single out what we might call "defining moments." The basic idea behind this term is that there are remarkable moments in our lives that determine our actions and our being. These moments shape the development of our individual stories in ways that are clearly distinguishable from the mass of lost minutes and hours that pass by almost unnoticed and fade away in our minds. This implicit, if not well-developed, theory of "defining moments" suggests that whereas forgotten moments are of relatively little importance, "defining moments" forge us into something new or set our lives on different courses.

So-called defining moments take all shapes. For the religious, such moments could be events or revelations that lead one to embrace previously rejected dogmas and practices, and to try to live in conformity with them. For those who thirst after political power, defining moments are perhaps introductions to certain personalities, or the first time that they believed themselves able to understand causes of problems which they wished to remedy through political thought and action. For those of customary ambitions, it could be finding a spouse or stable employment. In my few decades of life, to listen to the media that pander to and shape our whims and fantasies as consumers, one would believe that sexual events are the most defining moments of all. Perhaps these media are somewhat correct, as the toll of sexual congress on our consciousness is undeniable. Loath as I am to believe in neatly defined turning points in our lives, I tend to think that I had one of these shortly after my return to Nîmes.

It took place one Saturday morning during early spring in Arles, where for the first time I ate sausage made with horsemeat. In this action I crossed, definitively if unwittingly, a cultural and spiritual threshold away from the horse-worshipping Anglo-Saxon culture of my childhood and into those that sanction cutting up dead horses and turning their meat into sausage.

In my past experiences of riding horses in the United States and in England, people who loved and revered horses as almost divine beings surrounded me. Several times I heard remarks from horse-breeders and horse-riders that the French were "barbaric" because they ate horsemeat. The memory of such remarks tempted me one Saturday morning to travel to Arles to search out such forbidden flesh, a quest that I began with morbid determination.

For all that I had heard about French enthusiasm for horsemeat, it was surprisingly hard to find this unholy product in southern France. Indeed, I went to Arles that morning not for its Roman arena or ruins, not for its majestic situation on the Rhône, and not for its association with Vincent Van Gogh, but rather because butchers at the market in Nîmes had told me that Arles had the only local market where I could find horsemeat for sale.

For almost an hour I thought myself deceived as I wandered through Arles' market. No horsemeat was to be found, and the vendors whom I asked looked at me quizzically as I inquired about horsemeat or the nearest seller of it. I must have visited a dozen or so merchants of cured meats before one of them directed me to a truck on the *Boulevard des Lices*. Here at last I found horsemeat sausage for sale. I took a sample in hand.

There was no *frisson* of transgression within me as I put one slice of horsemeat sausage on my tongue for the first time that Saturday morning in the market at Arles. A mere ten euros was enough to buy a sizeable portion. The horsemeat was blended with pork to make a rather ho-hum piece of sausage. As for its taste, I only know that it was similar to sausage made from meat of mature bulls that was popular in Nîmes and in its surrounding countryside, easily found in any local market in that part of France.

However unremarkable the sausage's taste, I was satisfied to have found at last a place that sold horsemeat. The act of eating such meat was to do something that would have shocked and disgusted so many in the land and culture of my birth. I bought a bottle of youthful and strong Châteauneuf-du-Pape to accompany my new purchase. Later that afternoon, alone in my barracks room in Nîmes, slowly and carefully I ate slices of horsemeat on pieces of a baguette from my favourite bakery in the city, *Maison Villaret*. I took care to ensure that Châteauneuf-du-Pape bathed and washed down every slice. After consuming the wine and sausage, I lay down to a nap of sated sleep.

That afternoon of Châteauneuf-du-Pape and horseflesh probably did not change me on the spot, but I have since created from those moments of their consumption memories that represent my first conscious, deliberate rejection of Anglo-Saxon supremacy. Throughout my adolescence I had believed that English and British cultures, and the developments of British colonies in North America, represented unquestioned pinnacles of human political and cultural achievement. As so many still do in Churchill-worshipping lands, I believed that Anglo-American worldwide dominion was God-ordained, and I celebrated the British Empire and its legacy. In my heart of hearts, I longed for its revival, and I wished that I had been born in the age of British imperial glories, so that I could pursue and live out adventures "somewheres East of Suez."

Yet as the spring of 2010 matured and I prepared to leave the Foreign Legion to go back to the United States in pursuit of a career in the US military, already I had jettisoned these former beliefs. Never again would they hold dominion over my understanding. I fancy that they disappeared to tastes and textures of horseflesh mixed with young Châteauneuf-du-Pape.

LXXXVI

February 2010

Before my own military experience, never would I have been able to believe, and much less to understand, how much military life relies on patient teaching. Indeed, I would now argue that the quality of any military force is related as much to the expertise and professionalism of its teachers as to the bravery of its soldiers or the deadliness of its weapons. From my first day at Castelnaudary, the Legion's unique education instilled in me not only military skills, habits, virtues, and vices, but also new ways of understanding the world.

One of my foremost teachers in the Legion was a relatively young *caporal-chef* from Hungary. With almost fifteen years of service in the Legion, this corporal maintained the thin, fit, and youthful appearance of a man in his late twenties. The only feature that betrayed his age was his balding head. He had served mainly in the Second Foreign Infantry Regiment, but had also enjoyed two tours in French Guyana, where he had become one of that regiment's foremost runners—no small feat. An untimely injury to his lower back had robbed this man of his passion for running, but he had enthusiastically taken up biking and other cardiovascular activities in its stead. With him I shared a room throughout our deployment, first at Camp Warehouse and later at FOB Tora. Throughout our deployment he was also my direct supervisor when it came to matters of discipline and daily life.

Over six months in Afghanistan, the *caporal-chef* and I had many conversations as we shared meals and drinks together on most days, both at the task force's bars and in our confined rooms. I came to know him better than anyone in the regiment. Had we met in different environments, he probably would have treated me as a social superior and therefore curbed his behaviour and his conversation with me. In the Legion, he was my superior and therefore he had few reservations about speaking his mind to me, sharing his thoughts, and giving me wanted and unwanted advice.

A few years from retirement, this was meant to be his last deployment. Married to a Peruvian woman and with three young children by her, he took no excitement in this military adventure and saw it as a mere job to finish. Indeed, he spoke to me frequently about his plans after the Legion, since at this time legionnaires received a full pension after fifteen years of service. For most of the deployment his plan upon retirement from the Legion was to sell chicken products from a "food truck" in Nîmes. Soon after the deployment his wife put a stop to this fancy, insisting that she had married a legionnaire, not a man who makes chicken sandwiches. At her nudging and thanks to the encouragement of his superiors, he served the Legion for several more years than planned.

This *caporal-chef* claimed to have had a long career of seducing women both in metropolitan France and especially in French Guyana, but at that time he loved his wife madly and spoke of her every day for six months, so much that it was almost vexing to listen to him. One thing that he often stressed to me was the absolute necessity of showering immediately after defecating. In his words, you could never know when the "demon of love" would strike, and one must always be ready to satisfy its possibilities. I have no reason to believe that he had any inclinations to acts of sodomy, so with these words he probably meant to convey the idea that it is important to eliminate the lingering smells of recently expunged human waste through showering. I thought this practice wholesome, prudent, and worthy of emulation.

Pushkin once wrote about how friendship develops between men from "doing nothing." *Так люди (первый каюсь я) / От делать нечего друзья.** From working and from doing nothing together, the *caporal-chef* and I became friends, such that he invited me to dinner at his house in Nîmes many times. For some years we even kept up correspondence through electronic messages after I had gone back to the United States. Of necessity we had shared experiences and confidences. Indeed, there are probably few people in the world with whom I have shared more, and in such an open way.

Whereas women have unconditional love only for their children—their lifelong burden and their most extreme emotional events—for men the fullest examples of love usually take place in the realm of military service. This is why men without substantive military experiences are often missing a psychological and emotional completion that mothers do not lack. This love forged between men in martial environments, unique as a mother's for her own children, is what David captures for time sempiternal in his lament of Jonathan:

Your love for me was more wonderful / Than the love of women.†

Notwithstanding my shared experiences with the *caporal-chef*, we never developed a lasting bond based in such love. Once I moved away from France and became an officer in the US Army, our friendship first faded, and then ended. We no longer had anything to talk about other than to remember the deployment to Afghanistan and to share brief updates. I owed him more loyalty, since I had learnt many things from this man.

Like many citizens of the United States in the late twentieth century, I had grown up believing in my country's self-proclaimed "exceptionalism." I thought that my country was superior to any that existed then or that had ever existed,

---

* A.S. Pushkin, Eugene Onegin, Chapter IV, Stanza LII: "Thus people—I am the first to admit—become friends from doing nothing together."

† 2 Samuel, 1:26: פְּלְאַתָה אַהֲבָתְךָ לִי, מֵאַהֲבַת נָשִׁים

and that as its citizen I enjoyed, as my birthright, a degree of privilege and standing beyond those of other mortals. Before joining the Foreign Legion, I would have seen this Hungarian *caporal-chef* without university education as someone worthy of my polite disdain.

Instead, to this day I would argue that I learned more from this Hungarian than I ever did from all but two or three of my professors at Princeton.

LXXXVII

March 2010

In our company we had a small break room with an automatic coffee dispenser. One Sunday afternoon, probably after a siesta, I walked down to this room and sat at one of its tables to drink the machine-made coffee to which I had become accustomed in the Legion. Affixed to the wall in this room was a report that impressed me and that has since shaped my perceptions of soldiers and of military service in lasting ways. I wish that I had possessed the foresight to make a copy of this report, since I would be interested to read it again today after almost ten years of military experience as an officer.

This report's intent was meant to guide Legion officers about how to think about their soldiers' motivations for service. Put on display in our company room for coffee breaks, it was clearly meant for public consumption. The paper argued that most soldiers in today's Western volunteer armies—some 60 to 75 percent—had undertaken military service for reasons that were basically mercenary. In exchange for military service, they sought perks and privileges that were financial and social in nature: stable salaries, increased respect in society, cash bonuses, discounts, pensions, opportunities for education, and upward social mobility for themselves or for their children.

A sizeable minority of 15 to 20 percent of soldiers, so argued the report, joined out of fundamental spiritual, mental, and emotional needs. These men had so-called "guardian personalities" that, if unable to find a suitable place in military ranks, would seek out similar professions such as policing and firefighting. The core psychological desires and urges of such personalities include service to and protection of their local and larger communities.

According to this paper, a smaller minority, sometimes as much as 10 percent, were so-called "psychopaths" or "sociopaths." The paper's terms for such soldiers were vague, but its idea was clear. Many men joined the military so as to be able to kill other people legally and to enjoy the opportunities to wield far-reaching power over subordinates—power that exceeded almost any known to normal civilian professions in our era. These men were addicts to power, the most seductive and addictive drug of them all. To kill and to wield power over others, they would undergo great hardships.

After giving some necessary data and statistics, the paper's argument was that officers should understand that the motivations of most soldiers were economic and social and mould their leadership styles and tactics in accordance with this reality. Likewise, the paper argued that officers should try to recognize, to support, and to promote soldiers with "guardian" personalities that formed the spiritual backbone of professional armies. Last, the paper argued that while "psychopathic" or "sociopathic" soldiers would often seem to be skilful and motivated personnel with a "warrior ethos," their long-term effects on any military organization were destructive. It argued for the careful identification and elimination of such personalities from the ranks.

At the time, I read this report with interest, but I do not remember it having an immediate impact on me. Memory of the paper's contents and arguments nonetheless stayed with me and came to mind when I began basic infantry officer training at Fort Benning in the spring of 2013. Throughout my career as an officer in the US Army, this paper's core ideas have shaped my perception of my subordinates, my peers, and my superiors.

My experience with "psychopaths" or "sociopaths" in the US Army perhaps began on the first day that I explored joining it. On the night before my initial US Army medical examination, I shared a room at a hotel in New Jersey with a fellow Princeton graduate, whose father was a professor at Princeton's Classics faculty. This young man had served a tour in Iraq, left the Army, and now thirsted to join it again as a member of the Ranger Regiment. His words to me that night as we chatted in the hotel room reminded me of the report that I had read not long before at my company in Nîmes. He stated that the only thing in the world that came close to the thrills and the excitement of combat was sexual climax. He matter-of-factly observed that he could attain the latter anywhere in the world by himself, by manipulation, or by payment, but that in today's pacified world there were only few legal avenues for seeking out the thrills and comradery of combat.

As it turned out, the Army denied this young man the opportunity to join the Ranger Regiment since he had "flat feet." A few months later I saw him at a party in Princeton, where he was with a young woman who was probably satisfying his sexual needs at the time. He congratulated me then on my already successful manoeuvring to join the Army as an officer, noting that by becoming an officer I would live out the dreams of so many men.

With almost a decade of service in the US Army under my belt, and most of this time with prestigious and decorated units, I remain impressed by the prescience and the accuracy of that paper that I read in the spring of 2010, as I prepared to leave the Legion. Almost everything that I have seen in the US Army has confirmed what that paper outlined, and I believe that there are essentially three basic military archetypes: the mercenary, the guardian, and the murderer. Of these, the mercenary is the most predictable, and probably the most professional and loyal when all is said and done. Guardians are often too idealistic and taken up by their own supposed noble-mindedness, and their disappointments can lead them to take embarrassing actions and decisions. Many of them cannot thrive in today's professionalized and bureaucratized services.

Murderers are the most determined to remain in military uniform, since life for them would become unbearable without the pleasures of the military's more arbitrary powers, and its opportunities for violence and killing.

LXXXVIII

March 2010

While working at the regimental headquarters, that spring I had many chances to speak with Captain Michel, who took great pleasure in sauntering about the hallways and talking with passing legionnaires, whether to banter lightly with them or to upbraid them. It was typical of Captain Michel to raise his voice and to affect annoyance whenever a non-commissioned officer shook hands with him without first removing his gloves. On such occasions Captain Michel would let the entire hallway know that shaking hands while wearing one's gloves was uncivilized, filthy, and insulting.

Given my academic background, Captain Michel liked to spell out his theories about history to me. He believed that Arabs were taking over France and that French culture had already been destroyed, and along with it, European civilization. He did believe that "the West" would survive in the United States even as it died away in Europe, where it had been washed out to history's high seas by successive waves of Middle Eastern and African immigrants. According to Captain Michel, the version of the West surviving in the United States would be an adolescent "McDonald's civilization," or *civilisation McDo*, but still better than anything else in the world. To me, his world-weary disgust with France's end and petulant optimism about the United States reminded me of Gervase Crouchback's bemused observations about cocktail onions in *Sword of Honour*, when he described US citizens as a "remote and resourceful people…whose chief concern seemed to be the frustration of the processes of nature."

Captain Michel's theories about France's decline and fall, not uncommon among the Legion's officers and enlisted alike, was but *die ewige Wiederkunft* of points of discussion and conversation that had loomed over my youth. Ever since my first years at university, when I began reading journals and magazines about contemporary politics and culture, I have probably read few combinations of five English words so much as "the end of Western civilization." Almost all writers of conservative leanings indulged in woeful and dire observations about "the end of Western civilization," most often without belief in any remedies.

Since many people whose writings I found interesting had discussed "the end of Western civilization" as a given, for a long time I accepted this proposition's basic premises; to wit, that there was something that we can clearly label as "Western civilization," that noteworthy elements of that Western civilization persisted in our times, and that we could save "Western civilization" through right action, thought, and policies. Self-assured champions of Western civilization often quoted Werner Keller's phrase "East minus West equals zero," usually to assert this idea's basic correctness, notwithstanding inevitable qualifications, bandied in thoughtful remarks, offered to this absurd assertion.

As I have studied more and as new knowledge and experiences have bowled over my previous attempts to understand history, increasingly I have come to doubt the usefulness of talking about "Western civilization" or "European civilization." To my mind, many if not most of Europe's greatest cultural achievements came in times when European political bodies still competed against other cultural realms such as the Ottomans, the Mughals, and the Chinese on terms of relative equality, and before Europeans really thought about the West or Europe as unified cultural spaces. In any event, this eternally returning discourse about Western civilization's decline seems to be the bastard child of European colonial powers' experiences as they held sway over most of the world during the past few centuries. For most commentators, the "decay" or "decadence" that worried them had more to do with political, economic, and military might than with religious, social, cultural, or spiritual achievements. Few would question or condemn sacrificing the latter for the former's sake.

In any event, the whole world's crazed reactions to the outbreak of an ill-understood and relatively mild virus in late 2019, a reaction inspired, driven, and enforced by Western civilization's collective organs of power that acted together in remarkable concert, convinced me that we would be better off trying to create new cultures and civilizations than working to resurrect a dead civilization from the walking corpses of today's zombified "Western" nation-states.

Long before I had joined the Legion, I believed that T.E. Lawrence had aptly captured in his *Seven Pillars of Wisdom* a fundamental feature of modern Western self-conceptions, one that I continue to seek to understand. To this day, I recall the forty-ninth chapter of Lawrence's work at least once a week, if not more often, which records a conversation between Lawrence and his Arab hosts one night as they encamped out in the desert under its open skies. In this conversation, Lawrence answered the question of his friend, Auda:

> "Why are the Westerners always wanting all?" provokingly said Auda. "Behind our few stars we can see God, who is not behind your millions."
> "We want the world's end, Auda."

Lawrence here uncovers a fundamental drive of Westerners, cloak it as we may in the trappings of various religions and philosophies, or now in rejection of religion altogether. Most probably given added emphasis by Christianity's tenuous victories, but already present among Europe's pre-Christian religious systems, there is in the West a drive for the world's destruction—a yearning that must not be given licence now that man has the power to destroy most of the world.

Our latent urge for self-destruction and world-destruction seems to go beyond the disenchantment and dissatisfaction with life that is universal to all men. Over the past centuries we have seen regular manifestations of such drives in our great upheavals—French revolutionaries, Bolsheviks, and National Socialists to name but a few. All wished to build a new world characterized by what they believed to be a more just or a more theologically or ideologically correct organization of society. All these movements, however, at some point of crisis relished in wanton destruction. They were all inspired by powerful visions of the world's destruction and of its end.

Whether to a whimper or a bang, it is true: we Westerners want the world's end.

LXXXIX

April 2010

Before long Easter was upon us. I had not yet received word about my request to leave the Legion, but I expected an answer any day. Owing to the regimental commander's endorsement, it was unlikely that the Legion's commanding general would deny my request, especially as it was grounded in a logic that appealed to any right-minded legionnaire. However surprised they were at my leaving behind "Great Expectations" in the United States to join the Legion, my commanders respected my choice to do so. They likewise understood that my wish to leave the Legion was not based on enduring and remarkable disappointment with the institution itself, but rather owing to restrictions imposed by the French Army's medical bureaucracy.

The decision about my future was all but a foregone conclusion, but still these were weeks of uncertainty when my fate depended on the deliberations of others whose thinking I had no power to shape. This is common enough to us all, but this was the first time for me to understand that I was in such a helpless situation. Hitherto the importance of hierarchy had remained hidden to me. My culture and my educators encouraged me to believe that we lived in a world of radical egalitarian principles, where hierarchies are largely things of the past—perhaps worthy of some nostalgia, but not things that define us. It was thanks to the Legion that I first began to understand *rôles* and forms of hierarchy, to see hierarchies previously hidden to me, and to understand that behind its easy-going pretences of levelling individualism, I had grown up in a society whose hierarchies were far more exclusive and insidious for their very invisibleness.

For Easter my friend Jean-Paul invited me to spend some of the holiday with his family. Notwithstanding his impeccable credentials in Paris, Jean-Paul had once confessed to me that he considered himself an outsider in the Métropole and that certain elements in the city would never accept him as one of their own. Seeing him for the first time in Lyon rather than in Paris, I remarked that he breathed more freely in his birthplace. I spent some time touring it by myself, but Jean-Paul took pride in showing me many parts of the city, especially *La Croix-Rousse,* from which some of his family hailed. As usual, I learned many things from Jean-Paul. As he explained to me that many politicians once had planned to raze Lyon's handsome old city to build a highway—an action stopped only by the intervention of France's Minister of Culture at the time, André Malraux—I needed no further evidence of modern society's continual temptation to embrace the insane in the name of progress and to follow the latest wisdom of popular economic and scientific theories.

Jean-Paul's immediate family revered Paul Bocuse more than any other divine or human institution. Since his earliest youth, his family—he only had one younger sister—went out together to eat at the restaurants of Michelin-starred chefs at least four times a year. Of modest means, his father and his mother sacrificed other luxuries in order to ensure that they and their children partook of France's finest tables. Jean-Paul's sister, an aspiring actress who lived in penury in Paris, once remarked to me without any hint of irony—as one would comment on the quality of bread at a local bakery or how one's neighbourhood has improved over the years—that she had grown so accustomed to restaurants of chefs with three Michelin stars that she inevitably found disappointing the creations of those chefs with only two stars. "You can immediately taste and smell the difference," she assured me.

As Jean-Paul matured as a young man, his stated ambition in life was to eat at the restaurant of every chef in France with three Michelin stars. By 2010 he had eaten at over one-third of those then in existence, of which his favourite at the time was Jean-Georges Klein's restaurant in rural Alsace. Long before meeting Jean-Paul, I had a nose for restaurants, and I took great pains to find good ones. It impressed Jean-Paul's family that I had already found by my own devices *Abel Comptoir*, one of their favourite *bouchons lyonnais*. Yet, without Jean-Paul's friendship, I would have been more inclined to view chefs with Michelin stars with suspicion rather than with keen interest, and instead to seek out unknown or obscure restaurants of populist reputations. I confess here that I owe my enduring love for *les étoilés* to Jean-Paul's almost limitless enthusiasm for them. For me, it was a meal several years later at Massimiliano Alajmo's *Le Calandre* that cemented my own esteem for the demanding system of Michelin stars. Although circumstances of life and work have long divided us, I hope one day to eat with Jean-Paul at a restaurant that we both have long coveted, but which for one reason or another neither of us has yet visited: Fontjoncouse's *L'Auberge des Vieux Puits*.

I spent much of that *triduum* at the Cathedral of Saint John the Baptist in Old Lyon, where priests celebrated the liturgies according to traditional 1962 rubrics of the Latin Rite. Such lengthy ceremonies allowed for relatively little site-seeing, and Holy Week was not the appropriate occasion to eat at one of Paul Bocuse's restaurants. On Sunday after Mass, I enjoyed a lengthy lunch with Jean-Paul's family. At table, conversation centred almost entirely on food and on chefs, only occasionally straying to past and planned holidays, and his father's upcoming months on a sailboat in the Mediterranean.

Had it not been for the Foreign Legion and for the time I had to spend with Jean-Paul, I doubt that I would have ever developed the love for Michelin-starred chefs that I keep to this day, and whose reputations I steadfastly defend against naysayers and know-it-alls.

So, when it comes to *haute cuisine*, in the Legion I lived out in a remarkable way the celebrated Latin motto: *per aspera ad astra*.

XC

April 2010

As we approached 30 April, my second Camerone in the Legion, summer's warmth finally began to infuse our early-morning formations. One morning we were no longer allowed to wear our company sweatshirts. For a few days it was unpleasant to greet the morning's chill in our skimpy summer sport uniforms, but before long we stopped noticing this. Summer was almost at hand.

In the days leading up to Camerone, preparations for the holiday's specific rites took precedence over everything else. Above all we prepared for the Camerone ceremony—a long, formal event set to strict, almost liturgical rubrics. To get our uniforms ready and to undertake repeated rehearsals for this ceremony took weeks of work for almost every legionnaire in the regiment. We also had to prepare the regimental grounds for public scrutiny. The festivities following our Camerone ceremony marked the only time of the year when citizens of Nîmes or from farther abroad were allowed to enter the regimental grounds. For the benefit of such guests, every company manned kiosks and booths that served food and drink and offered to the outside world rare glimpses into the Legion's unique culture and composition.

No regiment could go without a *crosse de Camerone*. For ours that year, the regimental commander had chosen rugged but relatively flat terrain in the Garrigues training area outside of Nîmes. It was a modest run, not exceeding twelve kilometres or so, and we undertook the race in our normal sports clothes. Among my many duties as I awaited discharge from the Legion, I served as a driver for regimental staff officers, among whom I had already gained a reputation as a legionnaire who liked to drive *de manière sportive*. That day I was assigned to drive our regiment's new deputy commander, a short, balding man who had not been with us on the deployment. He had spent a lot of time in French Guyana, and unlike our circumspect and intellectual commander, he had plastered his office with photographs of himself smeared with camouflage and engaged in various training events, missions, and operations.

The deputy commander and I spoke little during the drive to our *crosse*. In this event I did relatively well, especially considering the weight that I had gained over the deployment. Two years before I was a sorry specimen of a runner, and a year before I was a middling runner at best at the Fourth Foreign Regiment. In this *crosse* I ran past my company commander in the last kilometre of the race and ranked among the regiment's top third. This was hardly an impressive feat in general, but for me this represented a vast improvement. I had also run faster than our deputy commander, which pleased him as it showed that I was taking seriously my responsibilities as a legionnaire and staying true to the fifth article of the Legion's carefully crafted code of honour: *Soldat d'élite, tu t'entraînes avec rigueur, tu entretiens ton arme comme ton bien le plus précieux, tu as le souci constant de ta forme physique.**

Once done with the race, the deputy commander had to return to the regiment as soon as possible to dress for a lunch in Nîmes. After we parked near his office, he asked me to sit in the running car until he finished showering and changing, whereupon we would promptly leave. I had not remarked it before,

---

* French Foreign Legion, "Legionnaire's Code of Honour" (*Code d'Honneur du Légionnaire*), Article 6: "An elite soldier, you will train with rigour; you will maintain your weapon as your most precious belonging; you will have constant concern for your physical fitness."

but someone had tuned this car's radio to *France Culture*. I turned up the radio's volume.

As is customary on French radio, a woman's voice of uncommon sensuality explained the upcoming broadcast. She gave a brief history of Gustav Mahler's compositions. Since I had never taken a liking to Mahler, I did not pay much attention to her discussion of his life and of his work. Perhaps since it tickled my darker sensibilities, my ears perked at her mention of *Kindertotenlieder*. As the music began, and a mezzo-soprano began to sing the first lines of "*Nun will die Sonn' so hell aufgeh'n*," I forgot entirely my past indifference to and criticism of Mahler's work. The mezzo-soprano's voice overpowered the running diesel engine of the regimental car, a loud Peugeot, and for brief moments I lost awareness of where I was and what I was doing.

In a lifetime of enthusiastic concert going, I can think of few musical moments that have captured me so much as *France Culture*'s airing of the *Kindertotenlieder* late that morning of 29 April 2010. The only concerts that surely outdid this moment in a Peugeot were two unexpected and unexpectedly spectacular performances in Venice that I heard a few years later—one a Schubert quintet at the *Scuola di San Giovanni Battista* and the other an impromptu performance of Shostakovich's Second Piano Trio at *La Fenice*. These moved me in ways that no radio presentation ever could do. Seldom if ever has music so absorbed me, however, as it did that morning after our regimental *crosse*. The performance of "*Oft denk' ich, sie sind nur ausgegangen*" had just finished when the deputy commander returned to the vehicle in his full dress uniform. As I drove him to his lunch with the regimental commander and with other local dignitaries, we both listened in silence to "*In diesem Wetter*."

Frenchmen might take it for granted, but as a young citizen of the United States, I found this colonel's respect for culture remarkable. This unlettered type who projected images of someone who loves the terrain and his terroir did not come back into the car and demand that I lower the overpowering volume to which I had set our vehicle's radio.

Instead, he quietly asked me to drive to the next address and remained in silence, in a nod of respect to the artefact of culture, *brisé en mille éclats de voix*, to which we listened on the way to his next business.

It bears remarking that it was not I who had chosen *France Culture* for our vehicle's radio station in the first place.

XCI

April 2010

The day before Camerone, my leaders told me to report to the regimental commander the next day after our *prise d'armes* on the regimental parade grounds. Of the many military ceremonies that mark any Foreign Legion regiment's calendar, Camerone's pageantry outdoes them all. Christmas in the Legion is unique, but nonetheless a holiday shared with broader French society and with larger Christian and secular worlds. Camerone is specific to the Legion, and its week-long celebration marks the organization's high holy days. More than anything else, this holiday celebrates self-sacrifice and abandon as well as willingness to give one's life for fellow legionnaires and for the mission, as immortalized in Captain Danjou's example at Camerone itself and enjoined in the sixth article of the Legion's *code d'honneur*: *La mission est sacrée, tu l'exécutes jusqu'au bout et, s'il le faut, en opérations, au péril de ta vie.**

For the ceremony of Camerone, we all donned our full dress summer

* French Foreign Legion, "Legionnaire's Code of Honour" (*Code d'Honneur du Légionnaire*), Article 4: "The mission is sacred, and you will execute it until its accomplishment, and, if necessary in operations, risk your life to fulfil it."

uniforms. Our white shirts were freshly ironed with their distinctive creases, our kepis scrubbed to immaculate white, and the red tassels of our epaulettes combed straight. We had scrubbed and polished our boots and our rifles with care and coated our bayonets with glistening lubricants. After marching into the *place d'armes*, we stood at alternating positions of attention and of parade rest according to the orders of the officer in charge of this Foreign Legion solemnity. Once the ceremony's lengthy script finished, we marched off the regimental parade grounds to the bouncy music of "*Tiens, voilà du boudin*." Our marching was hardly perfect, but when it comes to regular combat-arms units in nations of European military traditions, Foreign Legion regiments probably have the highest standards on the parade ground. Decried as such ceremonial practices are nowadays among rank-and-file and military enthusiasts, I do believe that in the Legion they represent and foster unique attachment to tradition, and a remarkable *esprit de corps*. Foreign Legion drills and ceremonies are excellent without being obsessive, scripted but permissive of artful imperfection.

After turning in my weapon to our company armoury after the parade, I walked up to the waiting area outside of the regimental commander's office. Once informed that I could enter the room, I followed protocol by knocking on the door and asking: "*Permission d'entrer*?" I walked into the room along a prescribed path, stopped at a designated spot in front of his desk, saluted, and recited the legionnaires' formulaic presentation while standing at attention. The colonel told me to stand at ease. I understood that he had received the decision from the Legion's commanding general about my request to leave the Legion on medical grounds. As I stood before the colonel, who looked at me good-naturedly but without smiling, I knew that I stood at a proverbial fork in the road.

Here the colonel could have told me that my request was denied. In this case, I would have remained in the Legion for an additional three years. Most probably I would have deployed to Senegal, to the Ivory Coast, to Chad, and possibly back to Afghanistan. I never would have been able to finish my doctoral studies in Princeton, and never would I have been able to join the US Army. Instead of looking back fondly now at my time in the Legion after almost a decade in the US Army, perhaps I would have remained disappointed and frustrated by the experience in the Legion and by my constraints within the organization, dreaming with ill-informed regrets and with embittered longing at what could have been back in the nation of my birth.

As it was, the colonel informed me that the Legion's commanding general had approved my request to leave the Legion. His instructions were that in the coming week I should report to Aubagne to begin out-processing. He thanked me for my service to the organization and expressed his regrets about the medical constraints imposed on me when I first joined the Foreign Legion owing to mild hearing loss in my left ear.

I obtained what I had requested from the Legion, but I felt no elation at the news. It relieved me nonetheless that the waiting and uncertainty about my future had ended and that I could proceed with my budding plans to seek out a commission in the US Army as soon as possible. The colonel bade me enjoy my last Camerone at the regiment and said that he hoped to see me again one day. As it turned out, I saw him and spoke with him much more often outside the Legion than I ever did or could while within it.

At that point in my life, to leave the Legion was one of the hardest choices that I had ever made. No matter what my disappointments with the organization, to my surprise and contrary to all expectations, I found that I loved many aspects of the military vocation. Part of my motivation for joining the Foreign Legion was that I believed that every man should have some military experience, and that the Foreign Legion was one of the most extreme ways to pursue such experience in today's world. Whatever my vague ambitions about becoming an officer and my fanciful daydreaming about military glories, I did not know if I would be suited for military life and if I would find it bearable and *idoine* for me for the longer term. To leave the Legion for an uncertain future was to leave a sanctuary where I felt that I could live truly as a man, and partake of a manly life and profession, in a world where most options available to me seemed pathetic and emasculating.

Soon I would face the world again as an individual, without institutional backing and without community and fellowship with soldiers who were indeed men, whatever their individual shortcomings. This prospect of undedicated independence troubled me, and perhaps this is part of why I felt such haste to join the US Army immediately after discharge.

XCII

April 2010

A consolation of the digital age is our ability to rediscover cultural artefacts with relative ease. I first experienced this boon of internet search engines when looking for a French popular song that I heard on the radio in the summer of 2000, as I rode in my Israeli host's car from Tel-Aviv to Netanya. For years I remembered wistfully this song's melody and the often-repeated words, *sur la plage abandonée*. One day I thought to put these four words into the Google search engine and discovered that the tune of my teenage memory was Brigitte Bardot's *"La Madrague,"* which has since become one my favourite *yé-yé* songs.

Of many songs and passages from books and articles that have impressed me or whose memory has stayed with me for whatever reason, the internet has helped me to find all but one: a Soviet-era song that I heard in early 2007, playing on the radio in a supermarket near Saint Petersburg's Belinsky Bridge. The brooding chorus held me spellbound, and for a long time I believed that this song was by Vladimir Vysotsky. I have not yet found its name.

I am thankful that the internet has helped me to put together my fragments of memory and to bring cultural and artistic creations back into my life. One of these fragments was a line that I had read late one evening at The Johns Hopkins University's Hutzler Library when I was an undergraduate—an exclamation attributed to Gustave Flaubert: "*Ils sont dans le vrai*!" According to the story that I read that night in the library, the aged Flaubert, who mocked bourgeois lifestyles and mores and eschewed traditional paths of family life, was walking along the Seine one day with his niece, Caroline Commanville. They had just visited one of Caroline's friends who was surrounded by her children, and whose family exuded bourgeois wholesomeness. After this visit, Flaubert remarked to Caroline: "*Ils sont dans le vrai*." He repeated these same five words with gravity. Without the internet, "*ils sont dans le vrai*" would have remained for me a hazy memory. Thanks to the internet's search engines, however, it was not hard to rediscover Flaubert's exclamation.

I thought of this exclamation for a long time that evening of Camerone Day in 2010. After meeting with the regimental commander, I changed into my normal duty uniform and walked out to the festivities. At some point in the early evening, I ran across a legionnaire with whom I had joined the Legion some twenty-one months ago, and with whom I had also completed basic training. His *nom de guerre* was Lawrence, and we had become relatively well acquainted for several reasons. Firstly, he had remained in Aubagne with me for a while, as officers sorted our various medical issues. Second, he was from the United States, so there was a national affinity between us in this foreign environment. Third, he was one of few legionnaires taller than me in our platoon at Castelnaudary. Since the Legion made us assemble in order of height for all formal formations, we often stood next to each other and shared many chats.

From our occasional conversations over the course of the deployment, I knew that Lawrence had found a French girlfriend about whom he had grown serious. She and her parents came to the regiment for Camerone, and Lawrence enthusiastically introduced me to her. I enjoyed hearing about how they had met. After talking with this young lady at a bar in Nîmes, Lawrence, a prudent sort, knew that she would never have anything to do with him if he told her that he was in the Foreign Legion, whose soldiers' reputation among women in the city could hardly have been worse. He lied and told her that he was a foreign exchange student. Only halfway through the deployment to Afghanistan did he confess to her his secret, but by this time she had grown to like him so much that his being a legionnaire, instead of frightening her away, only made her adore him more. Although almost every non-arranged relationship between man and woman begins with some concrete deception, this was one of the more amusing examples that I have witnessed.

It was impossible to mistake how proud Lawrence's girlfriend was of him and of his recent deployment to Afghanistan. They already planned to marry. From meeting her and her parents, I could tell that she came from a respectable working-class family and that, all things being equal, she would probably make a devoted wife for Lawrence. She was undeniably charming, thin, well-built, simply dressed, and graced with thick black hair, but not quite *de mon genre.*

As Lawrence drifted away for a time to speak with passing colleagues, his girlfriend and I remained alone in conversation. She admitted to me that she would never have had anything to do with Lawrence had she known at first that he was a legionnaire, but now she was actively seeking out good-natured and handsome legionnaires for her own friends. She entreated me to come out one evening soon to meet one of her friends whom, she promised, I would find beautiful and who would surely find me handsome and interesting. After promising to meet her and Lawrence again, we parted ways that evening—forever. I did not tell her, Lawrence, or anyone else at the regiment that I would be leaving early the next week for Aubagne, where my service in the Foreign Legion would end honourably, but well before its customary five-year term.

As I left Lawrence and his girlfriend, embracing and ogling each other naïvely and filled with undaunted confidence about their future together, I looked back at them and reflected on vaguely remembered images from a short poem by Paul Verlaine: a park, a pedestal in the shade, an alley filled with leaves and rubbish, and the words: *un avenir solitaire et fatal.*

And I mused on Lawrence and his girlfriend: "*Ils sont dans le vrai!*"

XCIII

May 2010

Late one morning in the first week of May, after a weekend of modest Camerone celebrations and thoughtful walks through Nîmes, I made my way to Aubagne. Father Gaël was kind enough to store several duffle bags of my belongings at his apartment in Nîmes until I could figure out how to ship them to the United States. My superiors from the regiment arranged to give me a ride to Aubagne in one of the regiment's vehicles, and soon I was at the *maison mère* for out-processing. At Aubagne, I walked into its ordinary for the first time since I had been in the selection process not even two years before this. As I ate dinner alone, I watched lines of *engagés volontaires* busy with *corvée*, thinking back to those recent days when I was in their shoes.

The next day I began the administrative process of leaving the Legion. As this process began, I ran across an intimidating Moldovan corporal who was at Aubagne when I joined the Legion. Blond-haired, enormously built, and with ominously pointed canines, in August 2008 he had filled me with anxiety and awe. He did not remember me as we ran across each other while drinking coffee at a company bar that morning, but the sight of him filled me with memories of the fears, doubts, and uncertainties that had once absorbed me. Whereas once I had imagined fantastical things about his experiences and past, now I could rather easily guess that he was either injured, on his way out of the Legion, or else in some administrative or disciplinary trouble—otherwise he would not have been at Aubagne.

As I went to the first office to begin the paperwork that would sanction my departure, the *caporal-chef* in charge of this procedure was curious about why I had asked to leave the Legion before the end of my contract, and even more nonplussed about why the Legion's commander had approved such an outlandish request. Once he saw my medical file and the restrictions that had been placed on me, however, he immediately understood and even congratulated me for having the courage to take steps to leave the Legion.

The Legion always shows tact and considerable respect to its legionnaires who have served their five-year contracts *avec honneur et fidelité*. As I proceeded with the paperwork, I often joined five corporals who were likewise in the process of leaving the Foreign Legion. One of these was a Mexican corporal whom I had known from Castelnaudary. He was surprised to see me departing the Legion early, but he wished me luck. Together our small group visited the Legion's museum, where we beheld for ourselves the fabled wooden hand of Captain Jean Danjou. We were given the whole afternoon to visit the museum, and I appreciated the chance to learn more about the organization's history and to see many of its relics from decades past.

To me it was important to leave the Legion in good standing, so I took pains to ensure that I would receive its official discharge certificate, or *certificat de bonne conduite*. Usually this was given to legionnaires who had completed their five-year contract, and it entitled them to seek permanent residency, and eventually citizenship, in any territory belonging to the French Republic. Given my unusual circumstances, and since commanders knew that I had already turned down the possibility to pursue French citizenship quickly within the Legion, the Legion honoured my request to give me a *certificat de bonne conduite*. A few months later I received this document in the mail in the United States. It was a carefully made certificate on fine paper that included many flourishes painted by hand, crafted by legionnaires whose main job it was to make these attestations.

The corporals who had finished their contracts received one-way train tickets to any destination of their choosing within Europe, and all their military licences and qualifications were converted to civilian equivalents. The Legion took pains to ensure that they were ready for integration back into civilian life after five years of service, and in France if they chose to remain there.

My departure was different. Unlike the corporals, there was no formal ceremony to honour my end of service, no fanfare or meeting with the Legion's commanding general, who took time to greet every departing legionnaire who had finished his five-year contract and to wish him well. Instead, one morning I signed a sheet of paper, took off my Legion combat uniform, dressed in civilian clothes, and walked out of the base and onto the roadway that led down to Aubagne. Before doing so I took one last look at Aubagne's massive *place d'armes* and admired its *monuments aux morts*.

It was an unclimactic and quiet ending to what was for me a life-changing engagement, and the last time that I have seen the *maison mère*.

As I walked down to Aubagne, I passed places that jogged memories of my first walk to the Legion's *maison mère*, including the Red Lion pub and the expansive sports park where a *caporal-chef* had once made us new recruits do push-ups in front of laughing schoolgirls from the nearby *Lycée Joliot-Curie*. Since I had never actually visited Aubagne, I took the afternoon to walk through its centre and to visit the city for which we recruits had once longed when confined to our enclosed pen at the First Foreign Regiment. Caged, desirously we had looked southward toward the city, framed by the mountains behind it that were decked with cedars and maritime pines.

Now a civilian, I took the train back to Nîmes to meet Father Gaël. For the next ten days he hosted me at his apartment in Nîmes and also at his country house at Montréal in the Aude, as I planned my return to Princeton before June. Without his kindness and generosity, the process of leaving the Legion would have been much more difficult, and I remain thankful to him.

XCIV

May 2010

I had spent quite a bit of time with Father Gaël in Afghanistan, but in France I came to know him in his native element. He kept a small apartment in Nîmes near the arena, which I found in a state of disorder that would have been scandalous to the most incorrigible bachelors. A cat, left free to run wild indoors, ensured that almost every surface in the apartment was covered with its hair.

Before this time with Father Gaël, I had never taken to the habit of drinking pastis with a splash of soda before dinner, but thanks to his influence I began and kept up the practice until I wearied of pastis' inexplicable ability to intoxicate me more readily than other liquors. During dinner with Father Gaël, I enjoyed listening to countless stories about his life as an Army chaplain, which, over almost thirty years of military service, had taken him throughout former French colonial possessions. Some of his stories were so scandalous that I do not really believe them today, even if they might have been true. One of my favourites was his tale from the island of Réunion, about how he had rescued an intoxicated bishop who had passed out in a swimming pool during a party and almost drowned.

One story that I did believe was Father Gaël's tale about a party in Paris, whose description conjured up images of Monsieur de Charlus *en fête*. It turned out that a younger brother of Father Gaël was an accomplished Parisian *coiffeur* who had embraced a metropolitan lifestyle that prized participation in the capital's many social activities for those with tastes for homosexual licence. Divergent as these two siblings' characters were, Father Gaël's brother invited him to attend a large and libertine *soirée*, and Father Gaël accepted the invitation. At this party Father Gaël encountered an *intégriste* Catholic officer from the Foreign Legion—a father of five and one with whom he often bickered owing to this officer's angry espousal of traditionalist Catholicism and not altogether uncommon blend of royalist and fascist political ideas. Father Gaël upbraided this officer for his hypocrisy, but never mentioned the episode to anyone at their regiment.

In this and in similar ways, Father Gaël filled whole evenings with continuous tales of scandal, intrigue, and gossip, which betrayed his taste for the salacious as well as valuable insights into human weaknesses, dispositions, and needs.

Owing to his vast experience as a confessor and counsellor to military wives across the world, Father Gaël had experienced thoughts about the female psyche. Despite his flamboyant airs, he was only attracted to women, and I believe that he had several intimate associations with women before seminary. I never asked about temptations after his ordination, but I have no reason to think that he would ever have broken his vows. He did tell me one thing that I had hitherto never heard about women, and that has since coloured and shaped my understanding of their desires and of their actions. He summed up his theory in one sentence: *Elles ont besoin d'éblouir*.

His basic theory was that no matter what her station in life, every respectable and well-appointed woman needs a means to dazzle others, to shine before them, and to earn their admiration. To his mind, a woman with no means of "dazzling" would invariably become an unhappy and disordered woman, mother, and wife. Since that day I have never forgotten these words, nor have I ever met a sensible woman to whom his theory did not apply. I imagine that I must have read similar observations in a novel or work of psychology over the years, but it was not until those dinners with Father Gaël that I took the idea seriously.

During these ten days I also enjoyed taking several day trips with Father Gaël throughout the surrounding area, as we drove through the Gard and visited Saint-Gilles and Saintes-Maries-de-la-Mère in the Camargue. At Father Gaël's house in Montréal, we enjoyed dinners with his delightful neighbours. For Sunday lunch we ate one of the village of Bram's awe-inspiring *cassoulets*, caressed by a splendid red wine from Fitou. Together we also travelled to Mirepoix, where I had once walked to attend Mass while working at the *ferme du Cuin*, and enjoyed several glasses of Suze on its main square.

On one of these mornings I ran through Montréal, whose population was smaller in 2010 than it had been at any point over the past millennium. As I traversed this small town that intersects a route of Saint James Way, I stopped in its *Jardin Jean Vidal* and admired its *monuments aux morts*. Before joining the Legion, I probably would have walked by such a monument without giving it a second thought. After even twenty-one months of military service, however, to do so was impossible for me. As I examined its construction and its mournful dedication *à nos héros victorieux*, I read through all the names of the village's men who died during the Great War from 1914 to 1918. It occurred to me to count the names on this commemorative plaque. They totalled 134. Given that the village's population was about 2000 in 1914, I guessed that close to half of its male population from eighteen to thirty had perished in the Great War.

Whenever I hear bombastic, ill-informed criticisms of France's military history, I almost immediately think back to this monument and to that day in Montréal when I understood for the first time how much the Great War had devastated France and gutted its villages of their lifeblood, the young men who would have one day been its farmers, fathers, priests, professionals, and leaders.

On this dour list were two military chaplains. Ten days with Father Gaël had convinced me that being a military chaplain was indeed one of the world's most interesting jobs, as it conjoined two of Baudelaire's three professions—poet, priest, and soldier—in which man can realize his greatness.

XCV

May 2010

Like so many others before and after him, Father Gaël wanted to find me a wife, or at least he wanted to see me in love. For this reason, when I was still a legionnaire, he invited me to several events where he felt sure that I might attract the attention of the women present. Had I stayed in France that summer under Father Gaël's tutelage, he would have embroiled me.

It was my ambition and *Wanderlust* that spoiled his plots. Owing to my few involvements with women and general reluctance to entertain new ones, many associates believe that I have impossible expectations that have kept me from marriage. I argue instead that I have only wanted what every man wants: someone beautiful to me, intelligent, responsible, prudent, and plausibly virginal. Buxomness has never been a need for me, and I only demand excellent proportionality and comely thighs. I know for a fact that there are millions of such women in the world, even in times of supposed sexual deviance—deviance whose lack of true decadence and absurd prurience have always shocked me more than any of its fleshly transgressions. Also, from my earliest years I have been willing to put aside some of my standards of feminine beauty, admittedly classical and high, for Semitic women of superior wit, cosmopolitanism, and obedience, so long as their nose be celestial or button, their builds dainty, and their hair dark and luxuriant. Here I confess to talking of women like Pechorin did, as one would of an English horse. In so doing I am only showing the responsibility that any self-respecting *shadchan* or pious continental aristocrat with care for his family would enjoin. With them and Pechorin, I count myself in kindred company.

It is not expectations of the daughters of men that have kept me from wedding, I think, but rather a combination of circumstances that make finding a suitable spouse most unlikely unless I were to make this search my foremost business for at least a year—something not in my character. All the same, given enough time and opportunity, Father Gaël would probably have been successful in his matchmaking quests. For he had privileged access to one feminine demographic that bewitched me in those years—French *bourgeoises*.

I do not know the cause of their former powers over me. Perhaps it was the tang of illicitness that accompanies ideas of congress with a class enemy. In any event, such unquestionable powers were in evidence one evening shortly after my departure from the Legion, when Father Gaël invited me for drinks with some of his friends at a lousy and loud "Irish" bar near the centre of Nîmes.

It turned out that one of his friends was none other than our regiment's chief operations officer, whom I had got to know some during the deployment to Afghanistan. I admired him almost as much as our regimental commander, even if he had kept us from roasting our prized pig on the supposed grounds of a former mosque at FOB Tora. From conversations in Afghanistan, I knew that he had five children and that he positively doted on his wife.

When I met his wife that evening, I understood his unslaked desire for the bride of his youth. I do not remember her name, but she was a spectacular specimen of a woman. The second couple comprised a French Navy pilot and his equally stunning wife, Camille.

The six of us spent much of that evening talking over bad drinks. The two *bourgeoises* probed me for comparisons between the Anglo-Saxon cultures of my upbringing and their own *aisé* French world. The most obvious comparison to make was the only one that I did not make, even if I implied it to them as much as I could without violating my sense of good taste.

Both in their middling or late thirties, these two women at table had each given birth to five or more children. Yet their bodies and their faces appeared to me more vigorous, youthful, and attractive than those of most European women in their twenties. The little make-up that they wore was applied to remain unseen. Their hair, if artificially coloured, was tinted with utmost discretion. Their clothes were casual but elegant and their demeanour combined feminine submissiveness and tenderness with confidence and aplomb. Had I given myself licence, I could easily have felt as much desire for these mature mothers as for nubile young creatures in their early twenties. Whereas many women from elsewhere become shadows of their former selves by their late thirties, at the same ages these two French women before me seemed not even to have reached the peak of their feminine beauty.

Far be it from me to praise without reservation the French *bourgeoise*. There are many faults to them, as our two lovely examples too willingly confessed in their seducing self-criticism that merged obligatory French irony with utter confidence about their attractiveness. Of all such faults, perhaps their provincialism is the most remarkable—something that my Bolivian godfather learned too well when he married into the family of Maxime Real del Sarte, the sculptor of dozens of *monuments aux morts* in France and a devoted partisan of *Action Française*.

The following Sunday began with a Mass in Montpellier, where the Archbishop of the French Armed Services presided over the confirmations of the children of military officers, including Camille's eldest daughter. After the ceremony we gathered together at the pilot's house. As the hours-long festive lunch began, the eldest daughter was the centre of attention. She blushed charmingly as she drank her first glass of champagne with us to celebrate her confirmation.

I spent most of the afternoon in conversation with Camille's parents. It was a day of that bourgeois wholesomeness that unsettled Flaubert toward his life's end. At some point Camille walked outside with several other ladies to enjoy a Sunday cigarette in the afternoon's sunlight, in which her blonde hair glistened.

XCVI

May 2010

During my stay with Father Gaël, at last I had the chance to enjoy Nîmes' *Feria*. Like many surviving Roman amphitheatres, the well-kept structure in Nîmes remains in use throughout the year and hosts concerts, civic events, and occasional Foreign Legion *prises d'armes*. The events of the *Feria* bring bullfighters from across Spain to Nîmes, whose artful struggles make for some of this arena's most remarkable events—even if they no longer slay the bulls. I spent an afternoon watching these fights before I left Nîmes to travel for several weeks in Italy, which I had not visited since joining the Foreign Legion.

I had already bought my aeroplane tickets to go back to the United States in the middle of June. In the meantime, in my short life I had yet to see Northern Italy's renowned cities, so I took needed steps to make right this wrong before leaving Europe. From Nîmes I went to Marseilles and then to Nice, where I took the train to Ventimiglia, which skirts the coast.

As soon as I arrived in Ventimiglia, I immediately recognized the train signs and standardized looks of the Italian *Ferrovia Statale*. Glad to be back in Italy, I resolved at that time to try, as an experiment, to speak only Italian throughout the coming weeks. To steel me in this resolve, I had several French-published books to help me to learn Italian. I had also brought several books about Renaissance painting, about which I wished to learn as much as possible while visiting many noted museums throughout Northern Italy.

After arriving in Genoa, I settled into a hotel near the train station. Money was not an object, since I had saved plenty of it during our deployment, but back then I was wont to travel with frugality. As I walked from the train station toward the city centre, one of the first churches at which I stopped impressed me in that it clearly offered liturgies and, more exceptionally still, all other Roman Catholic sacraments, according to the forms in use worldwide until the liturgical reforms implemented after the Second Vatican Council. As I walked through many churches that evening, I remarked that there was a surprising number of them that offered Mass in this extraordinary form, which made me suspect that the local bishop was an unusual Italian prelate, who used all tools at his disposal to support traditional liturgical forms and those attached to them.

The city was lively that evening. By a happy coincidence, I had come to Genoa on the "night of museums," the one night in the year when most of the city's museums and churches remain open into the next morning with free entrance to the public. By midnight I had seen so many paintings by Paris Bordone in so many palaces that I could never hope to forget his name. After spending the night with remnants of *Cinquecento* glories, I went back to my hotel and prepared to board a train for Florence the next day.

The following morning I arrived at Florence's *Santa Maria Novella* train station and walked to my tidy rooms at a *casa per ferie* in a quiet neighbourhood just north of *Piazzale Libertà*. In Florence I spent the next week visiting the great museums that later became so familiar to me when I lived in the city a few years later. I spent at least part of every day at the *Uffizi*, and of all Florence's museums I grew especially fond of the *Palazzo Pitti*. In Florence I fed that greedy appetite for plastic arts that I had whetted in the Foreign Legion, and quickly I gained a visual appreciation of the unique characteristics of Florentine painting. It was also during this week that I developed a lifelong dislike of Andrea del Sarto,

one that I still cannot explain.

I spent Sunday in Florence and went to Mass in the extraordinary form at the church of the *Ognissanti*. As I sat down in the pews, I did not take the time to look at the church's artwork. It was only as I looked up to my right during prayers at Mass that I saw Sandro Botticelli's fresco of Saint Augustine. At first I did not know whose fresco it was, but it seized my attention as few frescoes have ever done. It did not surprise me to learn that this was Botticelli's work as I spent half an hour after Mass admiring it as well as the pendant fresco of Saint Jerome by Domenico Ghirlandaio, on the opposite side of the nave.

I took the days slowly and made sure to eat at places recommended by one of my Tuscan friends who was a Dante specialist. I also made day trips to Pisa, Lucca, Sienna, and other areas easily reached by train. And last, I made it a point to visit San Gimignano. Since my prior trips to Italy had centred on Rome and its surroundings, my exposure to the richness and variety of Italian cuisine remained limited. During these days in Florence, therefore, it was hard for me to make heads or tails of the food. To walk into good Italian restaurants was still as challenging to me as would be walking into the *Uffizi* with little knowledge of Renaissance history and painting. Of course, one can appreciate the beauty and the goodness of its collected works, but without context it is hard to anchor these in one's memory.

As impactful as all these visits to cultural landmarks were, few matched the life-changing importance of my first proper Italian *aperitivo* at *Caffè Rivoire*. In those days Rivoire's *capo barman* was still Lucca Picchi, whose passion for the Negroni is unmatched. There I had my first Negroni cocktail, made by Signor Picchi's own hands, out of Campari, Cocchi Americano, and Bombay Sapphire gin. I knew little about cocktails at the time. This was my introduction, and since that day the Negroni has been my favourite mixed drink.

XCVII

June 2010

Until I started preparations to join the French Foreign Legion in 2007, I had not gone jogging or running since I quit all sports at the age of sixteen. My twenty-one months of service in the Legion left me, however, with a need to run every day simply to feel at ease.

It was in menacing, rainy mornings in the countryside of the Aude in autumn, in its almost Tuscan colours in summer, on Marseilles' *corniche* and Canebière, and in the Pyrenees, in the dusty fog of Kaboul, and in Surobi's unkempt beauties, in sunny mornings in the Gard's countryside, and in Nîmes' discrete gardens—it was in all these places and more that running became a morning rite for me, as obligatory as brushing my teeth, showering, or shaving.

Although I had just left the Legion, I kept to this rite with obsessive rigidity. To this day, I still put this rite over my friends, my family, and many pressing obligations. I left the Foreign Legion over a decade ago, but I still need my morning runs, where memories of what I perceive passing by me fade into the almost dreaming state of my organs of perception, still foggy from sleep. To these soft consciences I add the recitation of a Rosary, prayers interrupted by immediate impressions and by the flux between memories, perceptions, and imagination. In this way, every morning becomes for me a crossroad of time where the past, each moment, and the future unveil themselves to me with such speed that I cannot anchor myself in one dimension. In this state of entwined and interacting memories and impressions:

> *...tout est fécond, tout est dangereux, et on peut faire d'aussi précieuses découvertes que dans les Pensées de Pascal dans une réclame pour un savon.**

In unfathomed ways the memory of each run joins a pool of all those past. Having spent my mornings running in cities and countrysides worldwide, memories of them have gathered into a store that deepens with every run, and from which I fuel my actions each day. In this way all my morning runs shape my daily consciousness as it develops into wakefulness.

In Florence I began the habit of running through the centres of Italy's great cities, whereby I have discovered so many churches, historical sites, and restaurants that otherwise I never would have seen or known to visit. I took this practice with me when I travelled to Verona, and enjoyed my morning runs along the River Adige.

Based at a bed and breakfast in Verona, I took trains to visit many nearby cities about which I had so often read. One of these first trips was to Trento in order to see where its fateful council took place. The Council of Trent loomed large both in my studies as well as in my own religious practice and attitudes, so it was not without some awe that I walked into the rooms where it took place, and where the council's many leaders and fathers shaped the future of the Roman Catholic Church for the next five centuries.

---

* Marcel Proust, *Albertine disparue*: "At a certain age our memories become so entwined with each other that what one is thinking about, or the book that one is reading, has almost no importance . . . everything is fruitful, everything is dangerous, and one can make important discoveries in an advertisement for soap as easily as in Pascal's *Thoughts*."

About the middle of this week, one morning I took a regional train to Venice for a day trip. I had travelled to this city for the first time in late summer 2001. Of this first trip I had only bad memories, as I was exhausted after a night journey from Vienna and taken aback at Venice's light, noise, and crowds in late August.

Nine years later, as I walked out of Santa Lucia Station for the second time in my life, a monumental advertisement for the fashion designer Michael Kors covered the façade of the church of San Simeone Piccolo, the only parish in the city at the time that regularly offered all Roman Catholic sacraments according to the extraordinary form of the Latin Rite. From the station I walked through the city for much of the day, taking care to visit the one square behind the *Accademia* that I remembered from my first visit. I did not know the square's name, but it was easy enough to find it and to uncover its identity after wandering about *Dorsoduro*—it was the *Campo di Sant'Agnese*. Here I sat down on the same bench where I had sat nine years before and admired this *Campo*, one of several in Venice without any shops.

I spent the afternoon wandering about this part of the city. Of all the paintings that I saw that day in Venice's churches, it was Titian's *Descent of the Holy Ghost* in Longhena's church of the *Salute* that impressed me the most, recalling as it did the recent Pentecost that I had spent with Father Gaël and bourgeois French families.

I could not have foreseen how important Venice would become to me once I went back to it for the third time, in December 2011, to live at the Cini Foundation's residence on the *Isola di San Giorgio*. On my second visit in 2010, I had no reason to imagine that I would have the chance to return to Venice soon, and I regretted not having visited the *Accademia* and the Ducal Palace.

After the week in Verona, I took a train to Bologna to spend one night in the city, since I would be taking a morning train that would lead me back to Nîmes. After touring the porticoes of this university town the day before my departure for France, I was standing near the intersection of Via Giacomo Matteotti and Via de' Carracci when I saw a man with plentiful tattoos bestriding a Harley-Davidson motorcycle. I cannot explain why I took notice of a tattooed man on a motorcycle—a common enough sight. Yet something compelled me to examine his tattoos carefully as he stopped at a traffic light.

I barely had the time to make out that his arms were covered with tattoos from the Foreign Legion before the traffic lights changed colour and he sped off.

XCVIII

June 2010

By this trip's end I was able to carry out most daily business in Italian, and it was with some regret that I boarded the train in Bologna which began my journey back to France. Once at Nîmes, I spent only a few nights to prepare and to collect my bags at Father Gaël's before leaving for Paris, and thence for Princeton. Father Gaël was pleased that I had brought him back a subtly embroidered cassock from Florence's well-known vestment-maker, *Ceruti*. We shared a few last dinners before I made my way to the United States.

In Paris, I stayed for several days with Jean-Paul. It was with subdued ruefulness that we discussed my premature departure from the Legion. Such disappointment aside, he was glad that I would be continuing my doctoral studies at Princeton, if sceptical about my stated plans to join the US Army. We arranged for him to visit me in the United States, as he had already planned to spend two weeks in New York City and on the North American East Coast later that summer.

During those few days in Paris, I had two other meetings. One of these was with a young assistant professor at the business school in Fontainebleau whom

I knew from Princeton, and who had once confirmed me in my quest to join the Legion with tales of his time as an *aspirant* at the Legion's First Foreign Cavalry Regiment. After twenty-one months of service, I understood how delicate his situation in the Foreign Legion was as an *aspirant* from the *École Polytechnique*. As we met over coffee near *Place d'Italie*, he, too, was disappointed to learn that I was leaving the Legion. As we ended our conversation, I mused about the possibility of my coming back to the Foreign Legion in the future. He declared that this possibility seemed most unlikely.

The second meeting was with René, founder of Radio Surobi. One evening I joined him at a wine bar in Montmartre, from which we walked up the hill to a restaurant close to *Sacré-Coeur*. I had few expectations of this meal, but it turned out to be one of the more interesting ones that I have had in Paris.

At table I was seated next to a man in his eighties. He was in Paris visiting his daughter, one of René's friends. This man of posh British origins was born in Hong Kong and had spent his whole life in Asia, aside from his few years at one of England's ancient universities. As dinner progressed, I sat almost spellbound by his stories about travels throughout Asia and especially in China. I knew little about China's modern and ancient history, and his studied observations about China's linguistic and ethnic diversity impressed me so much that they color my views of that great country even today.

At dinner I also had the chance to meet René's girlfriend, a German woman of remarkable beauty who had left behind her career in Germany to be in Paris with René and with her son by a different man. After so many months with conservative officers in Afghanistan, René joked to me about his "living in sin" with his girlfriend and invited me to their wedding scheduled to take place the next year, by which act he would "regularize his canonical situation."

René's experience with the Legion had changed him. He had already volunteered to go back to Afghanistan to continue mentoring his team at Radio Surobi, which still received support from the commander of the Second Foreign Parachute Regiment who was then in charge of France's main task force in Afghanistan. Like so many of us, René believed in his work and in its goodness, and he wanted to continue doing something that he thought would help the peoples of those valleys near Surobi.

Unlike most of us, while in Afghanistan, René had prolonged daily contacts with his Afghan reporters; he knew their families, and he kept up with news about their well-being and about the valley. Later that summer he went back to Afghanistan for a time. He did his best to keep Radio Surobi alive and true to its founding principles for as long as he could. He succeeded in doing so for a few years, I think, before the French made it clear that they were leaving Afghanistan. I believe that Radio Surobi had already lost its unique character before the French handed over FOB Tora to units of the Afghan National Army.

After these few days in the Métropole, I flew back to the United States, landing in Newark. I arrived at Princeton in the middle of the night and walked to its security department, where the keys to a new apartment awaited me. From there I went to this apartment, my residence for that coming academic year, within a house next to where I had once lived on University Place.

Before going to sleep I walked through the campus grounds, quiet and deserted since most students had already left for the summer. Three years before, my efforts to join the French Foreign Legion began as determined dreams in these very places. Since then, I had successfully enlisted in the organization and adapted to it, living and working within what was reputed to be one of the world's most extreme and demanding military environments. Contrary to my expectations, I had grown to love the profession of arms.

What had the past twenty-one months done to me? What remained of the graduate student who had walked these grounds at night so many times before, usually brooding and at times intoxicated? Where would my newfound drive to join the United States military take me? Would my efforts be successful? Had I taken the right choice to leave the Foreign Legion?

As such questions floated through my tired mind while walking the campus' well-lit, faux-gothic grounds, I could repeat to myself in earnest that unofficial motto of the Legion: *Je ne regrette rien.*

XCIX

June–September 2010

In June 2008, I had signed out of Princeton's Graduate School at its administrative building, an idiosyncratic, white-stuccoed building in the form of a Greek temple. Since that month I had been on "leave of absence." The week after my arrival at Princeton's campus in summer 2010, I walked through the same building's six Ionic columns and signed back into Princeton University. On this occasion I sat down briefly with the Graduate School's dean. He appeared perplexed about what I had been doing over the past two years, but he welcomed me and wished me all success in my renewed studies.

My first step to renew my doctoral studies was to finish the history faculty's general examinations. These examinations were relatively straightforward events, but they still needed much preparation. For each of three separate examinations I had to read at least one hundred documents and scholarly books, and even more articles. After speaking with my professor, I chose to take general examinations in three fields: Erasmus of Rotterdam and the Northern European Renaissance, Julius Caesar and his *Commentaries on the Gallic Wars,* and the Florentine Renaissance. We devised a plan for my preparatory studies, and I began work.

That summer I had time for little else aside from studying. I did, however, continue exercising with the goal of losing weight that I had inadvertently gained in the Foreign Legion. I bought an electronic scale, and I began weighing myself daily. Before leaving France, I had bought two books about training for marathons, as recommended by the Hungarian *caporal-chef* who was my supervisor in Afghanistan and in Nîmes. At Princeton I began training according to these manuals. It was over these three months at Princeton that I came to understand my body and my limitations as a runner. I would never become one of great speed, but I did have remarkable capabilities of endurance.

In addition to running, I began lifting weights again carefully at Princeton's athletic facilities. Over these three months I whittled my weight down from eighty-six kilogrammes to approximately seventy-eight kilogrammes, and then to seventy-five kilogrammes. Once at these levels I made a pact with myself never to exceed eighty kilogrammes, whatever it might take to remain under this threshold. To do so over the past decade has required daily monitoring and the careful, progressive adjustment of my diet to the greater exclusion of calories and the gradual incorporation of what we now call "intermittent fasting."

Since that summer I have kept to my goal of not weighing more than eighty kilogrammes for any extended period. This *idée fixe* has created an all but constant struggle for me, but a productive one. The patterns and the expectations that I set for myself that summer in 2010 are the same that regulate my exercise regimes and dieting today. If I ever weigh more than eighty kilogrammes, my heart and my spirit are not at peace until I see a lesser number on the scale. Because of my obsessive attention to this number, many have told me that I have what are labelled "eating disorders," or perhaps a different psychological condition. At first, I found such observations perplexing, coming as they usually did from overweight people. I have since learnt to accept such amateur diagnoses with tact and thankfulness for whatever "eating disorders" keep me thin and in relatively good physical shape for my age.

That quiet summer was a blessed one, in which I fashioned what is for me the most productive possible rhythm of life. I liked to claim, with some fancifulness, that this rhythm was based on older ways of living common in Rome and in the Vatican before prevailing "global" customs managed to supress characteristic local ways of organizing daily life. Today Southern Italy, Spain, and a few Greek islands are the main bastions of resistance to these destructive trends.

To follow this rhythm, I woke up every morning about five o'clock and took a few hours to read and to study as my consciousness gradually returned to me. About seven o'clock, I went out to run for about ninety minutes, depending on the exercise programme specific to that day. After stretching and showering, I continued studying at the university's Firestone Library until the early afternoon. I took a small lunch at one of Princeton's colleges, usually Rockefeller College or Mathey College, before heading back to my room for a substantial siesta. After this I went back to Firestone and I read until about 1930, when I would go into the town of Princeton for dinner. Thereafter I studied until midnight.

As I built this rhythm, I found that something had changed my mind and my spirit in remarkable ways. Two years before I found the luxuries of life at Princeton uninteresting and deadening. Study though I did, these studies did not fill me with curiosity or respect, but rather had led me to unpierceable walls of the mind, into which I rammed my head ever more desperately with each passing month. Twenty-one months in the Legion had razed these walls. I had learnt to love to study again, and never again would I take for granted the enviable opportunity to spend hours, days, weeks, and months devoted wholly to reading classical and Renaissance texts. Shoved back into a world of books, I devoured these with an enthusiasm that I had lost during my time at Oxford.

By early September I was ready for my general examinations. One Monday morning I walked to the history faculty and picked up my tests. These comprised nine questions, three about each of my "fields." Over the next week I spent all day in my room writing responses to one question for each field, taking breaks only to eat, to go for morning runs, and to sleep. I turned in the examinations that Friday. The next Monday I learned that I had passed them.

I was then free to begin a new chapter of my life—one rooted in Italy.

C

September 2010

With my general examinations complete, I turned my attention toward trying to join the US Army. I did not know anyone in the Army, so I did what anyone else in my situation would probably have done—I travelled to the nearest Army recruitment centre in downtown Trenton, New Jersey.

An Army recruiter greeted me. He was a pudgy black man in his late thirties. To my legionnaire's eyes, his baggy combat uniform, made of the "Universal Camouflage Pattern" used by the US Army at that time, looked like pajamas. I found his boots sloppy and his overall appearance unkempt. I spoke to him about my wish to join the infantry and to become an officer by going to Officer Candidate School. He admitted that he knew little about the process of recruiting officers. Moreover, he did not care to learn more about it since officer recruitment was such a small fraction of his office's activity. In any event, he told me that I would have to go to Army basic training no matter what path I chose, so he helped me to begin the process of enlistment.

The recruiter warned me about US Army basic training, which, he assured me, would "test my limits." I knew little about the US military, but I doubted that its basic training could even approach the Legion's "limits." Already I worried that my experience with this recruiter would not end well.

One evening we travelled to a lifeless hotel near Fort Dix, where the next day I would join other recruits at the base's Military Entrance Processing Station (MEPS) for initial medical tests. I shared a room that evening with a recent Princeton graduate, that Princeton Latinist's son who thirsted for the thrills of combat.

When I began the medical examinations at MEPS the next day, I was nervous about my hearing loss, which might create problems with the US Army. I was hopeful, however, that I could get a waiver for this issue since standards for hearing in the US Army at that time were less rigorous than they were in the Foreign Legion. Otherwise, I did not expect any problems since I had undergone many thorough medical tests in the Legion.

My medical in-processing did not last more than half an hour. Upon my arrival at MEPS, the staff made me fill out a form filled with general questions about my medical history. At this time, I did not know that most official forms of the US military bureaucracy encourage dissembling or outright lying.

One of the questions on the form asked if I had ever been "hospitalized" or treated in an "emergency room" at hospital. I answered this question truthfully, noting that I had been to emergency rooms twice in my life. One of these occasions was when I was about five years old. I was walking through the woods in East Texas with my brother. By chance he hacked through a nest of hornets with a machete. In the ensuing chaos several dozen hornets stung me. Out of precaution, my parents took me to the nearest emergency room, where a doctor saw me, said that I was fine, and told my parents to give me a simple antihistamine that one could buy from any grocer. The second occasion was when, as a young boy, I crashed into a tree while recklessly riding an off-road vehicle with dubious brakes. I badly cut my head, which needed stitches.

Soon after submitting this form, I was called into an office to meet with a medic. He was alarmed at my reported "bee stings" and said that he would have to bring me to a MEPS doctor. According to him, the fact that I had reported hospitalization owing to "bee stings" on my intake form would disqualify me from service in the US Army.

In less than an hour I was back in my recruiter's car. He was exasperated that I had answered truthfully on the intake forms at this MEPS. He told me that one of the station's doctors had reviewed these forms and had declared me medically unfit for enlistment in the US Army owing to my hospitalization for "bee stings" when I was five years old. My only option now, he informed me, was to begin the lengthy and painful process of requesting a waiver for my allergies to "bee stings." He clearly did not want to undertake this process since he knew how much time it would entail.

I had no allergies to bees, and in any event the reported episode from my childhood had involved hornets, not bees. I found this whole situation hard to believe and as ridiculous as anything that I could have read in *Catch-22.*

Would my aspirations to obtain a commission as an Army officer, for which I had taken the painful decision to leave the Foreign Legion, be thwarted by this ridiculous episode about "bee stings"?

Back in my room at Princeton by that afternoon, I did not know what to do, or what I could do, to continue pursuing an officer's commission. Over the prior two years, the Foreign Legion had in many respects started to become part of my identify and of my being, and I had left behind this newfound *patrie* and France to join the military in the nation of my birth. Now I was faced with the reality that the US military would probably reject me for childhood "bee stings."

As it turned out, I found ways to circumvent this roadblock thanks to Princeton University's Reserve Officers Training Corps, through which I was able to earn a commission in 2012 and to begin an Army career.

A decade later, after much adventure, good fortune, and tribulation across the world as an officer in the US Army infantry, I resigned my commission and moved to Jerusalem. Abiding love for this city was my only youthful enchantment to survive the Foreign Legion and the psychic and spiritual consequences of my enlistment.

CONCLUSION

"The world is filled with males. It needs men."

I do not remember the priest's exact words from the other side of the confessional's grille in Tallinn's Saint Peter and Saint Paul Cathedral. His exhortation to this effect, however, inspired me such that confession with this unknown priest ranks among the three most remarkable of my life.

The first of these was with a traditionalist priest in Paris, who took no pains to avoid appearances of *gourmandise* during sales of oysters and other foodstuffs that took place after Sunday Mass at his parish in the Latin Quarter. The second was a general confession at Saint Peter's Basilica in Rome, after which I took the list of a lifetime of sins, mortal and venial, which I had carefully compiled, walked down to the embankment below the *Ponte Sant'Angelo*, set the list on fire with a Zippo lighter, and held it in my hand histrionically as I watched its embers and ashes fall into the Tiber. The third happened in Tallinn. After Michaelmas term in Oxford in 2005, I spent three days in Estonia before heading to Saint Petersburg for Christmas and for New Year's.

It was already dark when I had finished touring Tallinn's old city and walked to visit the city's Roman Catholic cathedral. I was not planning to go to confession, but as I looked about the nave, I remarked that a priest was present in one of the confessionals. I knelt at the grille and began my confession in our presumed common tongue, Russian.

Before long he stopped me and asked in English with a distinct North American accent: "Where are you from?" When I told him my nationality, he revealed that he was incardinated in the Archdiocese of Newark but now on indefinite loan to the Roman Catholic Apostolic Administration of Estonia. After my confession, he spoke to me for several minutes, expounding his theory that the world was full of biological males, but desperately short on real men. Before giving me penance and absolution, he exhorted me "to be a man." In his own way, I believe that he was coaxing me to understand a truth of our age that I encountered many years later in Pasolini's *Lettere luterane*:

> *La società preconsumistica aveva bisogno di uomini forti, e dunque casti. La società consumistica ha invece bisogno di uomini debili, e perciò lussuriosi.*[*]

That evening I did not make much moment of this priest's words. Yet as months and years passed, time and again I found myself recalling this unplanned confession. Believing that I was but a mere male, I wanted to become a man. Thus, long before I had ever read anything by Blaise Cendrars, I had already been seeking out what he claimed to have learned from the Legion in *La Main Coupée*: "*Être. Être un homme. Et découvrir la solitude. Voilà ce que je dois à la Légion…*"[†] It was this desire, above all others, that gave me the drive and the perseverance to quit Princeton, to fly to Marseilles, and to ask to join the Foreign

---

* Pier Paolo Pasolini, *Lutheran Letters*: "Pre-consumerist society needed strong men, and therefore chaste men. Consumerist society, on the other hand, needs weak men, and therefore promiscuous men." Napoleon also stands behind this idea in his maxim: *Les âmes fortes respoussent la volupté comme les navigateurs évitent les écueils.*

† "To be. To be a man. And to discover solitude. This is what I owe to the Legion."

Legion one August morning in 2008.

After almost two years in the Legion, did I uncover how to be man, or at least more of one? Had I discovered solitude?

The Legion was "fatalist" and broadcast few illusions about the legionary's condition. It did not promise happiness, which, in Nietzsche's estimation, only Englishmen seek in life. It promised instead pain, struggle, sacrifice, and death, possibly seasoned with some adventure and romance. If the latter two were lacking, prostitutes and alcohol were often enough in plentiful supply. Some of the Legion's unique spirit and culture became part of me. And I came to understand more truly the meaning of Hélie Denoix de Saint Marc's words:

> "*La guerre, c'est d'apprendre que l'ennemi est d'abord au fond de soi-même. Elle peut être une école de tueurs, mais aussi de renoncement et de fidélité.*"*

No journey of learning is complete. Today I would not make reckless claims of having become more of a man than any other *mingens ad parietem* owing to my twenty-one months in the French Foreign Legion. Much as one cannot label himself a "poet" or an "artist" without absurdity or compromising one's dignity, I would never dare to assign to myself any special qualities of manhood. No matter what my experiences and their results, from these I have learnt that any of my strengths are but a few faltering steps removed from pathetic weakness.

What I can say is that my time in the Legion dispelled many of my prior handicaps and gave me renewed zeal for study, for friendship, and for travel, and new motivations to seek out what I believed to be good, beautiful, and true in earthly existence's "brief crack of light between two eternities," eternities whose realities will necessarily surprise us. To me, Nabokov's statement about "two eternities of darkness" does seem childishly optimistic, and I have always been more partial to the observation in Benjamin Constant's *Adolphe:*

---

* "War, it is to learn that the enemy is above all within us. War can be a school of murderers, but also a school of disinterestedness and of faithfulness."

> *Ma surprise n'est pas que l'homme ait besoin d'une religion; ce qui m'étonne, c'est qu'il se croie jamais assez fort, assez à l'abri du malheur pour oser en rejeter une: il devrait, ce me semble, être porté, dans sa faiblesse, à les invoquer toutes; dans la nuit épaisse qui nous entoure, est-il une lueur que nous puissions repousser? Au milieu du torrent qui nous entraîne, est-il une branche à laquelle nous osions refuser de nous retenir?**

Dismissed from the Legion in May 2010, most of my prior fears, wants, worries, and pains had vanished by the time I walked out of Aubagne's gates, the same that I had entered timidly but determinedly in August 2008. I had become someone else.

To come back to the challenge that I gave myself at this undertaking's beginning, what story have my collected and distilled memories of twenty-one months in the Foreign Legion told?

As I type out my last allotted words, this is not my conclusion to make.

Jerusalem, 14 July 2023

---

* Benjamin Constant, *Adolphe*: "My surprise is not that man has need of religion. What surprises me is that he can believe himself so strong, so safe from tragic events that he would reject one. In his weakness he should, it seems to me, be more inclined to invoke the help of all religions. In the thick darkness that surrounds us, is there a light that we should spurn? In the torrents that sweep us away, is there a branch that we should refuse to grasp?"

L'ENVOI

Mi misi me per l'alto mare aperto
sol con un legno e con quella compagna
picciola da la qual non fui diserto....

Io e' compagni eravam vecchi e tardi
quando venimmo a quella foce stretta
dov' Ercule segnò li suoi riguardi....

"O frati," dissi, "che per cento milia
perigli siete giunti a l'occidente,
a questa tanto picciola vigilia

d'i nostri sensi ch'è del rimanente
non vogliate negar l'esperïenza,
di retro al sol, del mondo sanza gente.

Considerate la vostra semenza:
fatti non foste a viver come bruti,
*ma per seguir virtute e canoscenza."**

Inferno, Canto XXVI
Dante Alighieri

---

* "And so I set forth upon the open deep / with but a single ship and that small band / of shipmates who had not deserted me.... / I and my shipmates had grown old and slow / before we reached the narrow strait / where Hercules marked off the limits.... / 'Oh brothers,' I said, 'who in the course / of a hundred thousand perils, at last / have reached the west, to such brief wakefulness / of our senses as remains to us / do not deny yourselves the chance to know / following the sun—the world where no one lives. / Consider how your souls were sown: you were not made to live like brutes and beasts / but to pursue virtue and knowledge.'"

ACKNOWLEDGMENTS

For this composition's final form I am greatly indebted to my friend, Dr. Douglas Lewis (MA *Cantab.*, PhD Yale), who meticulously read the entire manuscript and made some hundred pages of detailed editorial suggestions. His efforts spared me from many mistakes in grammar and in content. I am also thankful to Jerusalem's Polis Institute for the excellent language instruction in Hebrew, in Arabic, and in Ancient Greek that accompanied my final compilation and editing of this document. To *Les Soeurs Blanches* in Jerusalem, at whose guesthouse I was able to complete this manuscript in peaceful and inspiring conditions, I am indebted. I also thank my *Doktorvater* at Princeton, who has always supported me in both my academic and military journeys.

Here I must also convey my abiding thanks to Mauro Mahjoub, Giorgio Fadda, Samuele Ambrosini, and Massimo d'Addezio for introducing me to and teaching me about proper cocktails and the peerless excellence of Italian barmen.

I have too many debts to various military personnel worldwide to mention here, and I am thankful for the many positive experiences and consequences of service both in the French Foreign Legion and in the US Army. I do owe special thanks, however, to my regimental commander in the Foreign Legion's Second

Foreign Infantry Regiment and to my brigade commander at the 173rd Airborne Brigade, each an exemplary officer and commander in his own unique way.

Whatever critical opinions I may voice about certain institutions to which I have belonged over the years, or about their members, I remain thankful to them all.

In keeping with established custom for written accounts about exploits in the French Foreign Legion, I have changed all names in this book save for a few cases where the person in question is already known to the public.

Last, I would honour my father and my mother.

ABOUT THE AUTHOR

Nicholas Tobias is a former legionnaire in the French Foreign Legion and a former infantry officer in the United States Army. Nicholas began his military career as an enlisted soldier in the French Foreign Legion (2008–2010), with which he deployed to Afghanistan. Following an honourable discharge from the Legion in 2010, he commissioned as an officer in the US Army through Princeton University ROTC while concurrently completing his doctoral studies in European history. From 2013 to 2022, he served as an active-duty infantry officer in the US Army, with assignments at various Airborne units and with the US Army Ranger School. During this time, he again deployed to Afghanistan. In addition to numerous military qualifications, he was a master-rated Jumpmaster, graduated from the US Army Ranger School, and completed the Colombian Army Lancero course. Proficient in eight languages (English, French, Spanish, Italian, Russian, German, Modern Hebrew, and Levantine Arabic), Nicholas has a strong dedication to reading and to studying Latin, and maintains a less intense interest in Ancient Greek.